Women Who Opt Out

Women Who Opt Out

*The Debate over Working Mothers
and Work-Family Balance*

Edited by Bernie D. Jones

NEW YORK UNIVERSITY PRESS
New York and London

NEW YORK UNIVERSITY PRESS
New York and London
www.nyupress.org

References to Internet websites (URLs) were accurate at the time of writing.
Neither the author nor New York University Press is responsible for URLs
that may have expired or changed since the manuscript was prepared.

Library of Congress Cataloging-in-Publication Data
Women who opt out : the debate over working mothers and work-family balance
/ edited by Bernie D. Jones.
    p. cm.
 Includes bibliographical references and index.
 ISBN 978-0-8147-4312-6 (cl : alk. paper) — ISBN 978-0-8147-4313-3 (pb :
alk. paper) — ISBN 978-0-8147-4505-2 (ebook) — ISBN 978-0-8147-4506-9
(ebook)
1. Working mothers—United States. 2. Wages—Working mothers—United
States. 3. Sex discrimination in employment—United States. 4. Women›s
rights—United States. 5. Feminism—United States—History. I. Jones,
Bernie D.
 HQ759.48.W65 2012
 331.4'40973—dc23
                                  2011043492

New York University Press books are printed on acid-free paper,
and their binding materials are chosen for strength and durability.
We strive to use environmentally responsible suppliers and materials
to the greatest extent possible in publishing our books.

Manufactured in the United States of America

c   10 9 8 7 6 5 4 3 2 1
p   10 9 8 7 6 5 4 3 2 1

This book is dedicated to the Center for Research on Families and the students over the years who made teaching feminist legal theory a fun experience.

Contents

Preface

I first became interested in this topic of "opting out" upon reading Lisa Belkin's October 2003 *New York Times* journalistic essay, "The Opt-Out Revolution." It was my first semester at the University of Massachusetts at Amherst Department of Legal Studies and I had recently finished a postdoctoral research fellowship with Martha Fineman's group on feminist legal theory and family law. The article intrigued me because it was the right piece at the right time from a pedagogical standpoint, seeming to embody the zeitgeist of certain American cultural anxieties. Belkin's piece gained a lot of attention in its controversial argument: successful young women had given up the struggle for feminist equality in the workplace; they were now content to retreat, stay at home, and raise families.

The article presented an opportunity for discussing gender in my spring 2004 class "Law and the Family," and the role of law in influencing women's abilities to balance work and family demands. There were various young women in the class who would enter the workforce upon graduation or go on to graduate school. They were intrigued by the topic and our discussions. What expectations would they have of themselves upon entering professional life? With more and more Americans marrying later in life, divorcing, or never marrying at all, they realized that as young single women they needed to work in order to support themselves. No woman is guaranteed marriage, and with one out of two marriages failing, marriage in and of itself is no guarantee of long-term stability, notwithstanding the optimism and hope with which most marriages begin. Nonetheless, they wondered whether life circumstances might change their relationships to the world of work. Were they interested in marrying at some point in the future? Did they intend to have children? What if life circumstances placed them (through no fault of their own, i.e., "waiting" or otherwise) among the population of women met often with surprise and curiosity, the child-free? Even though some might not have imagined having children in the near future, they were affected by certain cultural expectations nonetheless, the feminine gestalt found in the question often asked of married women and those of an age to be married: "Do you have any children?" But in general, those questions had yet not arisen for them; as young college students, they were not financially secure and most did not have long-term committed relationships that might lead to marriage.

Women are expected to fulfill social and cultural roles as the primary caretakers of children and quite often of elderly parents, at the same time as large numbers of them are in the workforce. Did my students believe Belkin's argument that work outside the home is irrelevant to highly educated women with advanced degrees, because they would be married to men who could afford to have them stay at home? How did my students imagine they would negotiate the different roles they might undertake, of caretaking in the home and working outside the home? Focusing upon other research projects in the meantime, I continued to address the topic in the classroom, developing over time assessments of workplace law and policy in light of feminist legal theory.

Teaching law and the family, I began with the presumption that the students would recognize, even on some visceral level, the significance of gender for understanding law and family policy, and that the two were not separate—law and the family are related to women, men, and the law. Putting aside the presumptions among a few students that any discussion of feminist legal theory meant "man-bashing," I realized that for some, gender, law, and family policy were not connected. One or two student evaluations of the law and the family class questioned the premise of assigning articles written by feminist legal theorists. Did some students believe that law and family policy could exist without a discussion of the significance of gender and feminism? Could it be that they had no inkling of the significance and influence of early feminist legal theorists (and their critics) in formulating many of the laws and policies that have become acceptable over time, such as family and medical leave? Was it a matter of believing that with the gains of feminism, the underpinnings of feminism in law and policy had become irrelevant? Or could it be that feminism was an "F word?"

Unwilling to see feminism as irrelevant and controversial, I reconfigured "Law and the Family" as "Women and the Law," a class in women's legal history, with an emphasis on feminist legal theories and their various applications, including families and the workplace. This book is dedicated in part to those students who matriculated in "Women and the Law" even as they knew they would face ridicule and derision from some of their peers who presumed that their study of women's legal history signified their status as militant feminists. These young women would not let the dreaded "feminist" label impede their education and growing self-awareness.

I thank Eve Darian-Smith and Ron Pipkin, former chairs in the University of Massachusetts at Amherst Department of Legal Studies, and most importantly, Sally Powers, Director of the Center for Research and Families, and Wendy Varner, Associate Director, for helping me conceptualize the October 2008 symposium "Women and Work: Choices and Constraints," that led to the publication of this book. It was amazing, all those hours spent in thinking, talking, strategizing, and meeting with people who could help realize my dream. There are too many of them to mention, but especially noteworthy are Karen J. Hayes of the Office of Research Liaison and Development that granted me the Research Leadership in Action award; Paul Kostecki, Vice Chancellor for Research and Development; the conference steering committee, including those who attended and participated in the symposium, and the sponsors and authors who contributed to the book. Thanks too to Steven Robbins, Director of Creative Services at the University of Massachusetts-Amherst Office of University Relations, Ben Barnhart, the photographer who worked with me on a conceptualization for the publicity, and the staff at Zanna's, Amherst. I have enjoyed working with you all. Thanks to all of you for your faith in me!

As for my goals in developing the conference and in editing this book, I was interested in assessing the literature on motherhood in the second half of the twentieth century, contextualizing the debate over "opting out" as one indicating the challenges posed to feminist legal theory in addressing women's greater presence in the workplace. So much of the popular discussions of feminism and "opting out" seemed superficial, indicating a serious lack; there was no nuanced understanding of feminism. Moreover, there was no assessment of the role of law in the debate, when law has been integral for determining women's entry into the workplace and whether they stay. Feminist legal theory was missing from the discussion.

Cultural and social forces in the latter half of the twentieth century led to workers experiencing more work-family conflicts, insofar as women have been encouraged by the push for legal equality in education and the workplace. But notwithstanding the existence of family-friendly laws and policies, workplace norms did not change to fit the realities of workers with families. The contributors to this volume, all of whom were participants in the conference, come from a variety of disciplines. They had been developing their own assessments and critiques of the "opting out thesis." Having the chance to learn from them was an honor. Editing their work was a privilege.

Thanks also to my colleagues at Suffolk University School of Law, who were supportive of me and this project once I joined the faculty, especially Marie Ashe, for her helpful comments. Thanks as well to Ilene Kalish of the New York University Press; the anonymous reviewers; Mary McClintock, copy editor; my husband, Daniel A. Perrault; my parents, Michael and Eliza Jones; Francis and Kelli Phillip; Elizabeth Noel and family; Evelyn Hercules and Magnola Purcell-Hunt; Louisa Hercules-Bauldock and family; Karen J. Francis, Dave Purcell, and Rhonna Ifill and family.

"Opting Out"

Women's History and Feminist Legal Theory

Women, Work, and Motherhood in American History

——————— BERNIE D. JONES ———————————————————

When Betty Friedan wrote *The Feminine Mystique* in 1963, she pulled a veil off the "merry homemaker" image ascribed to American women of the postwar era (Tyler May, 1988; Coontz, 2011). It was the problem that had "no name," women who asked whether being a mother and housewife was all there was to life. These were college-educated women who were told that they should not use their education and training in the workplace. The consensus was that well-educated wives were assets to their husbands as long as they remained in the home, because housewifery meant "true feminine fulfillment." Her book became a best-seller and rallying cry for women eager to escape the "gilded cage" of domesticity. She later became one of the founding members of the National Organization for Women. This new women's rights movement was developing a visible presence and institutions dedicated to the political and legal aspects of the struggle for equality.

Friedan described the nascent movement: "For those of us who started the modern women's movement . . . [t]he new paradigm was simply the ethos of American democracy—equality of opportunity . . . but applied to women in terms of concrete daily life as the theory and practice of democracy may never have been applied before. And how truly empowering it was, those first actions we took as an organized women's movement, getting Title VII of the Civil Rights Act enforced against sex discrimination" (Friedan, 1997, 5). This was about women tackling the next step after suffrage had been won in the earlier part of the century: women's economic citizenship (Kessler-Harris, 2001).

American society had long been conflicted over the very issue of women's economic citizenship, and the women's rights movement of the twentieth century brought these conflicts to the fore. Although the Industrial Revolution changed American society in that more men and women went into the workforce, "female workers' economic prospects" did not change (VanBurkleo, 2001, 136). Their work was seen as less meaningful and significant than men's work: "[W]omen could work and hold property, but not too seriously, not as a rule, and not for 'family' wages" (VanBurkleo, 2001, 137). Women worked for less pay than men and their failure to earn wages on par with male workers meant that their salaries were secondary, thus pushing women toward seeing their labor in the workplace as less important than domesticity. This trend persisted into the twentieth century, as the tensions over women's work took different manifestations.

Forty years after Friedan, Lisa Belkin addressed these tensions in her October 2003 article. Now that women have formal equality, what does it mean? Must formal equality equal substantive equality as the equal treatment feminists envisioned? Is all inequality the result of sexism? Can women who believe in equality and who call themselves feminists make choices that result in inequality for women in the workplace? The subtext to the article indicates a view among women of a younger generation of feminists that it is equal treatment ideology that is truly limiting by asserting that "choices" can only have one meaning, namely, that women must be absolutely equal to men. These younger women argue that feminism is meaningless without respect for women's individual needs as being separate and apart from equal treatment outside of ideology. Those who wish to eschew work outside the home should not be criticized.

The foundation for these contemporary debates lay in the late-eighteenth-century ideology of "Republican Motherhood," the notion that women's efforts in the new nation should emphasize the domestic sphere of marrying and raising children to become civic-minded citizens (Kerber, 1980). By the nineteenth century, the rhetoric became one of "separate spheres," that men belonged to the world of the public sphere—politics, commerce, and labor—while women belonged to the world of the private sphere. Women's protection from the public sphere meant that their domesticity would enable men's efforts in the public sphere. Continuing the duties ascribed to their foremothers of the Early Republic, they were to raise upstanding citizens (VanBurkleo, 2001).

Working women of the nineteenth century posed a challenge, though, to the idealism of domesticity and "separate spheres." Not all women could stay at home as the dependents of their fathers and husbands. These women had to work, in that their families depended upon their financial contribution. Some women had no choice but to work—those whose husbands were low-wage workers or those who suffered the losses of widowhood or abandonment (Vapnek, 2009). As policymakers were confronted with the reality that some women must work, reformers of the Progressive Era used protectionism to minimize the harsh effects of industrialization upon them and thus reinforce the domestic sphere. Reformers' efforts were predicated on the presumption that women were not as capable of negotiating their rights in the workplace. Women could thus be taken advantage of by unscrupulous employers; state legislatures aimed to intervene and take corrective measures. Thus, *Muller v. Oregon*, 208 U.S. 412 (1908), carved out an exception to the freedom of contract doctrine articulated in *Lochner v. New York*, 198 U.S. 45 (1905).

Both cases went to the heart of the newly developing regulatory state. What were its limitations? The Court considered a basic issue: which forms of regulations were legitimate and which were not? Comparing the two cases, the Supreme Court held quite differently when faced with similar gender-based protective labor legislation. Men had the ability to protect themselves, but women, as members of a protected and subordinate class, could not. Thus, some forms of legislation aimed at protecting the rights of male workers were unnecessary, because those workers could represent themselves well in the workplace and negotiate on behalf of their interests. Paternalism was rejected on their behalf; the state of New York in *Lochner* thus need not establish the maximum number of hours a baker could labor in a commercial bakery. Women, on the other hand, were not like male workers, in that they could not bargain on equal footing with men; their sex alone disadvantaged them. Moreover, protecting women workers served an important societal function: it protected women's reproductive capacities. Thus, the state of Oregon could intervene and assert policy rationales for limiting the number of hours a woman could labor in a laundry. Other forms of legislation excluded women altogether from certain types of jobs, "defined by the time and place where they were performed or by the nature of the task" (Kessler-Harris, 2003, 181).

The aspects of the women's rights movement of the twentieth century that focused upon gaining women equality in full economic citizenship jettisoned, in effect, the old protectionist trends that had long denied women access to certain types of jobs or which limited the number of hours that a woman could work. This movement made gains that turned American society upside down. The Civil Rights Act of 1964 specifically addressed gender-based discrimination in the workplace, with the EEOC acting in an administrative capacity, investigating and prosecuting employers who denied women equal opportunity, and Title IX further removed barriers to women's access to training in nontraditional fields.[1] As a result of these gains, women began entering into nontraditional fields of study and began taking professional jobs which had been foreclosed to them. They became doctors, lawyers, and business managers. They could become educated in their chosen fields, find jobs, and receive the lucrative salaries men earned. Greater access to birth control meant that women could control their reproduction as they pursued their new professional goals.

Nonetheless, as more women began pursuing their professional goals at the same time as they were raising families, they came up against a brick wall. The workplace changed to accommodate women, but norms in the home did not necessarily change at the same time. Notwithstanding the new "equality," women still undertook the bulk of the homemaking and childcare duties, while they worked outside the home just like men had always done. This was the brick wall of traditional sex roles: "[T]he career system inhibits women, not so much by malevolent disobedience to good rules as by making up rules to suit the male half of the population in the first place. One reason that half the lawyers, doctors, business people are not women is because men do not share the raising of their children and the caring for their homes. Men think and feel within structures of work which presume they don't do these things" (Russell Hochschild, 1997, xiii).

The goals of the women's rights movement as found in feminist legal theory, the aspect of the movement dedicated to using law for the purpose of improving women's status in society, was limited, some have argued, by its emphasis on equal treatment. Others have argued that the problem did not lie in feminism, but in society's failure to change. This equal treatment feminist legal theory has had a long history, dating back to suffrage. It presumed that women were exactly like men; without the legal impediments that enforced women's subordination—denial of suffrage, property rights, and employment, women would become equal in society (Levit and Verchick, 2006, 2–8). Critics responded that this feminist legal theory was inadequate in that it did not address the ways in which women are different from men: women bear children, men do not. Women tend to be caretakers of children, men do not. The workplace is predicated, though, upon norms that presume that men who work have no domestic responsibilities because their wives at home take care of those. Thus, the workplace did not address the needs of working mothers.

This debate became embodied in the sameness/difference debate which developed in the early 1980s, and which was signified by the notion of women's "voice" as distinct from men's (Gilligan, 1993). The adherents of "women's difference" argued that yes, women are equal to men, but they are also different, and that to focus upon sameness misses the mark. These cultural/difference feminists argued that women have to become exactly like men in order to become equal, for example, being driven to succeed in the world of work and careers, to the detriment of their interest in care-taking and nurturing roles in the home. But because they are not men, their differences are ignored, resulting in inequality. Levit and Verchick, in assessing feminist theory's development within the legal academy, explain the ostensible limitations of equal treatment: those who supported differ-ence proposed by the late 1980s that protectionism should be reinvigo-rated. Formal equality under the law did not result in substantive equal-ity. In order to reach substantive equality, women's differences should be addressed in law (West, 1988).

Although equal protection doctrine as it was developed by the Supreme Court showed some promise, for example in recognizing sex-based dis-crimination as actionable, formal equality only proved how women would be penalized. In *Geduldig v. Aiello*, 417 U.S. 484 (1974), the Court upheld Cali-fornia's denial of insurance coverage to state employees needing coverage for a normal pregnancy and childbirth. Asserting that a normal pregnancy was not a disability and not sex-based discrimination, even though only women were affected, the Court found that there was a rational basis for California to deny coverage. Women as a whole could get coverage—they were equal to men; they were not being especially targeted by the denial of pregnancy coverage. The Court held similarly in *General Electric Company v. Gilbert*, 429 U.S. 125 (1976), and upheld a private insurance plan's exclusion of preg-nancy-related disabilities. Cases like these led cultural/difference feminists to support the Pregnancy Discrimination Act of 1978 that broadened Title VII's reach to include discrimination against pregnant women in the workplace (Levit and Verchick, 2006, 55).

Cultural/difference feminists could thus support the Family Medical Leave Act.[2] Although women's work-family balance provided the impetus for legislation, the Act itself is gender-neutral; it nonetheless has become gender-specific by default. In *Nevada Department of Human Resources v. Hibbs*, 538 U.S. 721 (2003), the Court upheld the Act and made it applicable to the case of a man denied leave to care for his sick wife. The late Justice William Rehnquist wrote the opinion. The Act presumes, then, that men might have their own work-family balance issues to resolve, and accordingly this has enabled some men to negotiate family leaves with their employers as they coordinated child care responsibilities with their spouses. But this trend is not a common one, and as the Center for WorkLife Law has found,[3] men can experience discrimination when they seek to use workplace policies that were originally envisioned for women to use as they pursued their attempts to balance work and family.

The Act applies to public agencies, state, local, and federal, including schools and private employers who employ fifty or more people. Women employed by covered employers can receive a total of twelve weeks' unpaid leave during the year they give birth. But in order to be eligible, they must have been employed for a year prior to the time they request leave, and they had to have worked 1,250 hours during that period. This legislation was not easily won, though: "[F]or a long time the United States was the only Western industrialized country with no parental leave; after twelve years of lobbying, the result was the Family Medical Leave Act (FMLA). While the FMLA is a significant and important accomplishment, it is also a drop in the bucket: It covers only a small percentage of those employed in the United States, and offers only an unpaid leave that many women cannot afford to take" (Williams, 2000, 237). Once women returned to work, they used the means which had long been an option for upper-middle-class and upper-class women: they hired baby-sitters and nannies to care for their children, contracting out their home care responsibilities. By contracting out their responsibilities at home, they became on par with men.

But once women returned to work upon giving birth to their children, the FMLA did not help any, because the matter of "cultural caregiving," the tendency of women to be the primary caretakers of children, is not reached by antidiscrimination law (Kessler, 2005, 373). The FMLA only covers the extraordinary—mothers taking leave from work to care for young children—but it does not address the family-work balance issues of the mother who must juggle work with child care obligations long after she has recuperated from childbearing. It is about getting home from work in time to meet the baby-sitter, and managing with a sick child when one has limited vacation leave or sick days of one's own. Under those circumstances, both Kessler and Williams argue that Title VII does not help any if a woman loses her employment. Is it about discrimination against women because they are working mothers, or is it a matter of women failing to meet work obligations that any reasonable employer has come to expect? The tendency has been to see these cases as fitting into the latter, and not as involving gender-based discrimination.

At the same time as women were experiencing all these pressures upon their ability to negotiate work-family balance concerns, including the phenomenon of the "second shift" and the limitations of family leave policies, they were under even greater pressure to become "perfect mothers." This harkened back to the world of Betty Friedan's 1950s-era ideal of wifedom and motherhood: "In those days, a wife and mother who worked outside the home was supposed to be losing her femininity, undermining her husband's masculinity, and neglecting her children, no matter how much her paycheck was needed to help pay the bills" (Friedan, 1997, 5). Even though this orthodox view of 1950s-era families has been questioned for its veracity and its applicability to all postwar families, it persists as a social and cultural ideal (Coontz, 1992; Meyerowitz, 1994).

This mind-set became resurrected and reconfigured in the 1980s and beyond, with the rise of the "new momism": "the insistence that no woman is truly complete or fulfilled unless she has kids, that women remain the best primary caretakers of children, and that to be a remotely decent mother, a woman has to devote her entire physical, psychological, emotional, and intellectual being, 24/7, to her children" (Douglas and Michaels, 2004, 4). They argue, "[c]entral to the new momism, in fact, is the feminist insistence that women have choices . . . . The only truly enlightened choice to make as a woman . . . is to become a "mom" and to engage in "intensive mothering," bringing to child rearing a combination of selflessness and professionalism" (Douglas and Michaels, 2004, 5). Women "are in powerful competition with each other, in constant danger of being trumped by the mom down the street, or in the magazine we're reading (Douglas and Michaels, 2004, 6). They explain, "[T]he competition isn't just over who is a good mother—it's over who's the best" (Douglas and Michaels, 2004, 6).

Judith Warner adds that the pressure for middle-class mothers to become perfect became relentless, because "every decision we make, every detail we control, is incredibly important" to their children's future success in re-creating their parents' middle-class lives (Warner, 2005, 33). As a result, anything that might seem to undermine that possibility has to be pushed aside, like the job that might improve their family's economic situation. There is some evidence, though, that some women who choose to "opt out" experienced job-related stresses once they became parents, but did not feel conflicted about the pressure to become perfect mothers. Instead, they relished it (Moe and Shandy, 2009). These competitive women have been used to operating at a high level of competence all their lives. They did well throughout their school years and were successful at their prestigious jobs. They like that they are currently part of a coterie of mothers who are just as dedicated at using their skills in raising their children and managing their homes.

This popular focus on domesticity as being in conflict with working led to the "mommy wars,"[4] which seemed to pit "equal treatment feminists" against those within the "cultural/difference" camp. The proposition of the "mommy wars" set forth that mothers were either career women—mothers or childless women—who wanted to be like men in the workforce, or they were women who celebrated maternity and domesticity by giving up the working world to remain at home with their children. Each group apparently had contempt for the other: the working women seeing the stay-at-home mothers as losers who could not cope or as women stupidly buying into dependence and vulnerability. On the other hand, the stay-at-home mothers saw their counterparts as overly ambitious and uncaring of the needs of children in their desire to compete in the workforce on equal terms with men. The prevailing mind-set in favor of women becoming stay-at-home mothers is that children whose mothers stay at home are socialized under the best of circumstances: safe nurturing environments supervised by loving mothers who cater to their needs, as compared to children who are "institutionalized" in day care and after-school programs.

At stake here are a whole host of cultural and social anxieties not only about women and their roles in society, but the impact of women's individual decisions on the future of their societies. It has been quite clear over the past number of decades that birthrates in advanced and Western societies are falling. Apparently, as women become better educated, they become more "modern," that is, they enter the market economy and become less likely to have large families. As a result, more women have fewer children or none at all. Social conservatives, fearful of population decline and stagnation, worry about the future of Western societies and cultures if fewer women dedicate themselves to child rearing.

Social conservatives, developing their vision of the stay-at-home mothering ideal, took what appeared to be a cultural/difference stance, arguing that feminists like Friedan wanted to push American children into institutional child care and rip them away from their families, because they saw all women as victims of sexism. In the eyes of social conservatives, though, working mothers were seen as "victims [of failed social policies] forced into the labor force by feminist bullying and high taxes, and as villains who put their personal fulfillment above their children's well-being" (Young, 2000). They were "mugged by reality," according to Phyllis Schafly, the well-known antifeminist who was a stay-at-home mother of six (Young, 2004). Women have been hoodwinked, argue the policy analysts of the Independent Women's Forum, into believing that they can "have it all," just like men, pursuing high-powered careers at the same time as they raise families, when in reality they are not like men. They have different needs and preferences (Lukas, 2006). Or at least they *should* have them, and would recognize them, if not for equal treatment feminists' posturing.

Equal treatment became irrelevant, then, to those who adhered to this type of cultural/difference feminism. The artificial barriers had been removed, in their view. Women had opportunities equal to men. How could there be discrimination? Nothing barred women from getting into professional school, and nothing prevented them from getting jobs. When equal treatment feminists talked about discrimination, conservative women argued that they wanted "equality of results" through social engineering (Hoff Sommers, 1995). But these conservative women did not seem to recognize, in the eyes of their critics, that discrimination could still persist, regardless of the removal of the barriers.

Joan Williams, engaging with the debate between equal treatment and cultural/difference feminism, argued that those who celebrated women's "differences" were playing a dangerous game (Williams, 1989). Women's differences had traditionally been used to marginalize women, minimize their abilities, and limit their opportunities. Their differences stereotyped them, and yet cultural/difference feminists were using that same language of difference, but for a positive purpose, ostensibly to uplift women. Nonetheless, the stereotypical foundations persisted, resulting perhaps in some unintended consequences. Thus, she argued, *EEOC v. Sears, Roebuck & Co.*[5] pitted sameness/difference feminists on opposite sides of a divide, but the difference side prevailed, to the detriment of women.

This stereotyping arguably underpins the "opt-out" thesis and the rise of "choice feminism."[6] If women make choices because they are "different," does it then follow that employers don't develop policies supporting women in the workplace because they expect women to make certain choices? As Kessler-Harris suggested, this became, then, the long-lasting legacy of *EEOC v. Sears*: "Expectations and aspirations conditioned by generations of socialization and labor market experience would now be used to justify continuing discrimination against women" (Kessler-Harris, 1996, 595). Is it that women expect to make certain choices, so they don't request policies that might enable them not to have to choose career over family, especially when "opting out" might not be an option? Arguably, the answer is yes. Missing, then, from this discussion of women and their choices in the world of work was the recognition that the "mommy wars" were never that simplistic.

The focus here on the "opt-out" thesis and its emphasis on the needs of higher-income professional women is important not for the purpose of reinforcing the thesis but for demonstrating its perniciousness, in that the "opt-out" thesis reflects a popular perception of working mothers' experiences. This popular perception, in turn, minimizes any critique of workplace norms and policies. The rise of "choice" feminism among the demographic of women who comprise the "opt-out" revolution has contributed, then, to a mind-set that women no longer experience discrimination; they experience only a myriad of choices from which to choose. If a woman chooses an option that seems to deny her equality, she is not accepting discriminatory treatment; instead, she is just removing herself from the discussion. She should not be judged if she decides that formal equality, to be like a man in the workplace, has no meaning for her. Her choice to be selfless and put her children first is what matters more.

But this "choice feminism" has been met with criticism. Wendy Kaminer has argued that the cultural difference feminist perspective that underpins "choice" has always been based in stereotyping, that all women are the same, as are all men. This presumption about natural gender roles has truly limited men's and women's possibilities and choices: "sexual difference confused by a legacy of discrimination" (Kaminer, 1990, xv). Nonetheless, the rhetoric of "equality" must deal with "difference," and as in previous debates dating back to the 1920s and the 1970s over an Equal Rights Amendment, the two perspectives are not easily reconciled (VanBurkleo, 2001, 300–306).

For example, in debates over equal treatment feminism and over the Equal Rights Amendment of the 1970s, it was not uncommon for feminists who believed in equal treatment to be confronted with the topic of women in the military. The nation was already in turmoil over the war in Viet Nam, and many in the antiwar movement opposed the draft. What was going to be equal treatment feminism's response to the question of whether women should register for the draft? Women had long been able to join the military and serve in medical and other support roles during wartime. Putting aside the question of whether women might be drafted to fill those positions, if equal treatment feminists said yes, women should be drafted, then they had to deal with conservative traditionalist women and difference feminists who did not believe women were exactly the same as men when it came, for example, to women serving in combat. If they said that women should not serve, then they were accused of wanting "special treatment."

With respect to women in the military, current recruitment has reso-nated in "choice." Although only men must register for the draft, no one is currently being drafted. All those in the military serve because they want to. Women who see themselves as capable enough of serving in equal capacity with men can join the military if they choose. For example, when I was a young nineteen-year-old in the late 1980s, I received a notice from Selective Service that according to their records, I had not registered. Did they call due to my male-sounding first name? I'll never know. But the leg-acy of "choice" meant that I didn't have to join the military. I could reply that I need not register, because I was not a young man. If I wanted to volunteer, I could, but I was not interested, as current events reinforced my perspective that it was a mistake to imagine that women in the military are exactly equal to men. The Tailhook scandal shocked many, as did stories of female prisoners of war held captive during the first Gulf War. I wanted to go to law school instead.

Dominance theory might have an answer to the conundrum of equality's limitations in the face of a prevailing rhetoric of "choice." It certainly affected my lack of interest in joining the military. I found repulsive the macho and misogynistic culture that seemed to pervade it. In the context of women "opt-ing out," dominance theory might also bridge the divide between sameness/difference underpinning "choice." Instead of avoiding dominance, women might enable it, because the decision to leave the workforce upon having children indicates, in the view of Linda R. Hirschman, an insidious return to stereotyping. She argues that when the women with the most education and training "opt out," it means that those who could have been effective leaders in pressing for change for greater numbers of women have abdicated instead and removed themselves from the field, in a retreat to an earlier ideal: selfless domesticity. They relinquish their voice in the public realm and give up their economic power. The dark side to the bright and lovely romantic story of becoming a domestic goddess offers its own resonance, though. Women who opt out have in effect chosen dependence and vulnerability, and there are plenty of cautionary tales: from the housewife whose husband divorces her to the widow who has lost her primary means of support. This language of choice, then, masks the failures of workplaces to pursue family-friendly policies, and in effect places full responsibility on women to "choose" an option that leaves them vulnerable (Hirshman, 2006).

Linda Tarr-Whelan, former ambassador to the UN Commission on the Status of Women in the Clinton administration, explains that when women opt out, institutions can experience a dearth as they lose the significance of women's different voices. Tokenism marginalizes and leads to a tendency to follow traditional norms in the workplace, like for example those that require women to perform exactly like men. But there are measurable benefits, she claims, in having at least 30 percent women in positions of influence, for example, in various corporate governance sectors. She notes, "firms with one-third or more women as corporate officers and directors reap rich rewards: higher financial performance and better bottom lines, as well as more opportunity for upward mobility and improved policies for women and families" (Tarr-Whelan, 2009, 4).

Putting aside the argument Tarr-Whelan makes that it is good for society in general when women participate in the public sphere with men, those who presume that working mothers work solely out of selfishness ignore the fact that work might very well be obligatory for their family's support. Echoing themes dating back to "separate spheres," that presumption does them no good at all. Not all women can choose to leave the workplace, and working mothers' dedication to work does not mean they are any less dedicated to the well-being of their families. Some might actually be buying "insurance," protecting themselves and their children against the worst-case scenarios of divorce or widowhood. Yet, the perception of stay-at-home mothers as being "better" lay in a privileged view of the world of work, the same type of privileged perspective which lay at the heart of the "opt-out revolution," that because work is merely optional for many high-income women, women as a whole need not work. If a woman works, she must be doing so solely for her own personal edification or because of her selfish desires.

Considering this mind-set of "opting out," the work-family balance issue can be seen as irrelevant. Women who feel pressured by work and family conflicts are just not making the right choices. If they cannot or will not contract out their homecare responsibilities, these were their personal choices resulting in personal conflicts which they had created. The answer seems to be: either find a solution or quit the workforce. Betty Friedan assessed the raging debates: "I saw no real equality unless women could 'have it all' as men can. But they can't do it exactly as men do, can they, as long as women are the ones who give birth to children, and still take, or are supposed to take, most of the responsibility for raising them?" (Friedan, 1997, 7)

These debates over equal treatment feminism had other manifestations. The efforts of equal treatment feminism became equated exclusively with the efforts of professional and middle-class white women in the workplace. Indeed, this was the primary focus of Belkin's article: how middle-class and professional white women were dealing with work-family balance issues. She referred to the evidence: "[O]f white men with M.B.A.'s, 95 percent are working full time, but for white women with M.B.A.'s, that number drops to 67 percent." Yet, "the numbers for African-American women are closer to those for white men than to those for white women."[7] African American women thus tend not to opt out.

Traditionally, African American women have always worked, and yet even though there are numbers of African American women who are similar to their white female counterparts in that they have high-paying professional jobs that demand much of their time, there might be pressure on African American women not to quit working: "[T]he real conflict was in how to negotiate family and community expectations for educational and professional achievement while responding to the very real concern for the survival of black marriages and families" (Barnes, 2008, 189). Many African American women have been among the first in their families to obtain advanced and professional degrees. Their families sacrificed much for them to succeed; they were building on the efforts of earlier generations. To give up the gains of the professional world and remain at home seemed to fly in the face of their family histories.

At the same time, though, there were factors that could pull them home: many grew up in families headed by divorced or single mothers who were strongly career-driven, because they had to be. In order to raise their children, they had no other choice. Even prior to their divorces, their mothers believed that women should always be financially independent, as a means of ensuring safety in times of family crisis. But to these women looking back at their mothers' and grandmothers' lives, they wondered whether their foremothers' career focus contributed to familial stress and ultimately to their divorces. Their foremothers' career focus meant they did not focus on cultivating their marriages. In these women's views, this strategy precipitated marital strife. For some, their quest to balance work and family took a religious overtone; it led them, though, to the same conclusion as the secular arguments against working outside the home. Proverbs 31:10–31 provides guidance for conservative Christian wives and mothers aspiring to live biblically: they are called upon to remain in the home, focus on their families and submit to their husbands' authority.

Family stability required that these younger women give up their careers in order to take care of their families and support their husbands' career interests. This debate over African American women's career and family choices reached the national sphere, though, when First Lady Michelle Obama decided that upon moving to the White House she would focus upon raising her two daughters, Malia and Sasha. Moreover, she indicated quite clearly that she considered her mother, Marian Robinson, crucial for her children's transition. Hillary Clinton, a predecessor First Lady whose career trajectory more closely mirrored hers, came under attack in the early 1990s, on the other hand, when she was unapologetic about her career focus, as indicated in her comment about not staying home and baking cookies for her only child, Chelsea. Her statement was taken to be an affront against women who decided to become stay-at-home mothers for the benefit of their families. These stories of the First Ladies, former and current, only indicate that the "mommy wars" issue has been the source of long-standing debate within American culture: whether women's career fulfillment sacrifices their children's need for familial stability.[8]

This concern about familial stability did not seem to be a motive for the women in Belkin's article. For them, returning home was simply a matter of deciding that career interests were no longer important. Perhaps they were fulfilling roles their own mothers might have rejected when they went into the workforce a generation earlier. Their daughters, becoming mothers themselves, questioned what they grew up with. Others might have grown up with stay-at-home mothers and wanted to replicate what they had as children. Belkin explains this phenomenon of highly qualified and capable women leaving the workplace upon having families as what can be described as an unexpected side effect of equal treatment feminism's gains: "a revolution stalled."

Belkin assesses how the phenomenon developed. She found a common theme among the women regarding their social expectations. Women were supposed to be exactly equal to men; the women she interviewed for the article were the exact counterparts of their male peers, entering into law and business school at equal or even greater rates than their male peers. But something happened before they reached the upper rungs of their professions. They were recruited out of graduate school into the top firms and businesses. But they noted their disappearance: their numbers upon graduation and their entry into their fields did not match their numbers several years later; fewer of them became law firm partners or corporate officers.

Belkin's explanation is that these women rejected equal treatment feminism once they had children. They no longer wanted to be like their male peers. The drive for money and power came at a price they were unwilling to pay. Imagining what their lives would be like, they realized that in order to reach the upper echelons, they would have to sacrifice something dear to them: a balanced lifestyle and sanity. Gaining promotions would demand too much of their time and energy. The number of hours they would work for the increase in salary would not be worth it. Rather than live as workaholics, they decided to forgo the prestige and not rise to the top. As a cautionary note to those who might aim high, there were examples of women who pursued advancement but later came to regret it. They resigned once they felt the pressure of having to fulfill the demands of their very high-powered jobs. For these women, then, sameness was vanquished by difference.

Belkin's article garnered much attention and critique. Among them are the authors who have contributed to this edited collection.[9] The authors question the basic thesis of "the opt-out revolution." Are women choosing to leave the workplace because they are not interested in equal treatment in the workplace, or are they being pushed out because of workplace norms that are hostile to workers with families? Has the focus upon highly educated professional women led to presumptions that all women share the same work-family balance conflicts? How has a failure to consider the significance of class and race limited perceptions of women's workplace participation? Might "opting out" have implications for workplace policies that are harmful to working mothers?

Sylvia Ann Hewlett argues that there need not be a "brain drain" of accomplished working mothers leaving the workforce (Hewlett, 2007). If anything, she makes the case that in light of dire statistics about coming labor shortages as the baby boomers age, it is imperative that companies reach out to working mothers in the professions and reconsider the traditional career trajectory. Assure them before they quit in frustration or even after they have left, that there is still a place for them. Instead of questioning the dedication of women who want to "opt out," companies should think of working women's career trajectories in light of "off ramps" and "on ramps."

The presumption is that women who leave the workforce will never want to work again, when if anything, many might want to return to the workforce when their children are in school, and especially if they need to begin working again to support their families.

Of significance too is the possibility that women who opt out might not keep their skills current by pursuing part-time or volunteer opportunities; thus, their families might suffer during periods of economic downturn. A 2009 report explains that men make up "82% of the [current] recession's job losses,"[10] and especially hit were the financial and construction sectors. Both of these sectors were booming fields prior to the crisis, and gains in the financial sector in particular enabled many men to become high-earning primary breadwinners. Thus, numbers of white collar women who left the workplace to raise their families are now trying to get back in, since their husbands' incomes have decreased or become nonexistent. On the other hand, women who take maternity leave but who intend to continue working outside the home, are not protected from layoffs. Employers who harbor prejudices against working mothers might believe that high-achieving women will no longer be as dedicated; instead, they might become expensive liabilities. These employers thus view new mothers as the primary workers to fire in an economic downturn.[11]

Because the "opt-out" phenomenon is one that persists within the popular consciousness, and the desire to balance both work and family demands continues to be a point of unresolved concern for families and employers alike, the time is ripe for this book to address this "opting out" phenomenon and engage in both critique and assessment. The book is divided into three parts. This introduction comprises Part I. Part II asks whether the "opting out" assessment is an adequate explanation for women's decisions to leave the workforce. This section begins with Pamela Stone's chapter, a discussion of the results of in-depth life history interviews that shed light on women's aspirations, plans, and behavior with regard to work-family; their decision-making process; and reasons for labor force/career interruption. Instead of opting out, this chapter argues that women are shut out due to the existence of an effective "motherhood bar." The rhetoric of choice belies the reality of structural constraints and hides the class/race/gender intersectionality manifested within those constraints. The danger is that opting out will be seen as a solution to work-family balance, not a problem. Moreover, it could lead to arguments that will deter women's access to professional education and lucrative employment. If women "only leave anyway," why should they be hired?

Turning to the question of addressing the real-world needs of American workers, men and women, Ellen Galinsky and Kerstin Aumann argue the significance of a lifespan approach in thinking about the ways in which American workers—men and women—negotiate work, career, and caregiving. The development of this lifespan approach, a recognition that workers' interests and focus change over time, defines the real "opt-out revolution." While it is important for business and society to have talented people "in the pipeline" who are willing and able to move into positions of greater responsibility and leadership, not all workers are interested, or they might not be all at once. The challenge, then, is to encourage workplace realities that fit the factors predictive of success: demographics, employee values, work-and-family centrism, and child care and elder care responsibilities as they change over time.

Part III moves on to consider other authors who make an in-depth assessment of the race/class/gender axes as determining women's workplace participation, addressing issues not relayed by the "opt out" thesis—the women who can't afford to "opt out," or who find it difficult to "opt in." Susan Lambert considers the needs of hourly workers and their obstacles to full labor force participation. Low-level, hourly workers do not have a lot of choice with respect to the number of hours they work, and a growing proportion of Americans who work part-time (less than 35 hours per week) do so involuntarily. This means that they want to work and earn more but they cannot, because of workplace policies: instability is structured into many hourly jobs, making it hard for workers to fully access opportunities. Employers vary the number of hours needed on any weekly bases, the timing of individual employee hours, and the number of workers scheduled. Moreover, employers prefer those with open availability; these employees tend to be hired first and get more hours. Because worker availability determines whether an employee will be given hours, this can disadvantage working mothers who need stable work hours, days, and shifts.

Maureen Perry-Jenkins explores the work-family balance challenges faced by women who hold low-wage and low-skill jobs such as nursing assistants, waitresses, and retail clerks. At their level, entering and exiting the workforce is easy, because job turnover is high. Compared to more highly paid (and educated) women workers who tend to have both job flexibility and benefits of some sort, they have far less. For them, quitting is the only means of pursuing effective work-family balance strategies. They then look for work once they resolve their work-family conflicts. Yet, opting out of the workforce altogether is an impossible dream, which affects in turn their mental health and their relationships with partners and children.

Peggie Smith recalls the class privileges that have enabled many middle-class and professional women to "opt in." She focuses upon the constraints faced by low-income women who labor as home-based care workers: home care for the elderly and family child care. Care providers, especially home care workers and child care workers, have made it possible for many of the middle-class women highlighted in Belkin's article to seriously consider whether to work or not. The entry of women into the paid workforce and the changing structure of family life have fueled the demand for both types of home-based care workers. Many parents substitute paid child care for maternal care, especially when they prefer family child care to other child care options such as center-based care. Because more and more women find it difficult or impossible to care for young children and aging relatives while working outside the home, more householders turn to home care workers. Yet these workers cannot afford to leave the workplace and "opt out" because they tend to be women of racial and ethnic minorities who work very long hours but earn very low wages. They experience a high risk of on-the-job injury, but tend not to receive job-related benefits such as health insurance, medical leave, or retirement plans.

Joya Misra emphasizes that these issues of "opting in" are not limited to professional and middle-class women in the United States. All industrial nations are touched by the phenomenon of how to navigate the interests of highly paid workers to retain employment at the same time as they negotiate their need for child care. Once again, in order to pursue their lucrative careers, they need others to provide care work. This chapter examines the similarities among industrialized nations in the demand for care work (childcare, elder care, care for the disabled, and the like) as the result of women's rising employment rates, and the differences globalization and international policy impose upon outcomes: who provides care, where, and how are they compensated?

While most wealthy countries encourage women's employment outside the home, many European countries have shifted from supporting high-quality public sector care to a greater reliance on market-based solutions. New social care legislation has focused on creating low-paid service jobs in order to lower unemployment rates while also meeting care needs outside the more costly public sector. This chapter also examines where care work is most highly paid, showing that where care work is carried out within the public sector (for example, state-provided child care and elder care services), care work is more highly valued, better paid, and carries more social benefits. This suggests that while increasing women's employment rates may shift who does care work, with proper state support those who do care work can receive appropriate pay and benefits for carrying out work that is crucial to both society and the economy. Therefore, higher employment rates for middle- and upper-class women need not lead to greater inequality among women, but can instead lead to lower levels of inequality both among women and between men and women.

Finally, in Part IV Joan Williams and Jamie Dolkas conclude by highlighting an unexplored territory and pointing out topics for future research and policy—the work-family conflict among "the missing middle"—and argues that this is a new frontier for academics and policy makers to consider. Over the past few decades, a robust literature has developed about the work-family conflicts of professional women, including their need for reduced working hours and supportive workplace policies like paid maternity leave and on-site child care. In recent years, a parallel literature has begun to develop on work-family conflicts among low-income workers. This developing research has focused on the need for greater social supports for low-wage workers and single mothers to allow them to work more hours and earn a living wage while caring for their families. What is still lacking is a discussion of work-family conflicts among the middle and working class—those for whom the issue is neither opting in to more hours nor opting out of too many hours, but rather gaining some measure of control and flexibility during the old-fashioned forty-hour/week schedules they typically work.

Based on an ongoing study by the Center for WorkLife Law of work-family issues that arise in the context of union arbitrations, this chapter paints a vivid picture of work-family conflicts among the telephone operators, bus drivers, nurses aides, mineworkers, flight attendants, janitors, construction workers, and more, both men and women, who make up the American middle and working class. This chapter addresses how, when it comes to meeting competing work and family obligations, the needs of the "missing middle" both overlap with and differ from the needs of professionals and low-wage workers. It highlights key lessons for academics, unions, employers, policymakers, and the press—including how small changes in outdated workplace policies regarding scheduling, flexibility, and mandatory overtime can lead to important benefits for workers and employers alike.

Appendix

"Choice" Feminism and the "Opt-Out Revolution"

The contentious debates amongst feminists over sameness/difference and women's "choices" are at the root of the debate over "opting out." Belkin proclaimed that women are leaving the workforce in rejection of feminism, but perhaps women who leave are adhering to a cultural/difference feminist mind-set. They are merely rejecting the equal treatment norm in the workforce of women having to fulfill male-oriented norms of employment. Thus, although in some professional school settings, women comprise half or even a slight majority of those matriculating, they are not equally present in their professions several years later. Instead of focusing upon work at that point in their lives, they focus on the differences they have with their male colleagues, as they rediscover something more valuable: home and family.

Without question, cultural/difference feminism can be seen as a more conservative branch of feminist legal theory insofar as it emphasizes protection of women's traditional roles within the rubric of equality. What makes women unequal? According to the cultural/difference perspective, inequality is explained by a lack of regard for women's femininity. For example, under an absolute equality standard, laws and practices in the workplace that protect working mothers could be seen as irrelevant, because men don't need them and women are to compete in the workplace like men. It is not surprising that a number of feminist legal theorists teaching in Roman Catholic law schools find this type of feminism appealing, because cultural/difference, described as "complimentarianism," uses the same language of difference to justify some of the Church's positions, for example, on birth control and abortion. Thus, as Reva Siegel (2007) notes, conservative opponents of abortion argue that abortion harms women.

Feminists within the dominance school, like its pioneer, Catharine McKinnon, have argued that in a male-oriented and male-dominated system, women can't expect equality or even protection without changing the whole structure of the system. Thus, for women to have equality in the workplace, the male-dominant norms would need to be modified, since these were not created with women in mind. If anything, those norms ensure women's vulnerability and exploitation (lack of protection) as they ensure that men retain their dominance. Women who can't fulfill the norms of equality experience failure instead. The system is stacked against them but they are blamed, if they don't blame themselves, for failing to measure up. As for women's differences from men, these give women social value, but they are what also make women dependent and thus vulnerable. McKinnon believed that women pursue and celebrate "difference" because those traditions that make them different—childbearing and nurturing in the home, as examples—can give them greater social currency.

Thus, a dominance feminist might argue that it doesn't matter that women are in professional schools in similar numbers to men. Since the workplace norm is of a worker without domestic responsibilities who is thus capable of working long hours, women might leave eventually, because the workplace is set up for them to resign. Moreover, they know they will be applauded for it when they do. However, encouraging professional women to remain at home ensures both women's dependence and men's success and supremacy in the workplace. Notwithstanding women's gains, the men will benefit anyway because the social constructs are set up to ensure that women will never be in competition. As a result, when women depart from the workplace, their male colleagues will have a clearer field to access more lucrative employment opportunities. The gamble, of course, is that their husbands will be successful enough (and stay around long enough) to enable them to pursue their domestic endeavors.

Equal treatment feminists view with chagrin women's persistent failures to reach absolute parity with men. If women remain unequal men, what is the cause? Is it the result of institutionalized sexism—prejudice against working mothers? They argue that women's differences as found in childbearing should make no difference in the workplace. As long as mothers in the workplace are competent workers capable of negotiating work-family balance concerns with their employers and their husbands, women should be exactly equal and "opting out" should not be an issue. Whatever the cause—prejudice or "opting out"—women's failure to reach equality will only have dire consequences for women and society in the long run. Linda K. Hirschman's critique of "opting out" resonates here. For example, women tend to live longer than men but earn less during the course of their working lives. Not only do they tend to work in fields that don't pay as much as those where men predominate, but women are also more likely to leave the workplace for caregiving responsibilities to children and elderly parents, thus cutting short their lifetime of earnings.[12] They are more likely as a result to face impoverishment in old age.

By the 1990s, the existence of competing schools of feminist legal thought meant to some that feminism was fragmenting, the second wave of feminism had ended, and progress had stalled, especially in light of the backlash against feminism as the province of "man-hating lesbians" who rejected women's traditional values and interests.[13] Not only did many younger women eschew the feminist label as being too radical, but in the eyes of their critics, they were distinctly (and disturbingly) apolitical, as they seemed to take the gains for granted and thus to forget that they could be lost. With no uniform feminist theory, in what direction would feminism move? What policy initiatives would it pursue? Others saw this competition as pointing to the richness and vibrancy of feminist thought, and imagined that feminists could be pragmatists. A woman might face different issues at different times in her life, raising questions of gender, and thus, of feminism. Some situations might call for equal treatment, others for cultural/difference, or dominance. Thus, argued the pragmatists, developing fluency in different perspectives mattered.

This pragmatism marked the rise of feminism's third wave. The development of the "choice" feminism that underpins "opting-out" is also emblematic of this third wave gaining prominence in the 1990s, and especially among a younger group of feminists. Once the gains of the 1960s and 1970s had been made and the debates continued among the primary schools of sameness/difference/dominance in the 1980s, some younger women who were removed from the earlier battles began to think of feminism less as a political movement, more as a state of mind. They did so in rejection of what they saw as the rigid ideologies of the earlier schools. For them, feminism was about women pursuing whatever choices they believed empowered them. The personal was no longer as "political" as earlier feminists had once believed. But as Angela Onwuachi-Willig has imagined, "many women in this third wave age category, especially those of privilege, may more easily blind themselves to the barriers generally faced by women. They may think of themselves as making a real choice about work and home, even though their choices are arguably influenced heavily by gendered stereotypes and expectations."[14]

For example, this "choice feminism" "opt-out" mind-set has gained prominence not only among professional women who are already working, but among their younger counterparts as well, college-age women at elite colleges and universities who are expected to become highly educated professionals. A 2005 survey of Yale University students found that although the young women interviewed imagined they would pursue advanced degrees like their male counterparts, they fully expected that they would become stay-at-home mothers upon having children. Their education would provide them not only with a higher income before they had children, but they believed that they could return to their professions once their children grew up. But arguably too, their professions would put them in contact with men who could afford to have them remain at home. The "opt-out" mind-set seemed to be tailored to impress potential suitors who thought their interest in full-time motherhood was "sexy."[15]

The notion of "choice" seems to resonate especially among conservative women who argue that feminist law and policy initiatives undermine the goals of true liberty and free market economics. Policy analysts at the Independent Women's Forum fit into this category. They reject the feminism that they believe demands women make only certain choices, those affiliated more closely with a liberal or even radical political agenda. If anything, their goal has been to move feminism to the "right."[16] Some eschew the feminist label altogether because mainstream feminists have traditionally questioned the possibility that conservative women could be feminists. Rejecting feminism makes them "independent."

Critical race feminists and those interested in the international implications for feminism focused in turn upon race, gender, and class intersections. The work/family debate is one they have raised in their scholarship. They ask, "How does the traditional paradigm of sameness/difference/dominance mask the differences among women and emphasize instead the issues and interests of privileged women?" Moreover, "How have protection or equality for some women been predicated upon the domination of other women?" For example, those professional women who decide to "opt out" can do so because their race and class enabled them not only to access opportunities more easily, but they could see the decision to work as merely a matter of personal choice. Their exercise of choice—to work or stay home—is quite often tied to their ability to contract out their household labor to other women, including racial and ethnic minority women of working-class backgrounds.

Related to critical race feminism as well is the significance of global feminist legal theory/global critical race feminism, an approach to feminist legal theory that considers the impact of globalization upon women's rights and status internationally. Global critical race feminists consider, for example, the impact Western feminism has had upon women in developing countries. They wonder about the extent these contribute to competing interests amongst women and within women's cultures of origin. They note that globalization has highlighted the distinctions among women based upon class, culture, and country of origin. Finally, as in the critical race theory context, they observe that work/family conflicts among elite women can implicate the use of foreigners in domestic service.

For further discussion of the development of feminist legal theory, see Nancy Levit and Robert R. M. Verchick, *Feminist Legal Theory: A Primer*, NYU Press, 2006, and the following chart, which includes a sampling of various feminist legal theories. It is based (partially) upon the Levit and Verchick text.

TABLE I.1

Feminist Legal Theories: A Sampling	Examples:	Views of Various Adherents:	Views of Various Critics:
Equal Treatment Theory First wave--Suffrage Movement (Nineteenth century to 1920s)	Declaration of Sentiments (1848); the Married Women's Property Acts; Women's Suffrage, the Nineteenth amendment to the United States Constitution.	The social and legal orders of the Anglo-American common law contributed to women's subordination in society, especially with respect to their lack of legal protections and voting rights. Women had a right (and responsibility) to participate in the public sphere of work and politics, to represent their needs/interests and to improve society.	Drawing upon Blackstone as the standard for the Anglo-American common law, religious, social and cultural leaders objected to women's equality as undermining society and "family governance". They supported the notion of "separate spheres" and protectionist policies that denied women access and equality in the public spheres of work, politics and law.
Equal Treatment Theory—Second wave (1960s-1970s-today)	Equal Pay Act (1963); Equal Rights Amendment (proposed); Title VII of the Civil Rights Act of 1964; the National Organization for Women; Lilly Ledbetter Fair Pay Act (2009).	In law and policy, treat women exactly the same way men are treated; change the laws that denied women access and which resulted in inequality. Implement policies that will ensure women can become equal to men. Today, adherents discuss salary differentials between men and women, "glass ceilings" and "opting out" as harming equality.	Traditionalists like Phyllis Schlafly and F. Carolyn Graglia, along with religious conservatives, have been fearful of social engineering, upheaval, rejection of traditional morality, and women losing traditional protections; cultural feminists were concerned about women's differences not being recognized.
Cultural/Difference Theory (1970s-today)	Pregnancy Discrimination Act; Family Medical Leave Act; EEOC v. Sears. See as well, more conservative examples: Feminists for Life; Erika Bachiochi, Susan J. Stabile and Elizabeth Rose Schiltz as Catholic Feminist Legal Theorists.	Equal treatment does not account for women's differences; under equal treatment, women are treated equally only when they reject their differences from men. Use the law to protect women's differences and thus enable them to become equal.	It plays into paternalist stereotypes that had traditionally been used to deny women equality, in the name of "protection." It can be used to deny women legal protections or to deny them remedies under law, because "differences" can't be changed. Some opponents claim it advocates for "special treatment".

Feminist Legal Theories: A Sampling

Feminist Legal Theories: A Sampling	Examples:	Views of Various Adherents:	Views of Various Critics:
Dominance Theory (1970s–today)	Catharine McKinnon, criticism of domestic violence, rape and pornography; or Linda R. Hirschman, on the "opt-out" revolution.	Social, cultural, legal institutions all support patriarchy and contribute to women's subordination, if not their indoctrination; once these institutions are changed, women's status will change.	Some of its aspects have been seen by its critics as too radical, for example, in some of its strategies and in its critiques of institutions that many women value, like marriage and families—seen as "man-hating."
Critical Race Feminism (1980s–today)	Patricia J. Williams, Alchemy of Race and Rights (Harvard University Press, 1992); Patricia J. Williams, The Rooster's Egg (Harvard University Press, 1997); Adrien Wing, ed., Critical Race Feminism: A Reader (NYU Press, 2003, 2nd edition).	Race and the law issues presuppose a black male norm; gender and the law issues presuppose a white female norm. As a result, women of color experience inequality. Adherents can use equal treatment, difference, or dominance, but what is important, is that they address race in combination with gender, and often, class.	Critical race feminists were rejecting their racial loyalties. Other feminists argued that focusing on the race issue minimized the collective gender issues.
Global Feminist Legal Theory/ Global Critical Race Feminism (1990s to today)	Adrien Wing, ed., Global Critical Race Feminism: An International Reader (NYU Press, 2000).	Apply feminism to issues facing women internationally, and address the ways in which women's status in society is affected by globalization.	As with respect to critical race feminism, does "identity politics" within feminism detract from reaching the goals of women as a group? Is feminism too foreign for local tastes?
Lesbian Feminism (1970s to today)	Mary Eaton, "At the Intersection of Gender and Sexual Orientation: Toward Lesbian Jurisprudence," in Feminist Legal Theory: an Anti-Essentialist Reader, edited by Nancy E. Dowd and Michelle S. Jacobs (NYU Press, 2003).	Consider the ways in which lesbians' interest in equality coincide with, or differ from, heterosexual women's interests. Examples include lesbian parenting and "gay-baiting" of heterosexual women who are feminists.	Early critics like Betty Friedan were concerned that lesbians would taint the women's rights movement.

TABLE I.1 (CONTINUED)

Feminist Legal Theories: A Sampling	Examples:	Views of Various Adherents:	Views of Various Critics:
Third Wave (1990s to today): Pragmatic feminism	Margaret Jane Radin, Catharine Pierce Wells	With the rise of fragmentation, adherents argue there are various feminisms and advocate a pragmatic, situational approach.	Is pragmatism a real "theory," or is it an approach? Does it result in too many inconsistancies?
Third Wave (1990s to today) Choice feminism	Naomi Wolf, Fire with Fire (Random House, 1994); Regina Austin and Elizabeth M. Schneider, Mary Joe Frug's Postmodern Feminist Legal Manifesto Ten Years Later: Reflections on the State of Feminism Today, 36 New England Law Review 1-28 (2001); Lisa Belkin, "Opt-Out Revolution," New York Times, Oct. 26, 2003.	"Choice feminism" indicates the rise of "power feminism": reject orthodoxies of equal treatment, dominance and cultural/difference. Reject the notion of "woman as victim" and claim instead, that "whatever makes an individual woman feel empowered, is feminist."	"Choice/Power feminism" can result in feminism's trivialization. Is "choice/power feminism" sufficiently critical of institutions? Do choice feminists minimize the significance of social and cultural influences upon "choice?"
Third Wave (1990s to today) Conservative feminism	The Independent Women's Forum; as free-market conservatives, they have various concerns: feminist policies lead to bureaucracy, higher taxes, government control.	Conservative women claim the mantle of the first wave within "choice feminism". They critique the policies/approaches of mainstream feminism: equal treatment, cultural/difference and dominance. Since the law has removed the official barriers to access, they argue that women are not victims as much as they make choices that lead to inequality; and which thus make it appear that they are being discriminated against.	Are conservative feminists too complacent in their acceptance of the status quo, and in rejection of policies supported by equal treatment, cultural/difference and dominance feminists, policies which might be helpful to large numbers of women?

1. See, for example, Lenora M. Lapidus, Emily J. Martin, and Namita Luthra, *The Rights of Women: The Authoritative ACLU Guide to Women's Rights,* 4th edition (New York: NYU Press, 2009).

2. The Family and Medical Leave Act of 1993 was passed as Public Law 103-3 (February 5, 1993), 29 U.S.C. 2601 et seq. Information about the act can be found at: http://www.dol.gov/esa/whd/fmla/, http://www.dol.gov/esa/whd/regs/statutes/fmla.htm and http://www.dol.gov/esa/whd/regs/compliance/whdfs28.pdf. See, as well, Symposium: Respecting Expecting: The 30th Anniversary of the Pregnancy Discrimination Act, 21 *Yale Journal of Law and Feminism* (2009).

3. http://www.worklifelaw.org/RecentCases.html

4. Cathy Young has written frequently about this debate over motherhood: Cathy Young, "The Mommy Wars: Why Feminists and Conservatives Just Don't Get Modern Motherhood," *Reason Magazine,* June 2000, located at: http://www.reason.com/news/show/27765.html, or Cathy Young, "Opting Out: The Press Discovers the Mommy Wars, Again," *Reason Magazine*, June 2004, located at: http://www.reason.com/news/show/29157.html. For discussions of world demographics, see, for example, Robert Kunzig, "Population 7 Billion," *National Geographic*, January 2011, located at: http://ngm.nationalgeographic.com/2011/01/seven-billion/kunzig-text.

5. EEOC v. Sears, Roebuck & Co., 628 F. Supp. 1264 (N.D. Ill. 1986), aff'd, 839 F.2d 302 (7th Cir., 1988). The Equal Employment Opportunity Commission (EEOC) charged Sears with gender-based employment discrimination, based upon the theory of disparate impact, meaning ostensibly neutral employment policies resulted in discrimination: women were employed primarily in low-wage earning positions within the company and were steered away from the more lucrative opportunities which tended to be taken primarily by men. Were there policies in place, seemingly neutral, which led, nonetheless, to discrimination? The high court found none; Sears did not discriminate. The case exemplified the sameness/difference debate, insofar as each side relied upon expert testimonies from academic feminists in favor of its case. Rosalind Rosenberg argued in support of women's "differences," that women are more likely to be traditional and avoid certain types of jobs, while Alice Kessler-Harris argued that women in the workplace are interested in opportunities just like men, and tended to pursue them when discrimination did not hold them back. Rosenberg's view prevailed in court.

6. See the appendix for a discussion of the rise of "choice feminism" in the 1990s.

7. Lisa Belkin, "The Opt-Out Revolution," *New York Times Magazine,* October 26, 2003.

8. See, for example, Rebecca Traister, "Not Such a Long Way, Baby," *National Post,* November 13, 2008; Dahleen Glanton, "The White House's Working Mom," *Chicago Tribune,* November 6, 2008; Philip Sherwell, "Michelle Obama Persuades First Granny to Join White House Team," *Telegraph,* November 9, 2009; Ted Koppel, "Making Hillary Clinton an Issue," *Frontline,* March 26, 1992, http://www.pbs.org/wgbh/pages/frontline/shows/clinton/etc/03261992.html.

9. See, for example, *The American Prospect,* Special Report, March 2007: "Mother Load: Why Can't America Have a Family-Friendly Workplace?"

10. Bonnie Rochman, "Cash Crunch: Economoms. Many Who Opted Out of the Rat Race Are Scrambling to Get Back In." *Time,* March 23, 2009, 70.

11. Lesley Alderman, "When the Stork Carries a Pink Slip," *New York Times,* March 27, 2009.

12. The Women's Institute for a Secure Retirement is one group that has been at the forefront of addressing the dire situation for women who face impoverishment in their old age. Especially vulnerable are those who are single in their old age, whether because they never married, their spouse died, or they experienced divorce: www.wiserwoman. org. The bumper sticker offered by the Women's Institute for Financial Education (www. wife.org) puts it starkly: "A Man Is Not a Financial Plan." See, as well, Martha Albertson Fineman, *The Neutered Mother, the Sexual Family and Other Twentieth-Century Tragedies* (New York: Routledge, 1995); Martha Albertson Fineman, *The Autonomy Myth and a Theory of Dependency* (New York: New Press, 2005); and stories written by working mothers who opted out, only to have regrets years later once they divorced: Ruth Franklin, "The Opt-Out Problem We Don't Talk About: There's a Looming Economic Disaster for Stay-at-Home Moms Who Get Divorced." *The New Republic,* January 12, 2010, located at http:// www.tnr.com/article/the-read/81257/women-opt-out-economy-divorce.

13. Susan Faludi, *Backlash: The Undeclared War against American Women* (New York: Anchor Books, 1991).

14. Angela Onwuachi-Willig, book review: Megan Seeley, "GIRL, Fight! Fight Like a Girl: How to Be a Fearless Feminist." New York: NYU Press, 2007. *Berkeley Journal of Gender Law & Justice* 22 (2007): 254–273, 256.

15. Louise Story, "Many Women at Elite Colleges Set Career Path to Motherhood," *New York Times,* September 20, 2005. But note that this study has been critiqued as inaccurate: Jack Shafer, "A Trend so New It's Old: More on the *New York Times'* Career v. Motherhood Story," *Slate,* September 23, 2005.

16. See, for example, Ronee Schreiber, *Righting Feminism: Conservative Women and American Politics* (New York: Oxford University Press, 2008), and Kay S. Hymowitz, "Red State Feminism," *City Journal* (September 8, 2008), located at: http://www.city-journal. org/2008/eon0908kh.html.

Is "Opting Out" for Real?

1

The Rhetoric and
Reality of "Opting Out"

Toward a Better Understanding of Professional
Women's Decisions to Head Home

PAMELA STONE AND LISA ACKERLY HERNANDEZ

Introduction

Since the Industrial Revolution, when economic production moved out of the home, women have struggled to reconcile the roles, responsibilities, and day-to-day activities of productive and reproductive labor. They have used a variety of strategies, the parameters of which have been defined by their class, race, and immigrant status. Recently, attention has focused on a seemingly new work-family strategy, "opting out," which is identified with the most privileged beneficiaries of the women's movement, college-educated professional women. In this chapter, we deconstruct "opting out," first by providing the historical context in which to understand women's changing labor force participation (LFP) and the bases of difference that have historically defined women's paid work outside the home. We then address the media's claim that we are witnessing an "opt-out revolution" and provide evidence that challenges this claim, both with respect to the extent of "opting out" and its representation. Finally, we analyze the term as a mischaracterization at worst and exaggeration at best of actual trends, and as a potentially damaging euphemism that obscures the common dilemmas facing all women, even advantaged women, in their ongoing efforts to combine paid employment and family.

Historical Trends and Variations
Work, Family, Class, Status, and Race

Historically, more privileged women adopted and promulgated a work-family strategy based on the cult of true womanhood, elaborated on an ideology of separate spheres that maintained and glorified a strict divide between home and market (see Amott and Matthaei [1996] and Kessler-Harris [2003] on this point and for a comprehensive historical overview of women and work). Marriage to relatively affluent men with stable employment made it possible for them to remain almost exclusively on the home side of the divide until the middle of the twentieth century. By virtue of their class and race privilege, middle- and upper-middle-class white women were (and arguably still are) arbiters of gender norms, defining the male breadwinner model as the cultural desideratum and benchmark. White working-class women, aspiring to the middle class, but unable to forgo earnings, skirted the work-family divide by performing less visible work for pay at home, such as running boarding houses, or working intermittently as the need arose. To avoid the stigma attached to being a working wife or mother, they had jobs, not careers, and their employment was positioned as "pin money" secondary to that of their husbands. Their labor force participation was intermittent and episodic, often interrupted for family needs for which they had primary responsibility, the hiring of domestic help not being an option, as it was for even middle-class women well into the twentieth century.

The marginalized and outsider status of low-income white women, women of color, and immigrant women largely exempted them from strict adherence to middle-class gender norms. African American women, in particular, evolved an alternative conception of work and family which saw economic provision for their children as a central part of motherhood, not in conflict with it. Women in these groups worked, some almost exclusively in private households, doing acceptable "women's work" in the domestic sphere. They had relatively high labor force participation rates, even as mothers, but found their opportunities constrained by the double disadvantages of gender and race, which confined them to low-wage job ghettoes offering little in the way of job tenure or security. Facing limited job options and vulnerable to unemployment, as well as shouldering considerable caregiving responsibilities, often as single mothers, they moved in and out of the labor force.

During the latter half of the twentieth century, women of all backgrounds were increasingly incorporated into the paid labor market, a development that on its face would seem to signal an erosion of separate spheres ideology and blurring of the home-work divide. Yet in these more recent trends, the throwback to and tensions of separate spheres ideology can still be discerned, with persistent variations by class and race. Even as work became increasingly universal among women, their paid employment continued to observe the shapes and contours of family life, with the normative divide—

the inflection point at which it became unacceptable to comingle the spheres of work and family—being gradually pushed back to later stages of the family life cycle. Among the middle and upper-middle classes, single women could work until they married and, still later, wives could work after marriage, but not past motherhood. Only in the 1970s did this last barrier fall and mothers begin to work fairly continuously throughout their childbearing and childrearing years.

College-Educated Women, Work, and Family

Also during the 1970s, the women's movement and the growth of professional and managerial employment gave women, especially college-educated women, new options and opportunities. With these new options came new obligations, as professional careers, built on a male breadwinner model, required high levels of work commitment and continuity. Economic historian Claudia Goldin (1997) has documented the changing work-family configurations of college-educated women during the twentieth century. She has found that sequencing rather than simultaneity was the prevailing pattern for women seeking to combine work and motherhood. (Sequencing refers to a strategy whereby women pursue one or the other, typically working before having children, then leaving work in order to focus exclusively on childrearing, and possibly returning to work after their children leave the home). Goldin identified four distinct phases in the evolution of college-educated women's patterns of labor force participation (Goldin 2006). Phase 1 occurred from the late nineteenth century to the 1920s and was characterized by the young, independent, unmarried female worker who generally never expected to have a career and typically exited the workforce once she married. Phase 2, a transition era, lasted from about 1930 to 1950. This phase saw a marked increase in the labor force participation of married women, especially after the 1940s, when the marriage bar, which had prevented married women from working in many professions, had largely disappeared and part-time work options became more prevalent. Women in Phase 2, however, still did not intend to have careers, but rather to work only as the needs of their families permitted. Goldin characterizes Phase 3, from 1950 to the mid- to late 1970s, as the "roots of the revolution." During Phase 3, married women's labor force participation rates continued to rise, but they remained secondary earners. What distinguished women of this era from women in Phase 2 was the fact that they underestimated their future labor force participation while they were young, anticipating working only until they had families, but generally exceeding those expectations, working outside the home for a significant portion of their lives. She dates Phase 4, the "quiet revolution," as beginning in the late 1970s, when the birth cohorts of the late 1940s were in their early thirties, and continuing to the present. It was during this phase that women began to more accurately predict their future labor force participation and to anticipate combining work and family throughout their family formation and childbearing years.

Thus, it is only relatively recently (over the past thirty-five years) that women of the educated, professional class transcended centuries of adherence to separate spheres ideology and the male breadwinner model of family to envision, anticipate, and live lives in which they would simultaneously combine work and family. More recent research extends Goldin's, showing that for professional women with children, both labor force participation and employment are increasing across successive cohorts through Generation X, which encompasses women born between 1966 and 1975 (Percheski 2008). In fact, college-educated women, the group whose "quiet revolution" with regard to work and family is the most recent, now show the highest rates of labor force participation among mothers and nonmothers alike (Boushey 2008).

Convergence and Slowdown

The vantage point of the early twenty-first century makes clear that while the opportunities available to women of different statuses were (and remain) markedly different, their experiences with respect to engagement in paid work outside the home have increasingly converged, with the white middle and upper-middle class looking more and more like their less advantaged sisters—working more and more continuously, marriage and motherhood no longer a basis for work interruption. The changes Goldin describes among educated middle- and upper-middle-class white women can be seen in Figure 1.1. In the 1960s and 1970s, women worked at relatively high rates during their early twenties, their LFP rates dropping during the prime childbearing years (25 to 39), then rising again during their forties as children aged and nests emptied. Nowadays, women's LFP rates show more consistency and no marked "time out" for motherhood throughout their twenties to forties, the peak childbearing years; in fact, their age-LFP profile is quite similar in shape to men's (not shown).

Figure 1.1. Age-Specific Labor Force Participation Rates for Women 1960–2008

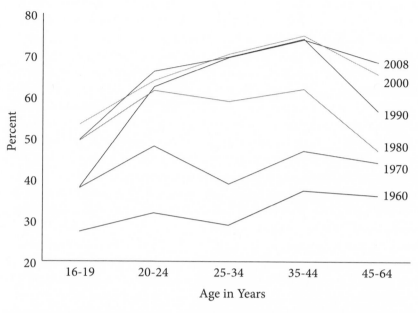

Source: U.S. Bureau of Labor Statistics, Bulletin 2217; and Basic Tabulations, Table 12

The mid-1990s, however, witnessed a slowdown in the decades-long increase in married women's, especially mothers', labor force participation (see, for example, Mosisa and Hipple 2006). The most pronounced drop (on the order of 9 percent) occurred among college-educated mothers of infants during a short period in the latter part of the decade, 1997–2000 (Cohany and Sok 2007). The reasons behind this change are as yet unclear, although there is an emerging consensus that motherhood per se played a smaller role than other factors, such as rising husbands' income, unemployment, and increasing workloads (e.g., Cohany and Sok 2007; Reimers and Stone 2007; Boushey 2008). Notwithstanding this dip, college-educated mothers continue to exhibit the highest LFP rates of all mothers. Dual-earner households also remain the majority (54 percent) among married couples and comprise almost two-thirds (64 percent) of married couples with children (Roehling and Moen 2003).

The Media Construction of "Opting Out" Backlash

Despite the fact that the period from the late 1970s to the mid-1990s saw mothers, especially college-educated ones who had been long-standing holdouts, working more and more continuously, as well as making significant inroads into formerly male-dominated fields, this period also saw the rise in mainstream media of stories about a supposed new and surprising counter-trend: these same women were said to be forsaking their newly gained and hard-won careers in favor of extended periods as full-time, at-home mothers. Well before women's labor force participation showed signs of leveling off in the mid-1990s, print media were reporting—and exaggerating the extent of—this purported new trend. A 1992 article in *Barron's*, for example, a leading business publication, proclaimed an "exodus" of women from the workforce (Mahar 1992). Faludi (1991) was among the first to note this developing story line, which she cited as one of the prime examples of media "backlash" against feminism in her book of the same name. The larger agenda of these stories, Faludi convincingly argued, was antifeminism, their "gotcha" point being that the very women who were supposed to be the greatest beneficiaries—as well as role models and standard bearers—of the feminist movement were turning their backs on some of its most dearly held goals: the erosion of separate spheres ideology; the integration of work and family; and the movement of women into professional and other jobs formerly closed to them.

Another feminist media analyst, Walters (1995), extended Faludi's critique to argue that these stories exemplified not only an antifeminist stance, but a dangerous "postfeminism" couched in the language of female liberation (i.e., choice), but antithetical to and undermining of feminist goals. Other feminist analysts, for example Barnett and Rivers (1996), who decried these stories as promulgating dangerous myths, as well as Williams (2000) and Crittenden (2001), took note of the increasing attention by the media to the phenomenon that would later be called "opting out." They noted too that the media positioned women's decisions in terms of "choice rhetoric" and as reflecting changing tastes and preferences in favor of domesticity (e.g., Williams 2000).

Analysis of "Opting Out" as Portrayed by the Print Media

These observations are supported by a systematic analysis of print media (Kuperberg and Stone 2008), which showed that numerous articles on the subject of women leaving careers for motherhood appeared in a range of high circulation, general interest publications such as major newspapers and newsweeklies during the sixteen-year period between 1988 and 2003 (the year the term "opting out" was coined in an article in the *New York Times* [Belkin 2003]). While the *Times* piece was notable for bestowing the phenomenon with a catchy and defining name, it was otherwise identical to earlier articles in theme and imagery (Kuperberg and Stone 2008).

Virtually all these stories focused on a clearly defined group. The "opt-out" demographic was white, college-educated, married women with children who had formerly worked in professional jobs. For the *Times* story, for instance, the majority of women profiled were white Princeton alumnae belonging to an Atlanta book group. Kuperberg and Stone (2008) found that among the 80 women whose prior careers were identified in the articles they analyzed, jobs included business executive, lawyer, vice president, journalist, CEO, economist, engineer, college professor, television producer, and even a member of the U.S. House of Representatives. Not surprisingly, given these backgrounds, articles on "opting out" typically positioned the women profiled as role models and cast their decisions in a favorable and approving light. Just over half of the articles took the form of editorials, advice columns, or other first-person accounts. The authors' authority and credibility were enhanced by their name recognition or the strength of their resumés prior to quitting.

These stories of professional, accomplished women leaving their careers to care for their children were indeed characterized by extensive use of "choice rhetoric" to explain and frame women's decisions to leave their careers. In addition to Lisa Belkin's (2003) "The Opt-Out Revolution" about women "opting," choice imagery appeared in earlier titles such as "Why can't you respect my *choice*?" and "More couples *choose* a one-job lifestyle" [emphasis added]. Finally, the articles illustrated what Douglas and Michaels (2004) have identified as the "new momism" in their preoccupation with motherhood. Motherhood, children, and families were repeatedly positioned in opposition to careers and as the reason, typically the sole reason, behind women's decisions to quit, illustrated by titles such as "*Mothers trade* paycheck for time at home" and "Top PepsiCo executive picks *family over* job" [emphasis added]. The defining *Times* article reflected both themes, choice and family, its cover photo showing a woman with a baby in her lap seated at the bottom of a ladder to nowhere and the line: "Why don't more women get to the top? They *choose* [emphasis added] not to."

A New Line of Feminist Commentary

The *Times* article galvanized renewed attention to "opting out" and reignited the earlier feminist critique. As before, much commentary questioned the existence of such a trend as well as the reasons attributed to women's decisions to leave their careers. This time, however, the slowdown in women's labor force participation, especially among college-educated mothers, had been registered, giving the thesis greater credibility and prompting new lines of attack. In an effort to minimize the impact of the *Times* story, "opting out," to the extent that it existed, was said to apply only to a small, elite group of women, and the article was criticized as "me and my friends journalism" (Graff 2007). A number of feminist observers accepted the depiction as accurate, attacking not the messengers (i.e., the media), but the women who were their subjects (see especially Hirshman 2006; Bennetts 2008). Former professionals, now at-home mothers, were denounced as traitors to the feminist cause whose "choices" and embrace of "choice feminism" betrayed naïveté at best and delusion at worst. The decision to stay home was criticized for creating a new, self-imposed glass ceiling, stymieing progress toward gender equality, and resulting in the loss of role models as well as the talents of these educated, high-achieving women.

Propelled by the backlash against second-wave feminism and the emergence of new "choice" feminism—which acknowledges the gains of the second wave, but is less focused on the goal of economic equality than on women having the freedom to choose among a variety of options—and, later, given limited basis in fact by short-term trends suggesting a slowdown in women's labor force participation, "opting out" is a media-created and media-driven phenomenon. It was given further plausibility by the ascendance, over roughly the same period, of intensive mothering practices—whereby mothers spend inordinate amounts of time and energy nurturing their children's developing senses of autonomy and self-esteem—a development recognized in both scholarly (Hays 1996; Lareau 2003) and popular literatures (Pearson 2002; Warner 2005). In combination, this mix gave the "opting out" narrative continuing durability. The counterintuitive turnabout by a group of women who had made significant investments in their careers and seemingly rejected "having it all" provided a newsworthy hook. And their actions appeared to dovetail with a political climate that saw the rise of conservative "family values" and efforts to promote traditional family forms. Women of the "opt-out" revolution were positioned by the media (typically favorably, except for the critics noted above) as being at the vanguard of a neotraditionalist resurgence, returning to an earlier era akin to Gold-in's (2006) third phase, during which women, especially educated women, "put away" their careers for motherhood in favor of a life of (at least tempo-rary) economic dependence on their husbands, a return to the sequencing and separate spheres of an earlier era. Further novel and newsworthy, their decision to "go home" was depicted not as a reflection of constrictive gender roles, but rather as a manifestation of lifestyle preferences that found fulfill-ment in domesticity over conventional definitions of professional success.

What is the reality of highly educated and professional women in the workforce? In the next section, we examine recent trends in "opting out" among the women who are said to be adopting this strategy. We then turn to an in-depth analysis of the reasons behind these women's decisions to "opt out," a characterization that is belied by the evidence.

Assessing Recent Trends in "Opting Out"
Operationalizing "Opting Out"

While there is no explicit definition of "opting out" in the media coverage of the phenomenon, the emerging definition is of a decision to take a pro-longed period of time out of the labor force in order to take care of children. As depicted in the media, "opting out" is, in its most basic form, a decision to allocate one's labor away from paid employment to focus exclusively on the unpaid work of caring or, to use the more pejorative language of labor economics, to "drop out" of the workforce. In the context of the educated, professional women who are portrayed as adopting this strategy, it is a deci-sion to interrupt or possibly terminate a career, with attendant costs in terms of forgone earnings and advancement. Positioned as a lifestyle choice, "opt-ing out" does not refer to the short-term interruption of parental leave dur-ing the months immediately before and after childbirth, typically around one to three months, but rather to a longer, more sustained interruption during which women devote themselves exclusively to domesticity, primarily child-care, making their husbands the sole earners in the family.

While most research on trends in "opting out" focuses on labor force participation (LFP, which indicates whether a woman was working or looking for work either last week or last year), it is a somewhat imperfect proxy. First, it references the allocation of labor exclusively to paid employ-ment and second, it fails to take into account alternatives to being in the labor force other than at-home motherhood. In fact, among women fitting the "opt-out" demographic, about 2 to 4 percent of those who are out of the labor force are students or disabled, as opposed to full-time, at-home caregivers (Reimers and Stone 2007). Thus, we use an alternative indicator, which we believe is a better and more direct measure of "opting out": whether or not women stayed at home in the prior year to take care of home and family. This indicator both references the behavior associated with "opting out" and reflects a sustained period out of the labor force. It also tracks LFP trends closely, albeit as a mirror image (see Reimers and Stone 2007).

It is important to underscore the extent to which "opting out" is a strategy identified in the media with privilege and discretion, both of which are typically afforded by women's own class backgrounds and professional accomplishments as well as by marriage to a professional or manager. Thus, as our media analysis revealed, "opting out" is a class- and race-specific strategy (as well as a heteronormative one). Merely being out of the labor force and taking care of home and family is not synonymous with "opting out." Whatever the faults (or merits) of the media depiction, our reading leads us to conclude that it does not apply to every mother, nor is any period out of the labor force for whatever reason equated with "opting out." For example, the high-school-educated mother who quits her low-paying job because she can no longer afford child care or the single mother who is laid off and unable to find another job is not positioned by the media as "opting out." As a result, we restrict our analysis to the group of women who are—white, college-educated, married mothers—in order to provide a more targeted and accurate look at trends in this behavior.

Recent Trends in "Opting Out"

An examination of national trends among white, college-educated, married mothers ages 22 to 59 using nationally representative data available from the Current Population Surveys (Figure 1.2) shows that "opting out" has unequivocally declined, from 25.2 percent in 1981 to 21.3 percent in 2005. The trend is complicated, however, because the period of the mid-1990s shows a turnaround like that seen for LFP: after a period of steep decline, hitting a low of 16.5 percent in 1993, "opting out" increases. Notably, fully 90 percent of the 4.8 percentage point increase between 1993 and 2005 occurred during the three-year period between 1999 and 2002.

The concentrated and abrupt nature of this turnaround seems inconsistent with the notion that it represents a lifestyle choice or preference shift in favor of domesticity, the story line favored by the media, because such

Figure 1.2. Rates of "Opting Out" among College-Educated
Married Mothers, 1981–2005

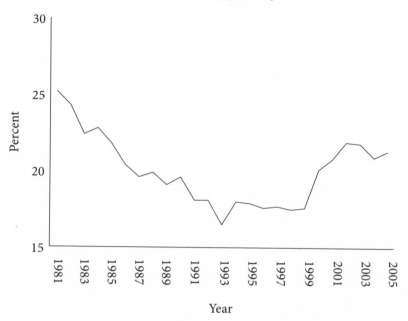

Source: March Current Population Survey, 1982-2006. For details, see Reimers and Stone (2007)

shifts typically occur more slowly and across successive cohorts, much in the way Goldin (2006) described changing work and family patterns for cohorts of educated women. Even though current levels of "opting out" are still considerably below those observed twenty-five years ago and appear to be stabilizing, this short-term reversal of the long-term decline in full-time caregiving among college-educated women provides fuel for media fascination and speculation, and raises intriguing questions about the reasons for the apparent slowdown. The media drumbeat, however, overlooks the fact that despite a hiccup in the long-term rise, this same group shows otherwise extraordinarily high labor force participation rates (on the order of 75 to 80 percent). Further, recent research suggests that much of the attention on high-achieving women heading home is misplaced: the typical at-home mother is not college-educated and white, but rather Hispanic, less educated, and likely a recent immigrant (St. George 2009).

While the foregoing analysis sheds light on the question of whether or not there is a long-range upward trend of college-educated women leaving the labor force for full-time motherhood—the answer being an emphatic no—it does not enable us to assess the more contested part of the media depiction of "opting out." The claim that those who are "opting out" are doing so as the result of a preference shift, eschewing the more recent strategy of combining careers and motherhood in favor of an embrace of domestic roles and a return to the earlier strategy of sequencing (and separation) of work and family, is not addressed by these statistics. Assessment of this claim requires a fine-grained analysis of the circumstances surrounding women's decision making, to which we now turn.

Understanding Why Women "Opt Out"
About the Study

To better understand why high-achieving women "opt out," Stone (2007) conducted in-depth, life history interviews with women who met the definition of that phenomenon based on prevailing media imagery (i.e., women who had quit a professional or managerial career and were engaged in motherhood as their primary activity, with no paid employment outside the home). Further consistent with the media depiction of "opting out," the women interviewed were college-educated, upper-middle class, and had formerly worked in a broad spectrum of professions, including law, medicine, science, banking, marketing, nonprofit management, publishing, and teaching. The goal of the study was to find out more about women's reasons for quitting paid work, how they felt about being stay-at-home moms, and their future aspirations, if any, for combining work and family. The study's qualitative methodology allowed for analysis of the complicated work and family histories of these women and a deeper understanding of their actions and the meanings they attached to them. More information about the study's design and a fuller analysis and discussion of its findings, aspects of which are summarized here, are available in Stone (2007).

The Language of "Opting Out"

Despite the fact that each woman's personal story was complex and multi-layered, significant similarities emerged. Typical of Goldin's (2006) fourth phase, "quiet revolution" generation, these women (about 90 percent) aspired to combine career and family. They had usually met their husbands in college or graduate school and began their marriages on an equal professional footing. Highly educated, highly credentialed, and high-earning, they enjoyed and took pride in their professional accomplishments, and identified strongly as professionals. As a result, for the vast majority the decision to quit their careers was a struggle, not a facile or easy "choice" or option. Wendy Friedman, a former editor, put it this way,

> I would think about like well, "How could I do this?" I mean the financial was one aspect of it, but there are other aspects. Not to minimize that, but my whole identity was work. Yes, I was a mother and a wife and whatever, but this is who I was. . . . And I really thought for a long time about it. And I would think like, "How could I do this?"

Elizabeth Brand, a former management consultant, echoed that sentiment: "I had never really envisioned myself being a stay-at-home mom. I think it's just not part of the persona that I ever had."

Seventy percent of the women framed their decisions to leave work in terms of their individual preferences, adopting the choice rhetoric pervading popular media reports on "opting out" and more typical of the post–second wave feminist rhetoric of the era in which they came of age. Melissa Wyatt, a former full-time fund-raiser, described her decision to stay at home in terms of choice: "I think today it's all about choices, and the choices we want to make. And I think that's great. I think it just depends where you want to spend your time." A closer look at these women's motivations for interrupting their hard-earned careers, however, revealed much less discretion and control, and the existence of considerable workplace pressures that narrowed women's true options, creating what Stone (2007) called the "choice gap."

Workplace Pushes

Defying the media depiction that women leave professional careers to embrace a return to domesticity and traditional roles, or because they believe it to be in their families' best interests, when women talked about their decision to quit, their narratives were dominated by comments about work, not family. Issues frequently mentioned included employers' inability or unwillingness to accommodate the needs of employees with dependent children. These women worked in highly demanding professions that required intense time commitments and were characterized by expectations of an ideal (i.e., unencumbered) worker model (Williams 2000; Moen and Roehling 2005).

The experience of Rachel Berman, a former investment banker and new mother, is illustrative:

> I nursed my child, but I never left the trading floor. I never left my desk. I never pumped during the day. I went from 5:00 in the morning until 6:00 at night without expressing milk, because this is an environment, where any time you leave the floor, any time you leave your desk, you have to tell people where you're going, so that they know where to find you, in case a client or somebody should call.

Although most employers provided maternity leave (typically paid), problems arose when women returned to work after childbirth. Many employers lacked policies that would provide parents with the flexibility to attend to their family responsibilities during the normal workday. When they did exist, they were so rarely used that women's requests for part-time or other flexible work arrangements landed them in uncharted territory. About 10 percent of those who requested some kind of flexible work arrangement (typically part-time) were denied. Meg Romano, a former trader at a large investment firm, had her request rejected: "I went back to talk to them about what was next, and a part-time situation presented itself in the sales area, and I got all gung-ho for that. I got all the childcare arrangements in place, started interviewing people to watch the kids, and at the last minute the big boss wouldn't sign off on it."

Two-thirds of the women interviewed were able to negotiate part-time work or more flexible work arrangements, but their stories demonstrate that in these types of work environments, flexibility was often in name only and carried with it unseen penalties. Part-time work, therefore, was often an illusory solution. Mirra Lopez, a former engineer, explained the problem this way: "There's no overtime pay. . . . So I would have been in a position where I might be 'working 20 hours' but really working 40." Another problem posed by part-time work was its negative impact on their career trajectories, as they became marginalized through the loss of interesting work or penalized through mommy-tracking. Diane Childs, a former nonprofit executive, explained the marginalizing effects of alternative work arrangements: "And I'm never going to get anywhere—you have the feeling that you just plateaued professionally because you can't take on extra projects, you can't travel at a moment's notice. . . . You really plateau for a much longer period of time than you ever realize when you first have a baby. It's like you're going to be plateaued for 13–15 years."

The short- and long-term penalties attached to alternative, flexible work arrangements that would accommodate their family needs, not least a desire to spend time with their children, led women to the conclusion, well-founded in their own experiences and by the absence of successful role models at work, that their jobs were "all or nothing." As a result, despite wanting to continue their careers, they perceived their options in equally stark and limited terms—continue working full-time plus or quit—and ultimately "opted" for the latter course.

Family Pulls

Although workplace pushes were the primary factors influencing women's decisions to interrupt their careers, family pulls also played a part. In this era of intensive parenting (read mothering), of all their household duties, children and childcare were most often mentioned. For about one-third of the women studied, the pull of babies was especially strong and immediate. Lauren Quattrone, a former lawyer, stated, "I was just absolutely besotted with this baby. . . . I realized that I just couldn't bear to leave him." The majority of women, approximately 60 percent, continued to work after the birth of their first child. For these women, the needs of preschoolers and school-age children, rather than newborns and infants, played a role in their decision to quit. School demands figured prominently, the intensity of homework assignments and complexity of balancing extracurricular activities requiring more time and energy than these working moms' schedules allowed. Marina Isherwood, a former HMO executive, noted,

> Our children come home and they have all this homework to do, and piano lessons and this and this, and it's all a complicated schedule. And, yes, you could get an au pair to do that, to balance it all, but they're not going to necessarily teach you how to think about math. Or help you come up with mnemonic devices to help you memorize all of the counties in Spain or whatever.

In addition to homework and scheduling concerns, the women interviewed often expressed the sentiment that a parent's care was necessary for the character development of older children. As her children got older, Denise Hortas, a former pharmaceutical executive with a Ph.D., had "a sense that they [her two school-age children] were needing what I can provide and what the babysitter couldn't provide." Whether it was the emotional pull of younger children or the increasing demands of raising older children, as women's childrearing responsibilities increased and job demands either ratcheted up or proved inflexible, the balancing act became impossible, further reinforcing the perception that their options were "all or nothing."

Husbands, specifically their absence, were another factor—usually overlooked by the media—in women's decisions to quit. For husbands, too, the nature and demands of professional careers circumscribed their ability to help out with childcare and related responsibilities. Women often functioned effectively as single parents. It fell to them to manage and oversee paid caregivers or other childcare arrangements, but beyond physical caregiving and household upkeep, women were responsible for the symbolic creation of "family" and for socializing their children into the values and traditions of their class. Very few husbands (slightly less than one-third) expressed an outright preference for their wives to stay home full-time. Instead, most removed themselves from the decision making process entirely, telling their wives that "it was their choice," while making no changes in their own jobs to help their wives better accommodate work and family demands. In this way, women's roles as mothers were solidified, and women's careers were relegated to the back burner and ultimately interrupted, potentially permanently derailed.

The fact that many women were significantly outearned by their husbands or perceived their future earnings potential as lower (an accurate perception, given what we know about the wage gap and the motherhood penalty; see, for example, Stone [2009] on the former; Crittenden [2001] and Budig and England [2001] on the latter) led them to privilege their husbands' careers over their own, which ultimately contributed to the decision to quit their jobs. Diane Childs said this about why her career, not her husband's, was expendable: "There's too much money at stake at this point in time that I couldn't approach his earning power." Tricia Olsen, a former trader, described how her career took a backseat to her husband's as their daughter got older:

My husband had taken a job three months earlier with a top investment bank, and we knew his life was going to go to hell because he was in the mergers and acquisitions department. . . . And we decided that somebody should be home to be more attentive to the kids because now we had a second child . . . and that somebody was me.

Plans for the Future

Having made the difficult and unanticipated decision to head home, women experienced a challenging transition, aspects of which further belie the idea that home was a preferred destination. Particularly hard was the loss of their professional identities, which they held on to, typically self-identifying in terms of their former careers. Women were concerned about the kind of role model they were being for their children, especially their daughters, and noted with consternation and resignation the extent to which their husbands had taken advantage of their being at home to ramp up their own careers and devolve even more of the work of the household to them. Teresa Land, a former telecommunications manager, explained it this way: "[My husband] feels that his contribution, a lot of men are like this, his contribution is making money. My contribution is keeping up the home front."

Two-thirds of women planned to return to work, further attesting to their continued identification with their professions. Looking ahead, however, they confronted the costs of their decision and worried that they would have difficulty reentering after their time at home, which was seen as a liability in and of itself and because of what it meant for skill loss and depreciation. Moira Franklin, a former engineer ten years out of the labor force at the time of the study, said, "It's kind of scary out there. What do you say you've been doing for the last ten years, painting my house? . . . But here I am with an engineering degree—and I don't have e-mail. . . . [Job-hunting] would be scary." Vita Cornwall, a former banker and nonprofit executive with two graduate degrees, explained her fear about returning to the job market: "I think I'd be seen as a stereotype, and I don't want to go in with that label on my forehead." Informed both by their negative experiences in their former careers as well as newfound perspectives afforded by their time at home, women typically did not plan to return to their former employers, nor often their former fields, instead planning either to freelance or consult or train for new professions entirely, teaching being an especially popular option.

Setting the Record Straight

A more in-depth look at the reasons high-achieving women leave hard-earned careers to return home belies the media depiction of a neotraditionalist embrace of traditional gender roles and family forms. These women's experiences with "opting out" show a much more complicated picture in which the organization of the professional workplace, built as it is on a male-breadwinner model of family inherently antipathetic to dual-earner (or single-head) families, played the central role, thus creating a de facto "motherhood bar" which effectively limited their options and shut them out of sustained careers. The motherhood bar forced them instead into a sequencing strategy involving significant redirection away from (and in some cases, termination of) their former careers. Workplace pressures reflect and are reinforced by gendered expectations about work and family roles, two aspects of which are especially notable among dual professional couples as compared to other dual-earner families. The first aspect is women's lower earning potential and bargaining power vis-à-vis their high-earning husbands and its corollary, the privileging of men's careers, which is more common among professionals (Pyke 1996, Walzer 1998, Coltrane 2004). The second aspect is the extraordinarily intense and time-consuming mothering standards distinctive of this group (Lareau 2003).

Women's adoption of choice rhetoric is inconsistent with their accounts of the actual circumstances surrounding their decisions to quit their careers, but resonant with the agency and privilege afforded by their class and race. Their use of choice rhetoric, however, is not accompanied by "new traditionalist" rhetoric; indeed, not only is their decision to quit and head home *not* occasioned primarily by family pulls, but women voiced concerns and reservations throughout the interviews about the extent to which their decisions appeared to emulate or reinforce traditional gender arrangements and dynamics (Stone 2007).

An analysis of national trends (macro evidence) and a fine-grained examination of women's lives and narratives (micro evidence) confirm the major critiques of the media construction of the phenomenon that has come to be called "opting out." Decades-long trends reveal neither a revolution nor an exodus, but rather a slowdown among a group of women whose labor force participation had until the mid- to late 1990s shown an especially rapid rate of increase. The overall trend in "opting out" among women fitting this demographic is downward, and at-home mothers are the minority of college-educated women (on the order of 20 percent). In-depth interviews with women who are at home, presumably having "opted out," refute the notion that their decisions are a reflection of, or motivated primarily by, motherhood, much less by a more expansive embrace of domesticity or of separate spheres ideology. Instead, educated women have moved beyond separate spheres in their aspirations, intentions, and behavior. Their "opting out" is a response to obstacles to the integration of work and family, not a "choice" among viable options.

In its focus on a small, elite minority and its accompanying story line of a return to tradition, "opting out" provides a narrative consistent with the work-family system characteristic of professional and managerial work and workers. In its emphasis on individual choices in favor of family, it deflects attention from the culture and organization of work. When properly contextualized, however, an alternative explanation emerges. This behavior, which appears on its face to be neotraditional, is better understood as a reflection of the workplace's failure to keep up with the contemporary realities of women's lives. "Opting out" rhetoric ignores the real problems even educated, privileged working mothers continue to encounter in the workplace and that undermine their career attachment. The true culprits are: the ideal worker concept of job commitment; a dearth of positive role models; inadequate policies to accommodate employees with dependent children; mommy-tracking; a persistent gender wage gap; and the ongoing gendered division of labor in the home that defines caregiving as women's work. All these problems are made to disappear in stories about "opting out."

"Opting out" imagery also misses the mark in terms of defining women's intentions. The media depiction of "opting out" has portrayed professional women as throwing in the towel as it relates to their careers, educations, and often highly specialized skills. They supposedly want out—out of their professions, out of the rat race, and back into the traditional role of mother. Most of the women interviewed, however, put forth significant efforts to make employment work, whether through requests for part-time work, job sharing, or other alternative work arrangements. In light of the commitment these women exhibited to their professions, the notion is deeply flawed that they "opted out" in order to escape the demands of the workplace and to eschew their financial responsibilities in favor of a leisurely life at home.

"Opting Out" as Controlling Imagery
Separate Spheres Redux

Despite the media's exaggeration and misrepresentation of this phenomenon, the ubiquity and persistence of the prevailing understanding of "opting out," rooted as it is in the dominant gender ideology of centuries, suggests that it is becoming what Collins (1991: 68) calls a "controlling image," designed to reinforce sexism by making traditional gender roles seem natural and normal. Reminiscent of separate spheres in its rhetoric of trade off and exchange, "opting out" embodies a highly polarized construction of work and family. With career and childrearing positioned as mutually exclusive, sequencing also seems "natural." Indeed, when the women Stone (2007) studied announced their decision to quit, they were typically congratulated by their bosses and colleagues, despite the loss their quitting represented to the women themselves and their firms. Younger generations of high-achieving women are said to anticipate "opting out" (Story 2005), seeing it as a solution to, not a problematic symptom of, the work-family dilemma. And while young adults desire more egalitarian arrangements around work and family, they are pessimistic about their ability to live them, envisioning that women's employment will take a back seat to that of their husbands (Gerson 2010).

Consistent with this notion that "opting out" is "natural," one of the most popular responses to the perceived brain drain of talented women in the corporate world is the policy known as on- and off-ramping, in which (typically) women take time off from work, generally for family-related reasons, maintain ties with their former employers, and then reenter the work force at a later date (Hewlett 2007). While there is a need for leave policies to address short-term, unforeseen, or emergency needs, a strategy that sidelines working mothers effectively removes the problem, undermines the impetus for change, and shifts employers' attention away from much-needed reforms that do *not* revolve around (or legitimate) interruption and trade off. Rather than sequencing or on- and off-ramping, a more responsive answer to the question of what women truly want would be policies that allow them to combine work and family and persist in their careers, such as shorter work weeks, enhanced flexibility and control, and better part-time options.

The imagery surrounding "opting out" and policies such as off-ramping reinforce the idea that women are marginal, uncommitted workers and provide an enduring rationale for statistical discrimination (women will "only leave anyway," the refrain that formerly shut them out of the professions) and more overt forms of discrimination such as the now well-documented motherhood penalty (Crittenden 2001; Budig and England 2001; Correll, Benard, and Paik 2007). By positioning women as taking "time out" during the prime years of career advancement, women's workforce exits and career interruptions clear the field for men to advance, the "leaky pipeline" of women's own choices further perpetuating the male breadwinner-dominated professional workplace unresponsive to caregiving and family.

The oppositional, separate spheres positioning implicit in "opting out" maps onto and reinforces the public-private distinction often associated with the work-family system, further exempting employers and the state from responsibility for workplace reforms that address family and caregiving needs. Thus, in the United States—the only wealthy, industrialized nation in the world that does not mandate paid parental leave, much less a host of other supports to working women and families (Gornick and Meyers 2003)—"opting out" provides an especially apt narrative and a compelling justification for a continued hands-off, privatized approach.

Euphemism and Doublespeak

"Opting out" and associated terminologies that have been used to characterize similar behavior, such as "sequencing" (Cardozo 1986) and "off-ramping" and "on-ramping" (Hewlett 2007), share the imagery of agency, discretion, ease, facility, and flow, making women's movement appear effortless as they go in and out of the labor force, between work and family. Waving the magic wand of "choice," such euphemistic doublespeak fails to reveal "opting out" for what it truly represents: difficult choices and jarring transitions followed by costly career interruption—a process not of self-realization, but rather of accommodation to the particular pressures of professional careers. Further maintaining this illusion, any mention of the difficulties of "opting in" or resuming employment is notably absent from the "opting out" narrative.

While the associated imagery is of ease of exit and reentry, limited research on the subject shows just the opposite to be the case. Women's fears and lack of confidence about returning to work appear to be well-founded, for reentry is typically lengthy and difficult, and women often transition back to the labor force via marginal jobs (McGrath, Driscoll, and Gross 2005). A study of highly qualified professional women who had taken a career break found that while 93 percent of them sought to return to work, only 74 percent were successful. From this vantage point, "opting out" loses the cachet of innovative choice conferred by the media depiction and can be seen more clearly as loss, disruption, and redirection.

Labels matter. Earlier generations of women who spent time at home and then sought to return to work (typically because of divorce or widowhood) were called "displaced homemakers." While the circumstances prompting reentry differ, the realities confronting women who "opt out" and seek to return to work are, in fact, fairly similar to those faced by displaced homemakers. By jettisoning a label that evokes economic dependence, vulnerability and victimization, "opting out" obscures the risks and costs attached to this strategy. Obscured too is another very real risk, that is, that today's "opt outers" may themselves become "displaced homemakers" through widowhood, divorce, or husband's disability.

Demonizing and Dividing

In its disproportionate and, in light of actual trends, misplaced attention to college-educated, high-achieving women, "opting out" imagery ignores the sweeping and pronounced changes in beliefs and behavior among elite women in favor of an inaccurate and trite understanding of work and family. It also overlooks their very real and pioneering efforts (even if sometimes unsuccessful) to challenge prevailing workplace practices in their prestigious fields. In the power of its story line, "opting out" positions high-achieving women not as the change agents they are, but as throwbacks, casting suspicion on their work and career commitment and undercutting their potential leadership in workplace reform.

More invidiously perhaps, by identifying white women of the middle and upper-middle class with the desire to be full-time mothers to the exclusion of having careers, "opting out" coverage continues a long-standing practice in the media of positioning elite women as arbiters of gender norms and of associating motherhood with class and race privilege. Motherhood, especially "good mothering," is at-home and identified with whiteness, while working and working motherhood, or "bad mothering," is associated with women of color. There is probably no more compelling illustration of this identification than the coincidence of timing that saw, over roughly the same period of the 1980s and 1990s, the rise of "opting out" stories—affluent white women eschewing work—coincident with the debate over welfare reform and the passage of the Personal Responsibility and Work Reconciliation Act of 1996, which demonized low-income at-home mothers of color as "welfare queens" who should go out to work.

This identification of "opting out" with a privileged elite also plays to long-standing divisions that balkanize women and obscure their commonalities. The exclusive focus of the "opting out" story line on white, middle and upper-middle class professionals leaves little room for attention to the work-family challenges shouldered by those who are less privileged and have fewer resources with which to fashion solutions. Less powerful, and deemed less newsworthy, their caregiving crises go unreported and unacknowledged.

Unfortunately (and ironically, at a historical moment when educated women look more like less privileged women than ever before with regard to work and family), some feminist critics unintentionally contribute to this balkanization by buying into the individualist rhetoric of "opting out" and/ or by emphasizing the exceptionality of women who have supposedly done so. Thus, the "choice" narrative and seeming abandonment of second-wave feminist goals implied by "opting out" also fuels gender wars: the "mommy wars" of "working" moms against stay-at-home moms and the ideological and generational wars of second-wave, typically older feminists against third-wave, typically younger ones. Less remarked on, "opting out" also sets the stage for a battle of the sexes, since "opting out" takes as unproblematic that well-educated women are entitled to quit lucrative jobs, stay home, and be economically dependent on their husbands' earnings, a bait and switch that increases pressures on men to be breadwinners.

Finding Common Ground

Real and consequential differences among women mean that different groups have different strategies available to them as they seek to integrate their work and family, earning and caring responsibilities. Elite professionals of the sort who are said to be "opting out" actually have more control over their conditions of work and experience greater access to work-family benefits than other workers, but in today's ever-escalating professional workplace (Jacobs and Gerson 2004), these advantages cannot offset the long hours and other requisites of these jobs, such as face time, travel, and 24/7 accountability, that make them difficult to combine with motherhood. Working-class couples use alternating shifts and tag-team parenting (Presser 2003). Workers in low-wage jobs, with no control over the conditions of work, no vacation or sick days, and little bargaining power, lose or quit jobs and cycle in and out of the labor force to meet their family needs (Heymann 2000, Drago 2007). While the options and strategies differ, they are symptomatic of the same fundamental problem, work-family incompatibility, and what Rosanna Hertz (2004) has called the "hegemonic culture" of the workplace, with families, especially women, bearing the burden of accommodation in the absence of public or employer-provided supports to working families.

"Opting out" plays into class and race divisions, generational disputes, and gender wars. It obscures women's common underlying struggle to be both worker and mother. The controlling imagery and mythic proportions of "opting out" focus attention on and glorify a return to traditional gender roles and to family the way we never were (Coontz 1992). Demolishing the myth requires that we see it for what it really is, and not be blinded to the universality of the problem it obscures—the still "stalled revolution" that Hochschild (1989) identified two decades ago. From "working for pin money" to "opting out," cultural constructions of women's work repeatedly embrace language that minimizes, devalues, stigmatizes, and marginalizes women's work outside the home. "Opting out" is but a new variation on an old theme, a correct understanding of which reveals the limits of even privileged women to challenge and change the interlocking institutions of work and family. It also opens up possibilities for cross-class and cross-race alliances to realize policies that would benefit working families across-the-board, such as child-care, reform of wage and hour laws, enhanced part-time and flexible work opportunities, part-time parity, and parental leave. While one could argue, by virtue of their advantaged position, that educated women have a special obligation and leadership role to play in these efforts, the realization of such policies will only be made possible by a coalition that transcends the kinds of divisions that "opting out" both rests on and perpetuates.

The Real "Opt-Out Revolution" and a New Model of Flexible Careers

KERSTIN AUMANN AND ELLEN GALINSKY

In recent years, there has been a great deal of discussion about the "opt-out revolution"—the notion that educated, professional women with small children choose to leave the workplace to focus on their families instead of their careers (Belkin, 2003). The basic thesis of the opt-out revolution has been challenged on a number of fronts, including whether it is an accurate reflection of the changes among women with and without children in their labor force participation (e.g., Kreider and Elliott, 2009; Graff, 2007; Boushey, 2005). In this chapter, we argue that the debate has missed a very important point. Because there has been a focus on women who *leave* the workforce, the opt-out debate has neglected a more significant trend with far-reaching implications among those who *remain* in the workforce. New data from the National Study of the Changing Workforce (NSCW), a nationally representative telephone survey of the American workforce conducted by the Families and Work Institute every five years, show that a number of employees—women and men alike—are "opting out" of wanting to move up the traditional career ladder to positions with increasing levels of responsibility. This presents a serious challenge for employers who continue to see career progression as a ladder and yet who need to develop and manage the talents of future leaders to ensure that their organization will both survive and thrive over the long term.

We propose that diminished career aspirations among American employees reflect a different kind of revolution that deserves attention and should redefine the opt-out debate. The discussion should be extended beyond women who choose to leave the workforce to include both women and men who are employed, but do not desire to advance to jobs with more responsibility. Further, it should focus on a notion of *flexible careers*, acknowledging that employees' career aspirations are fluid as individuals move through different life stages and are faced with different issues and tasks in their lives on and off the job. Thus, career paths should be viewed as dynamic and flexible as individuals negotiate work and personal responsibilities in various life stages—this might include increasing engagement and commitment at work, seeking advancement at some times while scaling back work hours and career aspirations or temporarily leaving the workforce at other times. A few forward-looking companies have noted this reality among their employees and one corporation, Deloitte, has replaced the notion of a "career ladder" with a "career lattice" (Benko and Weisberg, 2007). At the Families and Work Institute, we use the term "flexible careers."

We begin this chapter by presenting NSCW data from 1992 to 2008 on employees' desire to advance to jobs with more responsibility and showing that we can no longer assume that most employees generally have a desire to advance to jobs with greater responsibility. Given that traditional approaches to career development assuming a linear trajectory of jobs with increasing levels of responsibility no longer adequately seem to capture the reality of much of the American workforce, we then argue that a framework for thinking about careers and desire for advancement as flexible, dynamic constructs is needed. We argue that employees' career aspirations are ultimately a function of the interaction between individual and environmental factors. Thus, to understand how employees' career aspirations may change over time, we need to consider factors at multiple levels: the macrolevel sociocultural and economic context as well as the workplace and the individual level, examining their effects on the psychological processes by which individuals derive meaning from their experiences on and off the job and develop a desire for jobs with more, or the same, or less responsibility. After proposing a multilevel framework for flexible careers, we draw on NSCW data to examine emerging macrolevel trends in gender roles and their impact on individuals at work and at home. Further, we present some NSCW data to highlight relationships between the proposed psychological processes that shape employees' desired level of responsibility at work. We conclude by discussing how workplace effectiveness and person-organization fit can help make work "work" for employees at various stages of their careers and personal lives.

The Career Aspirations of Employees in the United States Have Changed over Time

A comparison of NSCW data from 1992 to 2008 on employees' desire to advance to jobs with more responsibility reveals that desire for career advancement, defined in the way that it is traditionally defined—as pro-

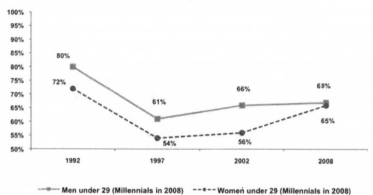

Figure 2.1. Young Men's and Women's Desire to Advance to
Jobs with Greater Responsibility, 1992–2008 (N = 598)

Source: 1992, 1997, 2002, and 2008 National Study of the Changing Workforce (NSCW),
Families and Work Institute (FWI).

motions to jobs with a greater scope of responsibility (Hall, 2002), has
generally and significantly decreased within the U.S. workforce (Galinsky,
Aumann, and Bond, 2009a). In 1992, when the NSCW first asked about
employees' desire to advance to jobs with more responsibility, the majority
(54%) indicated they wanted jobs with greater responsibility. By 2008, only
about 41% of employees did so. The pattern of decline held for employees
of both genders and among three age groups—under age 29 (Millennials in
2008), age 29–42 (Generation X in 2008), and age 43–62 (Baby Boomers in
2008).

A closer look at the data on employees' desire for career advancement
reveals two striking new trends. First, the data show that in 2008, young
women (under age 29) were just as likely as their male counterparts to want
to advance to jobs with more responsibility. This was not the case among
employees under age 29 in 1992, when significantly more men under age 29
wanted jobs with greater responsibility (80%) than women under age 29 (72%).
Figure 2.1 depicts a comparison between employed women and men under
age 29—Millennials in 2008—in their desire for jobs with more responsibility from 1992 to 2008. By 2008, the desire for jobs with more responsibility had declined among all young employees, with the lowest point being
recorded in 1997.

The Real "Opt-Out Revolution" and a New Model of Flexible Careers | 59

The highest drop in employees' desire for greater responsibility occurred between 1992 and 1997 at a time when there was a great deal of discussion about increasing job pressure. Research findings from the Families and Work Institute, for example, revealed that job pressure intensified in those intervening years (Bond, Galinsky, and Swanberg, 1998). Thus, as we explore later in this chapter, the decline may be a function of shifting values around work and family life in response to mounting job pressure. However, because we did not have questions in our study that directly asked employees *why* they did not want to move to jobs with more responsibility in 1992 and 1997, we can only examine reasons for this decline theoretically. Since 1997, there has been a slight increase. As depicted in Figure 2.1, the increase has been greater among young women (from 54% to 65%) than young men (from 61% to 68%). This finding challenges the central notion of the opt-out revolution as it is traditionally depicted—that young women who are employed want to leave the workforce. Instead it reveals that young women want to opt out of career progression as it is implemented in many workplaces. This finding also reveals that young women's career aspirations, in fact, are now not only equal with those of young men, but they also show a more marked increase. The real opt-out revolution needs to be reconceptualized and it needs to include men.

A second striking trend supports our challenge to the thesis of the traditional notion of the opt-out revolution. We find that young women with and without children are equal in their desire to move to jobs with more responsibility. This represents a significant change since 1992 when young women with children were far less likely than young women without children to want jobs with more responsibility. In fact, desire to advance among young women with children is at its highest level since we started asking this question in 1992. These findings are depicted in Figure 2.2. While our data include only women who are currently employed, it suggests that these young women do not become less likely to want to advance in their jobs when they become mothers.

In 2008, the NSCW for the first time asked those who did not want to advance to jobs with more responsibility *why* this was the case. Their responses point to some of the same reasons that are associated with the opt-out revolution—24% of Millennial, Generation X, and Baby Boomer employees who do not wish for jobs with more responsibility cite concerns about the increased job pressures that come with such jobs. Further, 19% say they already have a high-level job with a lot of responsibility and 8% are concerned about not having enough flexibility to successfully manage their

Figure 2.2. Desire to Advance to Jobs with More Responsibility Among
Young Women With and Without Children

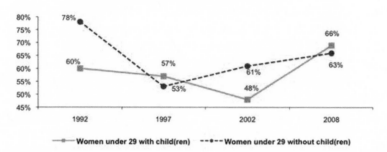

Source: 1992, 1997, 2002, and 2008 NSCW, FWI.

responsibilities at work and their personal or family lives. While the feeling
that they already have a job with a lot of responsibility does not differ among
the generations, Millennial women (under age 29) are more likely than others (31%) to say that they are concerned about increased job pressures and
are worried about not having enough flexibility to successfully manage their
work and personal lives (14%).

Perhaps surprisingly, men and women are equally likely (24% and 25%,
respectively) to cite concerns about increased job pressure as a reason for
not wanting more responsibility. This finding holds for men and women
of all generations. Employees with children under age 18 are more likely
to say they do not want jobs with more responsibility because of concerns
over increased job pressure (28%) than employees without children (21%).
All in all, the data suggest that employees today perceive jobs with high
levels of responsibility as less desirable—possibly because it is harder to
balance these jobs with personal or family lives now than it was a decade
or so ago. In fact, as we summarize briefly below and discuss in more
detail later in this chapter, both work and family life have changed in
ways that can make it more difficult for employees to successfully manage
a demanding job and personal responsibilities—at least at certain stages
in life.

Some of these changes in work and family life are dramatic. For example, over the past three decades (1980 to 2010), women have made strides
toward educational and occupational equality with men. According to the
U.S. Department of Education's National Center for Education Statistics,
women have been earning more bachelor's degrees than men since 1982 and
more master's degrees than men since 1981. In addition, findings from the

2002 NSCW study revealed that women were more likely than men to work in managerial or professional occupations (Bond, Thompson, Galinsky, and Prottas, 2003). Still, women have certainly not broken through the so-called glass ceiling, as is evident from the persistence of the gender gap in earnings and the scarcity of women in high-level executive management (e.g., BLS, 2006, 2009; Helfat, Harris, and Wolfson, 2006). However, a culture of egalitarian values around gender is emerging (Galinsky et al., 2009a). Dual-earner couples and employed mothers have become the norm and gender roles have changed and are converging at work and at home, presenting new challenges in managing work and personal life to both men and women. At the same time, the workplace has become treacherous terrain for many employees as a result of changing economic and technological conditions. Globalization has increased competitive and economic pressures on organizations. Job security and lifetime employment have all but disappeared for many American workers in the wake of organizational restructuring, downsizing, and outsourcing. Flatter organizational hierarchies have left fewer opportunities for employees to climb a traditional career ladder. At the same time, technology has increased the pace and demands of the workplace, making it virtually 24/7 (Bond et al., 2003).

These macrolevel changes have affected employees' workplaces and their families, making continuous employment and progress on a traditional, linear career ladder less and less feasible for many employees in the U.S. If linear, hierarchical models of career development no longer fit employees' reality, then it is not surprising that the assumption that the desire to advance to jobs with greater responsibilities is also less tenable among many employees. The question, thus, becomes: what are the factors that determine whether an employee desires more—or the same, or less—responsibility at work? What can employers, who need to manage the talents of employees interested and eager to advance to positions of greater responsibility and leadership, do to foster working conditions that encourage viable career paths and career aspirations among their employees? And what can employers do to affect workplace responsibilities themselves so that they do not foster a culture of overwork and burnout?

It is time for a new model of career development, one that captures the complexity of life today. Thus, we are proposing and describing a framework for flexible careers, depicted in Figure 2.3 below. This model illustrates the key influences on employees' career aspirations throughout their working lives.

Toward a Multilevel Framework for Flexible Careers

It is clear that individuals' responses to what happens to them are influenced not only by their own needs and desires but also by the world in which they live. This is a tenet of interactional psychology, which holds that one influence is not more powerful than the other, but rather it is how these influences "interact" with each other that make the critical difference (Magnusson and Endler, 1977). In Figure 2.3 below, where we depict our model of flexible careers, we build upon this concept from interactional psychology, specifying which personal and environmental factors we deem the most important in affecting individuals' career aspirations.

The personal factors are depicted at the bottom of Figure 2.3, beginning with the individual's career and personal/family life stage on the left side. Employees' career and personal/family life stage influence their motives, their needs, and their values, which in turn shape how they perceive and interpret their work environment. Because individuals have unique experiences of their work environment, we call this a "psychological climate" (e.g., James and Jones, 1974) which we propose affects their career aspirations—or desire for jobs with more responsibility in the organization. We further propose that "person-organization fit" (e.g., Chatman, 1989)—that is, the degree to which individuals' work environment is *aligned* with their life stage, values, needs, and aspirations—impacts the extent to which the psychological climate at work is conducive—or not conducive—to aspiring to a job with more responsibility.

Environmental factors are depicted at both the macro (societal) and organizational levels of analysis in Figure 2.3. At the highest level on the left side, macrolevel factors, including sociocultural norms and economic and marketplace conditions, affect both organizations and individuals. Macrolevel factors influence when and how individuals progress through different life stages. For example, sociocultural norms designate adolescence and early adulthood as the appropriate time to pursue an education. Young adulthood is considered the "right" time to launch a career and start a family. The senior years are deemed the appropriate time for retirement.

Macrolevel sociocultural norms and values impact individuals' personal values and attitudes through social learning processes (e.g., Bandura, 1986; Rokeach, 1973). For example, since the late 1970s societal values about gender have shifted toward egalitarianism. As a result, individuals today, in the teens of the twenty-first century, are more likely to value gender equality and

Figure 2.3. Multi-level Framework for Flexible Careers

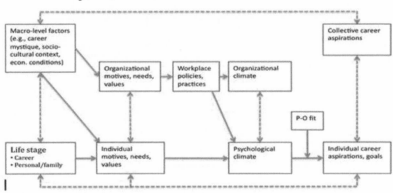

less likely to embrace traditional, segregated gender roles. Finally, macrolevel factors also impact organizational motives, needs, and values. For example, economic pressures define what an organization needs to ensure survival and effectiveness in a competitive, global marketplace. This in turn impacts workplace policies and practices designed to help the organization achieve its goals and compete within the current economic climate.

Similarly, sociocultural norms and demographic trends impact organizational values, which in turn translate into appropriate workplace policies and practices. For example, the influx into the workforce of women, people of color, and the aging has changed the demographic composition of the workforce in many organizations, thereby changing their needs, values, and, ultimately, their practices and policies with respect to managing a more diverse workforce. Thus, organizational motives, needs, and values inform workplace policies and practices, which in turn shape the organizational-level climate, that is, employees' collective experience of workplace policies and practices (e.g., Kopelman, Brief, and Guzzo, 1990). Workplace policies and practices and organizational climate drive the formation of the psychological climate at the individual level (Ostroff, Kinicki, and Tamkins, 2003), thereby influencing employees' career aspirations.

The framework for flexible careers we are posing includes a number of dashed bidirectional arrows that show the connections among the variables in our model. These arrows depict both top-down and bottom-up compositional processes (Chan, 1998; Kozlowski and Klein, 2000). For example, when a substantial proportion of employees within an organization hold similar individual values, a shared view of organizational values emerges, bottom up. However, this is not a one-way process. Organizational values also influence the individual values of employees through top-down processes. For example, socialization and social learning processes may influence an individual's values to make them better conform or be more similar to shared organizational values. Similar bottom-up and top-down processes also occur between the psychological and organizational climate. When a significant number of employees share similar views of the psychological climate—that is, they experience the work environment in similar ways—a shared organizational-level climate emerges (Ostroff et al., 2003).

Further, we propose that top-down, bottom-up processes occur between individual level and collective career aspirations. If decreased career aspirations are widely shared by a substantial proportion of individual employees, for example, because of widespread concerns over job pressure—and 2008 NSCW data suggest this is the case—we will begin to see this view becoming more widespread among the American workforce. These shared norms, in turn, influence the career aspirations of individuals, especially as they see others struggling to manage their work and personal responsibilities and indicating in subtle and overt ways that jobs with greater levels of responsibility are not undesirable.

Finally, our framework for flexible careers includes bidirectional horizontal arrows at the top and bottom of Figure 2.3 connecting individual career aspirations with individual life stage, motives, needs and values, and collective career aspirations with macrolevel factors. Over time, shared career aspirations may influence sociocultural norms. For example, a decreased collective desire for jobs with more responsibility may eventually alter social norms about career development and success. As norms about linear, hierarchical, and uninterrupted career progressions become increasingly unfit for the realities of contemporary lives, the normative belief that most employees want to climb the career ladder continuously and always want jobs with more responsibility may be called into question more frequently and, ultimately, begin to disappear in favor of more flexible norms about career aspirations, advancement, and success. Sociocultural norms, however, are likely to also impact collective career aspirations directly. For example, as employees change their perceptions of gender roles and as they increasingly prioritize their family roles over their work roles, the collective career aspirations of the American workforce are likely to be affected and lowered. Thus, we depicted the link between collective career aspirations and macrolevel socio-cultural norms as a bidirectional relationship.

Similarly, the relationship between individual level career aspirations and life stage is bidirectional. For example, employees in early life stages are more likely to desire opportunities for advancement simply because they are "starting out" in their career journeys, while employees in mid- or late career stages are more likely to have already achieved their desired level of job responsibility. However, career aspirations may also serve as a cue to individuals about their current life stage or when it is time to move to a different stage in their personal or career life cycle. For example, a new and exciting experience at work may give way to routine and boredom over time, signaling to the employee that it may be time for a change—a new job, a new career, or a new challenge in his or her personal life.

In sum, the present theoretical framework illustrates that employees' aspirations to jobs with a greater scope of responsibilities are influenced by myriad variables and processes at different levels of analysis—setting forth a number of propositions for future empirical studies. Two factors in particular—macrolevel trends and microlevel life stages—drive the dynamic and flexible nature of career development processes today. Both individual and environmental (macro- and organizational level) factors in the personal-environmental interaction are subject to change as employees move through life stages and cycles in a changing world.

A comprehensive test of the proposed model is beyond the scope of the NSCW data. The NSCW data are cross-sectional and a true test of our theory requires data from individuals within organizations over time. However, our cross-sectional data from the NSCW point to macrolevel and individual level trends that we think drive the need for a new career model—the model we are proposing of flexible careers.

Macrolevel Changes:
Converging Gender Roles at Work and at Home

Women's participation in the labor force has increased substantially since 1950, while that of men has decreased (BLS, 2009). Today, men and women are in the workforce in virtually equal numbers. Women are also catching up to men when it comes to educational level. Until the mid-1990s, men had an advantage over women in completion of at least four years of college by about six or seven percentage points (National Center for Education Statistics, 2008). The percentage of men completing four years of college or more leveled off in the late 1990s and decreased slightly in the the first decade of the twenty-first century, while that of women increased steadily. By 2007, 29.5% of men and 28% of women in the U.S. population had completed at least four years of college—a gap of only 1.5 percentage points. These increases among women will continue, given current graduation rates. For example, in the 2006–2007 academic year, women earned 57% of all bachelor's degrees, 61% of all master's degrees, and 50% of all first professional degrees (e.g., medical, law) (National Center for Education Statistics, 2008).

With the increase of women's educational attainment and participation in the labor force, it is not surprising that women play an increasingly important role as financial contributors to household income. According to our data, the percentage of dual-earner couples has increased significantly—four out of five couples (80%) were dual-earner couples in 2008 compared with 66% of couples in 1977. In 2008, women in dual-earner couples play a greater role as contributors to family income than ever before, earning an average of 45% of their family's income. This represents a significant increase since 1997, only eleven years earlier, when women in dual-earner couples earned an average of 39% of family income (Galinsky et al., 2009a). In fact, women's annual earnings have increased over the past decade compared with those of their spouses or partners, which have decreased slightly. In 2008, 27% of women living in dual-earner couples had annual earnings at least 10 percentage points higher than their partners or spouses—significantly more than in 1997, when 15% of women earned at least 10 percent more than their partner or spouse. Thus, women play a substantial role in their family's economic well-being—a trend bolstered by the recession of 2008–2009 which cost more men their jobs than women (BLS, 2009). This being said, however, as of 2009 (the time of writing) women continued to earn less than men—for example, by 2007, the average full-time employed woman earned 80% of what men earned on a weekly basis (BLS, 2009).

As a result of changing sociocultural norms and economic realities, employed mothers have become the norm. In 1975, employed mothers were a minority with only 47% of mothers with children under age 18 participating in the labor force (Cohany and Sok, 2007). By 2007, 71% of mothers with children under age 18 were in the labor force—a percentage that has remained more or less stable since the late 1990s. Even among mothers with infants, the majority participates in the labor force. After decades of dramatic increases, labor force participation among married mothers with infants peaked in 1997 at 59% and has remained relatively stable since 2000, currently (in 2008) standing at 56% (BLS, 2009; Cohany and Sok, 2007).

It is clear that women and men's lives at work have changed over the past decades. Thus, it is not surprising that attitudes in both genders about the proper roles of women and men have changed as well (Galinsky et al., 2009a). Both men and women are less likely to accept traditional gender roles in 2008 than they were in 1977. The percentage of employed adults of all ages who agree that it is better for all involved if "the man earns the money and the woman takes care of the home and children" has dropped significantly and substantially over the past three decades from 64% in 1977 to 39% in 2008—a decline by 25 percentage points. These data, however, do indicate that two in five employees still endorse traditional gender roles.

Changes in attitudes about proper gender roles have changed more dramatically among men than among women. In 2008, for the first time, women's and men's views about gender roles have converged to a point where they are virtually shared with no statistically significant differences between the two genders. The percentage of men who endorsed traditional gender roles fell from 74% in 1977 to 41% in 2008, while the percentage of women fell from 52% in 1977 to 37% in 2008. This change—the convergence between men and women on views about gender roles—is both striking and seminal. The attitudes of men in dual-earner couples have changed the most. In 1977, 70% of men in dual-earner couples thought it was better for men to be the breadwinners and for women to stay at home, but by 2008, only 36% of men in dual-earner couples adhered to this view. The fact that women in dual-earner couples are contributing larger amounts to the family income while men's annual earnings are declining, is likely to be contributing to the shift in men's attitudes about gender roles.

Similar to attitudes about gender roles, attitudes about employed mothers had shifted as well since the late 1970s. The percentage of employed adults who agreed that "a mother who works outside the home can have just as good a relationship with her children as a mother who does not work" had increased significantly from 58% in 1977 to 74% in 2008. Again, men's attitudes had shifted more than women's. In 1977, men who agreed with the above statement were the minority (49%), but in 2008, two-thirds (68%) of men agreed either somewhat or strongly. Not surprisingly, the majority of employed women held favorable views about employed mothers in 1977 (71%) and 2008 (81%). In spite of dramatic changes in men's attitudes about employed mothers since the late 1970s, employed men were still significantly less likely than employed women to believe that employed mothers could have relationships with their children just as good as those of mothers who were not employed—68% of men versus 81% of women believed so.

Women are not the only ones whose actual roles have changed. Men's roles and behaviors at home have changed significantly over the past three decades. Employed fathers with children under age 13 are spending more time with their children today than they did thirty years ago. The amount of time fathers report spending with their children under age 13 on workdays has increased from an average of 2 hours in 1977 to an average of 3 hours in 2008. At the same time, the amount of time employed mothers spend with their children under 13 on workdays has remained the same at nearly four hours both in 1977 and 2008. Thus, mothers still spend more time on average with their children than fathers, but fathers are catching up. Men are taking more overall responsibility for the care of their children in 2008 than in 1992, according to both self-reports and reports from their wives or partners. "Taking responsibility for the care of children" means not only providing care firsthand, but also managing child care arrangements.

In 1992, the majority of men (58%) reported that their wives took primary responsibility for child care. By 2008, however, men who reported their wives as taking primary responsibility for child care were no longer a majority (46%). Further, nearly half (49%) of men reported taking most or an equal share of child care responsibilities in 2008, up from 41% in 1992. Importantly, women's reports are in the same direction as their husbands' or partners' self-reports. The percentage of women reporting that they take most of the child care responsibility has dropped from 73% in 1992 to 66% in 2008. There is a discrepancy between women and men in their views, however. While 49% of men say they take as much or more responsibility for child care as their spouses, only 30% of women report men sharing in this way. Even so, there has been an increase among women reporting that their husbands or partners are taking an equal share or more of the responsibility for child care—from 21% in 1992 to 30% in 2008.

In sum, work and family gender roles have been converging since the late 1970s. Not surprisingly, these changes have affected the degree to which employees experience work-life conflict. Men, in particular, are experiencing more work-life conflict today than they did thirty years ago, while work-life conflict has remained relatively stable among women. In 1977, the proportions of men and women reporting some or a lot of work-life conflict were similar at about one-third for men and women (34%), respectively. By 2008, however, the percentage of men experiencing some or a lot of work-life conflict increased significantly to 49%, while that of women increased to 43%—not a statistically significant change.[2]

Fathers in dual-earner families are the most likely to experience rising work-life conflict—60% of fathers in dual-earner couples reported experiencing some or a lot of work-life conflict in 2008, up significantly (25 percentage points) from 35% in 1977. Among mothers in dual-earner couples, work-life conflict had not changed significantly since 1977. In fact, with 47% of mothers in dual-earner couples reporting work-life conflict, in 2008 fathers in dual-earner couples were much more likely than mothers in dual-earner couples to experience work-life conflict. In addition, fathers in dual-earner couples were also more likely to experience work-life conflict (59%) than fathers who were the sole breadwinners (49%).[3]

It is clear that these macrolevel changes in societal values and norms around gender roles, child care, and family life have made the interaction between work and personal life more complex and more challenging for many employees today. These changes have taken place at the same time that other macrolevel changes in the economy have occurred. For example, difficult economic conditions and fierce competition in a global marketplace have changed workplaces and the psychological contract between employees and employers in ways that make work and its rewards less stable and predictable for many employees. A psychological contract is an implicit, mutual agreement between employee and employer about what each side expects to give and receive from the employment relationship (Schein, 1978). For example, employees contribute their time, energy, and skills to help achieve organizational goals in exchange for challenging, rewarding work, good working conditions, pay, benefits, and an organizational future in the form of promises of continued employment and career advancement.

Traditionally, psychological contracts between employees and employers were geared toward what Moen and Roehling (2005) call the "career mystique"—employees are expected to work hard and put in long hours on the job in exchange for opportunities to advance within the organizational hierarchy along a clearly defined, linear career path. However, taking an organizational view, career ladders are precarious at best. As organizations adapt to competitive and economic pressures, organizational restructuring, downsizing, and outsourcing have flattened organizational hierarchies, reduced the number of advancement opportunities within organizations, and eroded the promise of job security that was traditionally implied in the psychological contract between employee and employer.

These changes are compounded by other macrolevel trends, such as technological advances. There is no question that technology has transformed American workplaces. New communication technologies have turned workplaces increasingly into fast-paced, 24/7 operations as many employees are able to work any time from anywhere. Needless to say, with increasing job demands and decreasing job security and advancement opportunities in many workplaces today, work has become more stressful for a large portion of the U.S. workforce. In fact, data from the 2008 NSCW offers some insights into the state of employees' mental and physical health, suggesting that the pressures of contemporary work and family life may be taking a toll.

Analyses of 2008 NSCW data on the health of U.S. employees reveals that physical health is declining (Aumann and Galinsky, 2009). Fewer employees report their current state of overall health as *excellent*—30% rated their overall health as *excellent* in 2008, down significantly from 34% in 2002. Further, employees are more likely to report minor health problems, including headaches, upset stomachs, and trouble sleeping, in 2008. The percentage of employees who reported *never* experiencing such problems in the last month dropped significantly to 29% in 2008 from 36% in 2002.

Our data reveal that men's physical health has declined more than women's over the past six years. This trend is consistent with findings that work-life conflict has increased more among men than women and is likely related to the challenges men are facing at work and at home. Moreover, 2008 NSCW data reveal that one-third of the U.S. workforce is experiencing one or more signs of clinical depression. In addition, sleep problems are pervasive among employees, with more than a quarter (28%) reporting sleep problems in the last thirty days that affected their performance at work. Finally, stress levels have increased significantly among employees in the United States from 2002 to 2008, with 43% of employees reporting that they experienced at least three out of five indicators of stress measured by the 2008 NSCW.

While the reasons for the declining physical and mental health of the U.S. workforce are multifaceted and complex, we do think that the challenging nature of contemporary work and personal or family life plays a significant role. Maintaining economic security and an uninterrupted career with a linear progression of jobs that have increasing levels of responsibility has become elusive for the majority of employees. Economic and sociocultural realities have led to significant increases in the labor force participation of women and mothers. As a result, the majority of couples and families in the early twenty-first century have both partners in the workforce.

Moen and Roehling (2005) also argue that changes within the personal and family lives of employees make the "career mystique" untenable. In fact, they show that the prevailing notion of a linear, three-phase lockstep regime of education, continuous employment in an uninterrupted, hierarchical sequence of jobs, followed by retirement as a final exit from the workforce has simply not been a reality for many employees today. Because the career mystique is based on the notion that employees will work hard at jobs with long hours to demonstrate their commitment to their jobs and earn rewards, including increases in pay, status, and job responsibility, this view of career development all but excludes the employee's personal or family life. In fact, as we discuss in greater detail below, the career mystique is predicated on traditional gender roles with men as breadwinners and women as homemakers because care giving responsibilities are presumed to inevitably detract from a person's time and energy for the job. And that is not life today, as we all know.

·Despite the fact that a career ladder has not been a reality for many employees, especially women, the notion of how careers are supposed to progress appears to be deeply ingrained into the fabric of American culture and, thus far, has been slow to change. Even in today's world of dual-earner couples, the career mystique assumes that one partner—usually the woman—will significantly scale back work responsibilities in order to care for the family. In other words, the career mystique does not leave much choice than for one partner to opt out—either entirely or in terms of reduced work hours and responsibilities. In fact, the article in which Belkin (2003) proposed the notion of an "opt-out revolution" was illustrated with a photograph of women turning their backs on a traditional career ladder when it appeared as a cover story in the *New York Times Magazine*.

Unfortunately, as Moen and Roehling note, the career mystique makes it difficult for those who temporarily opt out of its lockstep regime to return to resume their careers at similar levels of pay, responsibility, and status. Thus, it is high time to reconceptualize career development as fluid throughout an employee's life span, allowing flexibility in career aspirations and development through a diverse range of entry, exit, or modification points without permanently relegating those who do stop working for a time into a disadvantaged status. That is precisely why we argue that it has become more timely than ever to replace the career ladder with the notion of flexible careers.

Individual Level Processes: The Role of Life Stage and Psychological Climate

In line with developmental and life stage theories, we propose in the framework for flexible careers (see Figure 2.3) that employees' personal and career life stage influences their individual motives, needs, and values related to work and career development. Life stages play a substantial role in driving a person's work and career-related values, needs, and goals because each life stage comes with its own set of challenges and developmental tasks. For example, Super conceptualized career development as a process with five stages—growth, exploration, establishment, maintenance, and disengagement (Super, 1957, 1980).

The growth stage is the earliest in the career development process and begins in adolescence. During this stage, individuals develop their occupational self-concepts—who they are and what they want to do in the world of work. Growth is followed in late adolescence by the exploration stage, when individuals select a career, prepare for it with training and education, and begin employment. During the early career stages of growth and exploration, individuals' needs and values are likely to center on exploration, learning, and development.

During the midcareer stage of establishment beginning in early adulthood, employees seek to stabilize their position. During this stage, employees may place increasing value on rewards and recognition for hard work and achievement and opportunities for advancement. Establishment is followed by the maintenance stage, when individuals seek to protect the level and status achieved thus far. At this stage, individuals may value job security, stability, and sometimes opportunities for further advancement.

During the final career stage, disengagement, individuals' needs and values focus on preparing for retirement and exiting their occupational roles. Although Super originally conceptualized these five stages as occurring in sequential order over an individual's life span, he later conceded that individuals may cycle and recycle through these stages repeatedly throughout their working lives. Each decision point in an individual's career marks the beginning of a new "mini-cycle" with its own set of the five stages (Super, 1980).

Edgar Schein's work on career development also takes a life stage perspective. Schein (1978) argues that individuals develop and refine their career "anchors" throughout their life span. "Career anchors" represent the person's occupational self-concept and include the individual's perceptions of his or her talents, skills, and abilities, as well as motives, needs, values, and attitudes. These anchors change over time as the person moves through different life stages and is faced with different tasks, challenges, and learning experiences. Schein notes that the stages and tasks of career development are closely related with the stages of the biosocial life cycle, in that both are driven by age and cultural norms about what is considered age appropriate. Schein further notes that the interaction between an individual's work and personal life can be especially challenging during certain stages and situations. For example, dual-earner couples may face particular challenges around negotiating work and child care responsibilities.

Strategies for managing work and family life in dual-earner couples may include differentiation of roles with one partner focusing on work, the other on child care. Sharing child care responsibilities more or less equally among two working partners is also possible, but presumably requires both partners to accommodate the work needs of the other partner at times—in other words, both have to be prepared to shift their focus and energy from work to family as needed. According to Schein, it is virtually impossible for dual-career couples to negotiate linear careers through a traditional set of career stages when both partners are focused on advancing their careers without interruption or some scaling back during certain life stages—for example, when they have young children.

Similarly, Moen and Roehling's three-phase lockstep model of the career mystique is geared to employees' life stages, beginning with education at a young age followed by continuous employment until retirement. They note that while U.S. employees in the 1950s had often completed their education and launched both their careers by beginning employment and their family lives by getting married and having children before the age of thirty, today individuals tend to stay in school longer, delaying employment and often delaying marriage and parenthood.

As a result, employees in their thirties are often launching both careers and families at the same time, making their needs more complex with respect to managing work and personal responsibilities. In addition, employees' reality seldom conforms to the lockstep "regime" Moen and Roehling have observed as a social norm governing career development. Continuous employment has become difficult to achieve in the age of frequent organizational restructuring, downsizing, and outsourcing. The traditional rewards for hard work, long hours, and commitment—career advancement and job security—have become elusive for many employees in workplaces shaped by today's economic climate. As a result of decreased stability and frequently changing environmental conditions, employees today are more likely to move in and out of careers, education, and relationships than their counterparts several decades ago. The result is a greater diversity of life stages within a given age group—employees in their thirties may be well-established in their careers and be married with children, they may be working part-time to pay for graduate school, or they may be single and starting their first job in a new career in a new geographic location. Thus, it has become more difficult to predict employees' life stage and thus their career-related values, needs, and goals based on age alone. Still, qualitative information about an individual's life stage—above and beyond conventional assumptions about age-based life stages—can yield helpful insights as to the individual's career-related values and needs, which drive the individual level psychological processes that influence career aspirations, as depicted in the lower half of Figure 2.3.

In fact, data from the 2008 NSCW reveals some support for the notion that employees' work-related value priorities do differ according to life stage. The question of whether and how life stages influence employees' personal motives, needs, and values, thereby shaping the psychological climate and their career aspirations, should be explored in more detail in future studies that use longitudinal designs and more refined measures of both life stages and values. For the time being, however, we explored whether employees of different age groups—who are presumably in different career and life stages—have different value priorities. To this end, we compared employees under age 29 (i.e., Millennials, who are likely to be in early career stages), employees aged 30 to 42 (i.e., Generation Xers, who are presumably in early to mid-career stages), employees aged 43 to 62 (i.e., Baby Boomers, in mid- and late career stages) and employees age 63 and older (i.e., Matures, who are presumed to be in late career stages or working in retirement) on twelve value dimensions. Employees were asked to rate each dimension with respect to its importance in deciding whether to accept a new job.

We found that younger employees—Millennials and Generation X—are more likely to place high importance on dimensions associated with advancing to jobs with greater responsibility. For example, younger employees are more likely to rate opportunities for challenging work and learning new things as extremely important—37% of Millenials and 34% of Gen Xers compared with 29% of Boomers and 23% of Matures. Similarly, Millennials—those most likely to be in the exploration or launching stages of their careers—are most likely to place high value on being able to advance at a desired pace, with 40% of Millennials rating this dimension as extremely important compared with 35% of Gen Xers, 27% of Boomers, and 18% of Matures. Further, Millennials and Gen Xers are more likely to rate being well-paid for their skills and effort as extremely important—50% of Millennials, 48% of Gen Xers, compared with 40% of Boomers, 28% of Matures. Boomers and Matures are more likely to be in life stages where they have already achieved a certain level of occupational and financial success, while Millennials and Gen Xers are more likely to be in the early stages of launching their careers and family lives.

Perhaps surprisingly, Millennials are significantly more likely to express a high need for job security relative to older employees—57% of Millennials rate having job security as extremely important compared with 53% of Gen Xers, 45% of Boomers, and 32% of Matures. It is likely that for employees in early career and personal life stages, the stakes are higher when it comes to a potential job loss due to the fact that they have had fewer opportunities to establish their careers, build occupational skills and networks, and gain experience. This might make finding new jobs more challenging. It is also possible that financial stakes are higher for young employees who may be paying off student loans, saving up to buy their first home, or about to start a family. It is also likely that young employees have been influenced by witnessing macrolevel trends that have destabilized their parents' workplaces and caused widely held beliefs about the American career mystique to be shattered.

Finally, consistent with the notion that employees in their thirties and early forties were most likely to be in the launching stages of their family lives and have small children at home, Gen Xers are most likely to place high importance on having schedule flexibility to successfully manage work and personal life—45% of Gen Xers rated this dimension as extremely important, followed by Millennials (42%). Among Boomers and Matures, the percentages rating schedule flexibility as extremely important are lower in comparison (36% and 27%, respectively). Similar patterns emerged when comparing employees with children under the ages of 6 and 13 to employees without children. Parents are more likely to value being well-paid and having job security and schedule flexibility to manage work and family life as extremely important. These findings suggest that family life stage—for example, having small or adolescent children—plays a role in shaping employees needs and motives at work.

Life stage theory suggests that young employees, and especially those who do not have major family commitments (yet), should be more motivated to pursue advancement opportunities at work because they are still beginning their careers. Employees in more advanced career and personal life stages are more likely to have already reached certain levels of responsibility. Thus, they may be more interested in maintaining what they have achieved. They are also more likely to face significant commitments and responsibilities in their personal lives, for example, to a partner, small children, or elderly relatives. The 2008 NSCW data indicate that there are, in fact, differences between employees of different age groups in their desire to advance to jobs with more responsibility. In keeping with the tenets of life stage theory, Millennials are significantly and substantially more likely to desire more responsibility at work—two-thirds of Millennials express a desire for jobs with greater responsibilities compared with 46% of Gen Xers, 24% of Boomers, and 8% of Matures.

Making Work "Work" throughout the Personal and Career Life Span

Our framework and the data presented above illustrate that not all employees want to advance in their jobs at the same time. The dynamic nature of career aspirations presents a challenge for employers who need to have a pool of talented employees willing and able to move into positions of greater responsibility and leadership. Employers should not assume that all their employees are ready and willing to take on greater responsibility at all times. Then, what are the factors that predict employees' desire to advance to jobs with greater responsibility?

Our framework suggests that three categories of variables need to be considered: macrolevel contextual factors, including social norms, economic conditions, and technology; workplace characteristics, including organizational values, policies, and practices; and individual factors, including employees' current life stage, values, needs, and goals. Employers may have little or no direct control over macrolevel factors, but they should be aware of what is happening within the organization's context. For example, how do economic trends or new technologies impact their workforce and working conditions within their organization? Do these changes impact certain groups of employees more than others? Changing gender dynamics, for example, appear to have affected men more than women, as illustrated by rising work-life conflict levels among men. Similarly, employers have little control over employees' life stages or value systems. They can, however, implement policies and practices designed to address the needs, values, and goals of employees at different stages in their personal and career lives. Most importantly, employers must be aware that one-size-fits-all solutions will inevitably be ineffective for some portions of their workforce.

Effective workplaces recognize that employees are an organization's most important resource that makes a difference for sustained organizational performance (Aumann and Galinsky, 2009; Jacob, Bond, Galinsky, and Hill, 2008; Bond, Galinsky, and Hill, 2004). This implies that organizations need to have groups of some talented employees who are both able and willing to ascend to positions of greater responsibility (even though what this means may be redefined) and help lead the organization to future success. Thus, employers should strategically use their organizational cultures and human resources practices to build effective workplaces with characteristics that are conducive to career advancement for employees at a variety of life stages. Further, employers need to consider how their organizational values and practices affect the workplace experiences and perceptions of their employees. In other words, employers should understand how the characteristics of the workplace interact with characteristics of their workforce (e.g., the needs, values, and goals of employees at different life stages) to create psychological and organizational climates that facilitate career aspirations and development toward higher levels of responsibility.

The Families and Work Institute has explored the characteristics of effective workplaces for several years. Like career development and aspirations, effective workplaces are fluid—their criteria change as the needs, values, and goals of the workforce and of employers change. Based on past research on criteria of effective workplaces (Bond et al., 2004; Bond and Galinsky, 2006; Galinsky, Carter, and Bond, 2008), we developed and tested hypotheses about current workplace effectiveness criteria and tested these criteria using data from the 2008 NSCW. As a result, we identified six main criteria that distinguish highly effective workplaces from those that are less effective (Aumann and Galinsky, 2009). These criteria include job challenge and learning opportunities (e.g., having a job that is meaningful, requires learning new things, and makes use of the employee's skills and abilities), supervisor task support (e.g., the supervisor is supportive when there is a work problem and keeps the employee informed), autonomy (e.g., having a say about what happens on the job, having the freedom to make decisions), a climate of respect and trust (e.g., trusting what managers say and having managers who deal ethically with clients and employees), economic security (e.g., being satisfied with pay, benefits, and career advancement opportunities) and work-life fit (e.g., having supervisors who care about the effects of work on personal or family life and a work schedule that fits the employee's needs).

Data from the 2008 NSCW reveal that an index of overall workplace effectiveness based on the six criteria described above is associated with better outcomes for both the employer and the individual (Aumann and Galinsky, 2009). For example, overall workplace effectiveness is significantly related to higher levels of employee engagement, job satisfaction, and intent to stay in one's job. In addition, all six criteria individually are related to greater employee engagement and job satisfaction. Five of the six criteria, excluding climate of respect, are significantly associated with greater intent to stay in one's job. These outcomes—employee engagement, job satisfaction, and intent to stay—are important to employers because they contribute to an organization's overall performance and success (Gelade and Ivery, 2003; Huselid, 1995; Huselid, Jackson, and Schuler, 1997). Further, recent findings published by Families and Work Institute show that overall workplace effectiveness is linked to outcomes relevant to employee health and well-being (Aumann and Galinsky, 2009).

Employees in highly effective workplaces are more likely to report being in excellent overall health and are less likely to report experiencing minor health problems (e.g., headaches, upset stomachs), signs of depression, and sleep problems. Employees in highly effective workplaces also report lower stress levels than employees in workplaces with moderate or low overall effectiveness. Having an effective workplace also makes a difference for the interaction between work and home life—employees in highly effective workplaces are more likely to report that their work has a positive impact on their energy level at home and vice versa. With respect to the six workplace effectiveness criteria, economic security is by far the most important predictor of employee health and well-being outcomes, followed by work-life fit and having autonomy on the job.

Exploratory analyses of the relationships between workplace effectiveness and desire to advance revealed that employees in workplaces with low overall effectiveness are *more* likely to desire to advance than their peers in high effectiveness workplaces. This effect, however, disappeared when taking into account employees' turnover intention. In other words, employees in workplaces that rank as low on our effectiveness criteria may understandably want jobs with greater responsibility, but not necessarily with the organization they currently work for. As then expected, our exploratory analyses showed that employees whose current jobs fall short of their desired level of responsibility are more likely to look for a new job with a different employer within the next year than employees who have jobs at their optimal level of responsibility. In fact, employees who view the characteristics of their workplaces as ineffective are more likely to be motivated to seek changes in their employers because they are not very satisfied and engaged. Workplace effectiveness may also be implying a fit between an employee's current and desired level of responsibility; that is, employees in effective workplaces may be more likely to have jobs at their desired level of responsibility than employees in less effective workplaces.

When we statistically controlled for employees' turnover intentions—whether they plan to look for a new job with a different employer in the next year—we found that among employees who plan to stay with their current employers, overall effectiveness has a *positive* effect on desire to advance.

Among those employees, a more effective workplace is associated with a greater desire for a more advanced job within the organization. Clearly, the nature and design of the workplace—its policies and practices—affect employees' experience at work (depicted as psychological climate in Figure 2.3) in ways that can contribute to positive outcomes for the organization and the individual. Thus far, we have found that workplace effectiveness based on six criteria—job challenge and learning opportunities, supervisor task support, autonomy, climate for respect, economic security, and work-life fit—helps make work "work" for employers and employees. The impact of workplace effectiveness, however, can be even more powerful when the workplace effectiveness characteristics *align with* their individual needs and preferences for these characteristics. In other words, an effective workplace is not a "one size fits all" notion. Our theory specifies that the components of an effective organization are even more "effective" when they align with employees' values.

We have specified this dynamic aspect in our theory based in part on a recent study by the Families and Work Institute where we found that employees benefit more from effective workplaces when the characteristics of the workplace align with their individual values and preferences for these characteristics (Galinsky, Aumann, and Bond, 2009b). This finding, moreover, is consistent with insights from person-environment fit theory that specifies that when employees' needs and values go unfulfilled, they are more likely to evaluate this mismatch as a concern. For example, employees who value work-life fit may be more dissatisfied with a lack of workplace flexibility than those who care less about this issue.

Person-environment fit theory defines the interaction between person and environment as the extent to which individual attributes (e.g., needs, goals, values) match or align with those of the environment (e.g., characteristics of the workplace) (e.g., Kristof, 1996). In the workplace, fit is conceptualized as the degree to which employees and their work organizations match on a given set of criteria (e.g., values). A good match, or person-organization fit, is associated with a range of positive outcomes for employees and employer, including employee engagement, job satisfaction, performance, individual health, and organizational effectiveness (e.g., Adkins, Ravlin, and Meglino, 1996; Moos, 1987; O'Reilly, Chatman, and Caldwell, 1991).

The person-environment fit perspective has informed theories and research on occupational choice and career development (e.g., Holland, 1985). For example, the Theory of Work Adjustment (Dawis and Lofquist, 1984) proposes that individuals will seek out and stay in work environments that support their personal needs, values, and preferences. In fact, a plethora of studies have demonstrated that individuals are more likely to derive satisfaction and achieve beneficial outcomes, including longer tenure, in workplaces that are a good fit with their personal requirements (e.g., Bretz and Judge, 1994; Kristof-Brown, Zimmerman, and Johnson, 2005). Employees who perceive their workplace as satisfying and who have stayed there for a substantial period of time are more likely to understand the organization's values and norms with respect to career advancement. In other words, employees who are a good fit with their work organizations are more likely to understand what it takes to advance one's career in that organization. They are also more likely to have strong social networks, mentors, and sponsors within the organization that can facilitate occupational advancement. As a result, they may be more likely to get desirable assignments and recognition at work. Thus, person-organization fit indirectly influences employees' career success (Bretz and Judge, 1994).

Extending this line of reasoning, we propose that person-organization fit also plays a role in shaping employees' desire for career advancement. More specifically, we propose that the degree of what has been termed "needs-supplies fit," a type of person-organization fit in which the organization's characteristics meet employees' needs, specifically impacts the relationship between psychological climate—individuals' perceptions of the workplace—and career aspirations, as depicted on the right side of the individual level processes in Figure 2.3.

The needs-supplies perspective of fit conceptualizes an organization's workplace policies, practices, and resources as organizational "supplies" that interact with employees' needs and preferences (Kristof, 1996). Good needs-supplies fit occurs when the characteristics, policies, and practices of the workplace meet employees' needs and preferences. When this kind of fit occurs, employee motivation is maximized because the workplace facilitates needs fulfillment and the accomplishment of goals (Bretz and Judge, 1994). As a result, employees' psychological climate perceptions of the workplace are more likely to be favorable; that is, they are perceived as instrumental in helping the individual obtain needed or desired outcomes. Person-organization fit has a positive impact on the cognitive processes that translate employees' psychological climate into attitudinal responses, including motivation and career aspirations. When employees view their workplace characteristics as a good fit with their needs and preferences, they will be more likely to believe that the workplace will support their needs even in a higher level position. However, when the workplace falls short of meeting important employee needs, employees are likely to perceive this mismatch as frustrating and dissatisfying and, as a result, may be motivated to seek changes, including reducing their effort and engagement at work or planning to leave the organization.

Expectancy theory (Vroom, 1964) offers additional insights as to how person-organization fit may support employees' career aspirations. Expectancy theory proposes that individuals are motivated to engage in behaviors that are "expected" to yield desired outcomes. Thus when employees have a good fit at work and are able to meet their important personal needs at work, they may be more likely to expect that moving to positions with more responsibility will be a positive move for them. On the other hand, individuals who have a poor fit may be more likely to want to leave their organization rather than seek advancement, because they expect that advancement within their organization would not turn out to be a good move for them.

In addition, employees who fit the characteristics of their workplace may be more likely to understand the particular requirements of their organization and thus better understand what it takes to succeed in the organization (Bretz and Judge, 1994). As a result, employees who fit their organizations well are more likely to have "instrumentality beliefs," that is, to believe that their efforts will lead to strong job performance and facilitate career advancement. Employees without such instrumentality beliefs are less likely to be motivated and to aspire to positions with higher levels of responsibility. Affecting this process is the fact that employees with a fit with their organizations tend to have longer tenures and are more likely than employees with a poor fit to have historical knowledge of what is valued and rewarded in the organization, which again contributes to stronger instrumentality beliefs.

Finally, the "attraction-selection-attrition framework" (Schneider, 1987) is useful in explaining who is likely to desire career advancement in their employer's organization. The attraction-selection-attrition framework proposes that individuals tend to be attracted to, selected by, and stay in organizations that fit their personal characteristics. Individuals who fit their organizations poorly will either assimilate as a result of socialization and training processes until their values, needs, and preferences are consistent with the organization's characteristics or they will leave the organization, either by choice or by being terminated. The central premise of this framework is that fit is a dynamic process in which the employee's choice plays a major role (Schneider, 1987; Bretz and Judge, 1994). Essentially, employees self-select themselves into and out of organizations based on their fit; however, this may change among those employers that truly embrace and exemplify diversity.

The six workplace effectiveness criteria outlined above—job challenge and learning opportunities, supervisor task support, a climate of respect, autonomy, economic security, and work-life fit—actually embody a diversity perspective because they are not one-size-fits-all criteria. A closer look at each of these criteria reveals that they are rooted in individuality. For example, a climate of respect means that each individual is appreciated for who he or she is. And work-life fit is based on the premise that this fit will differ for different individuals.

Although more research is needed, our exploratory analyses do indicate that person-organization fit—using these six characteristics of an effective workplace—significantly impacts employees' desire for more responsibility at work. Those employees with a poor fit are more likely to desire jobs with greater responsibility than employees with good person-organization fit, but typically at different workplaces. For reasons discussed above, employees with poor person-organization fit are more likely to desire changes to their current work situation. Employees with good fit are more likely to have jobs at their preferred level of responsibility and are less likely to seek jobs with another employer.

A Word about Jobs with More Responsibility

Although the focus of this chapter has centered on the processes of career development, we would be remiss if we did not note that the outcome of "jobs with more responsibility" should change along with the notion of career ladders. A few leading employers are recognizing that the organizations may not be successful if they simply pile on more and more work. Thus efforts to reduce workload have been emerging. These include eliminating unnecessary or waste-of-time work, sponsoring team efforts and tools to create jobs that are reasonably—but not overly—demanding, and establishing workload coordinators and wellness scorecards so that management can spot employees at risk for burnout and intervene (Galinsky, Peer, and Eby, 2009; Benko and Anderson, 2010).

Conclusion—A Call for Reframing the Career Ladder Model into Flexible Careers

Employees want and need different things from their jobs at different stages in their life. Personal or family life stage, as well as career stage, must be taken into account in trying to understand an individual's career decisions and development. Life stages—both personal or family and career—no longer necessarily conform to the linear models of the past. Employees may go through a succession of minicycles throughout the life span of their careers or family life. Career aspirations are bound to fluctuate as employees' needs, values and interests change with progression through life stages and minicycles. Thus, the "real" opt-out revolution is not women leaving the workplace when they have children, but the diminished desire among all U.S. employees for the traditional career ladder with its lock-steps pattern of advancement and even its traditional definitions of "increased responsibility." We believe this is a clarion call for a newer and more relevant model of flexible careers— recognizing that career aspirations are affected by life stages, contextual factors, and workplace characteristics. The time for this change is now.

NOTES

1. Data presented in this section are based on the 1977 Quality of Employment Survey (U.S. Department of Labor) and the 1992, 1997, 2002, and 2008 National Study of the Changing Workforce (Families and Work Institute) unless otherwise noted.

2. Comparisons between 2008 NSCW and the 1977 QES include only employees working at least 20 hours per week because the 1977 QES is limited to employees working at least 20 hours per week.

3. These percentages include fathers working any numbers of hours per week.

Can All Women "Opt In" before They "Opt Out"?

"Opting In" to Full Labor Force Participation in Hourly Jobs

SUSAN J. LAMBERT

Rather than "opting out" or even being "pushed out," women in low-level, hourly jobs are often "kept out" of full labor force participation.[1] The practices employers use to contain labor costs in hourly jobs often serve to undermine women's prospects for sustained employment and adequate work hours. In this chapter, I first present national data suggesting that a greater proportion of women, especially those in hourly jobs, would prefer to work more rather than fewer hours per week. I then draw on research I have led on firms in Chicago to highlight practices found on the frontlines of firms that make it difficult for hourly workers to "opt in" to full labor force participation (see Lambert 2008 and 2009 for a full description of these studies).

Preferences for Working More Hours

The economic recession is drawing needed attention to the growing proportion of American workers classified as *involuntary part-time*, defined by the Census Bureau as working less than 35 hours a week for economic reasons (could not find a full-time job or work hours were reduced due to slack demand) rather than by choice. In September 2010, 9.5 million workers were classified as involuntary part-time, the highest level in recorded history (BLS 2010). The current recession did not, however, give birth to employer practices that foster underemployment. Figure 3.1 traces involuntary part-time employment over the past forty years (1970 to 2010), demonstrating that this is not the first spike in involuntary part-time employment. Millions of American workers do not get "enough" hours even during relatively good economic times.

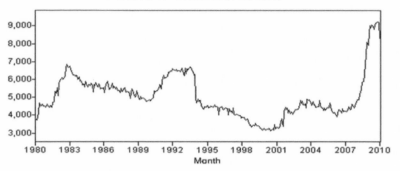

Figure 3.1. Involuntary Part-time Employment, 1980–2010,
Numbers in Thousands (BLS, 2010)

Work Hour Preferences

Census data on workers' work hour preferences provide additional support
that many workers are excluded from full labor force participation. Table 3.1
presents data from the 2001 Current Population Survey (CPS), a time period
prior to the recession of 2007–09 when, as shown in Figure 3.1, involuntary
part-time employment was technically at a forty-year low.[2] A nationally representative sample of U.S. workers was asked the question: "If you had a choice at
your main job would you prefer to work fewer hours but earn less money, work
more hours and earn more money, or work the same number of hours and
earn the same money?" Women's responses to this question are reported in
Table 3.1, men's responses in Table 3.2. These data provide an empirical, albeit
limited, assessment of some of the central assumptions of the "opting out"
thesis and insight into how the economy and changing gender roles may be
reshaping workers' preferences to opt in or out of full labor force participation.

Opt "Out" or "Opt In"?

Consistent with the "opt out" discourse, a greater proportion of women
(8.9%) than men (5.5%) did indeed report that they would prefer to work
fewer hours per week even if it meant sacrificing earnings (p<.05). Also, the
majority (61.9%) of women who worked part-time (less than 35 hours per
week) reported that they would prefer to continue to work the same number
of hours for the same earnings. And a greater proportion of women with at
least one child 5 or younger (10.9%) than women with older children (8.5%)
or no children (8.4%) reported that they would prefer to work fewer hours,
although these differences are not significant (p>.10).

TABLE 3.1

Percentage of Women Preferring to Work Fewer, More, or the Same Number of Hours Per Week ((N=20,558); 2001 Census Data)[a]

	Fewer hours & less pay			More hours & more pay			Same hours & same pay		
	Total	Hourly	Salary	Total	Hourly	Salary	Total	Hourly	Salary
Overall	8.9%	7.3%	11.6%	23.5%	27.4%	16.9%	67.6%	65.3%	71.4%
Race									
White	9.9	8.3	12.4	20.3	23.9	14.6	69.8	67.7	73.0
African Am.	5.3	4.0	8.1	34.3	38.4	25.0	60.5	57.6	66.9
Hispanic	5.6	4.3	9.2	34.1	35.9	29.4	60.3	59.8	61.4
Other	7.2	6.3	8.8	30.3	34.1	23.7	62.5	59.6	67.6
Work Hour Status									
Full-time	9.9	8.2	12.3	20.7	24.3	15.7	69.4	67.5	71.9
Part-time	5.7	5.2	7.2	32.4	34.6	24.5	61.9	60.2	68.3
Primary Wage Earner?[b]									
No	11.8	9.9	14.5	16.6	19.7	12.3	71.6	70.4	73.2
Yes	5.4	4.5	7.4	31.8	35.7	23.9	62.8	59.9	68.7
Any children?									
No	8.4	7.2	10.2	22.6	25.9	17.6	69.0	66.9	72.2
Yes	9.5	7.3	13.5	24.5	28.9	16.1	66.1	63.7	70.4
Child under 5? (n=9,802 women w/children)									
No	8.5	7.0	11.6	24.5	28.6	16.6	66.9	64.4	71.8
Yes	10.9	7.9	16.4	24.3	29.4	15.3	64.7	62.7	68.4

a. The census rotation that included the work hour preference question did not contain information on pay status (hourly, salaried) for 15,472 female workers (16,145 male workers). In these cases, when possible, information on pay status was taken from other rotations that included it. In order to ensure that the job referred to by respondents in the rotation was the same as that referred to in these 2001 data, jobs were matched on job seniority, occupation, and industry. For the 4,715 women (4,984 men) for whom there was no job match (that is, the respondent was reporting on a different job in other rotations), a regression procedure was used to predict the probability that the 2001 job was paid by the hour. Jobs scoring at the median and above were coded as hourly. Four different estimation procedures were followed to assess the sensitivity of estimates to different assumptions. These four estimations were correlated above .9, yielding proportions of hourly jobs that varied by under 1 percent from one another.

b. 'Based on Shaefer's (2009) definition, 'Primary wage earner' includes single heads of household plus workers whose earnings constitute more than half of their household's total income.

TABLE 3.2

Percentage of Men Preferring to Work Fewer, More, or the Same Number of Hours Per Week (N=21,369; 2001 Census Data)[a]

	Fewer hours & less pay			More hours & more pay			Same hours & same pay		
	Total	Hourly	Salary	Total	Hourly	Salary	Total	Hourly	Salary
Overall	5.5%	4.3%	7.1%	28.8%	35.7%	19.4%	65.7%	60.0%	73.5%
Race									
White	6.3	5.1	7.7	25.0	31.5	17.3	68.8	63.4	75.1
African Am.	3.4	3.2	4.0	38.6	42.8	28.7	58.0	54.0	67.3
Hispanic	2.3	1.9	3.7	45.3	49.4	33.1	52.4	48.7	63.3
Other	4.3	3.0	6.2	35.2	41.0	26.7	60.6	56.0	67.2
Work Hour Status									
Full-time	5.6	4.4	7.2	27.1	33.9	18.6	67.2	61.7	74.2
Part-time	4.1	3.8	5.1	45.1	48.0	35.1	50.8	48.2	59.8
Primary Wage Earner?[b]									
No	6.0	4.8	7.3	23.7	30.8	16.3	70.2	64.4	76.4
Yes	4.7	3.8	6.6	36.8	41.4	27.0	58.5	54.8	66.4
Any children?									
No	6.3	5.2	7.7	27.6	32.9	20.2	66.1	61.9	72.1
Yes	4.6	3.3	6.4	30.2	39.0	18.6	65.2	57.7	75.0
Child under 5? (n=9,929 men w/children)									
No	4.8	3.5	6.4	28.2	36.3	17.5	67.1	60.2	76.1
Yes	4.5	3.0	6.4	32.5	42.3	19.8	63.0	54.7	73.8

a. See Table 1, Note a.
b. See Table 1, Note b.

The comparison that is central to the issue of whether working women are seeking to "opt out" of employment or to "opt in" to fuller employment is between the proportion of women who say they would prefer to work more hours per week versus those who would prefer to work fewer hours per week. As shown in Table 3.1, overall over twice as many women reported that they would prefer to add (23.5%) rather than subtract (8.9%) hours to their work-week. This holds for women with children, even those with young children. Among women with children, fully 24.5% reported that they would prefer to work additional hours, compared to 9.5% who said they would prefer fewer hours. Similarly, among women with at least one child 5 or younger, 24.3% reported that they would prefer to work additional hours, which is over twice as many (10.9%) who reported that they would prefer to work fewer hours if it meant lower earnings.

Women in hourly jobs

The contrast between the proportion of women preferring more versus fewer hours is especially stark among women paid by the hour, who constitute the majority of women in the paid work force (61.9% in 2001; 60.7% in 2010). In 2001, almost a third (27.4%) of women in hourly jobs preferred to work more hours to earn more, whereas only 7.3% reported that they would prefer to work less if it meant earning less. Among women paid by a salary, on the other hand, 16.9% reported that they would prefer to work more hours while 11.6% would like to work less even if it meant lower earnings.

Women of color

Among women in hourly jobs, a preference for additional hours of work was greatest among women of color who were even more likely than white women to hold an hourly job (60.6% of white women, 69.2% of African American women, 72.2% of Hispanic women, and 63.4% of women in other race/ethnic groups who were members of the wage and salaried workforce were paid by the hour in 2001). Notably, 38.4% of African American women and 35.9% of Hispanic women in hourly jobs reported that they would prefer more hours of work. Thus, the data suggest that the rhetoric of "opting out" holds little relevance for women in hourly jobs, especially women of color.

Women in part-time jobs

Part, but not all, of the difference in work hour preferences among salaried and hourly women may be attributable to the greater proportion of women paid by the hour than by a salary and who work part-time (29.7% of hourly women worked part-time; 13.7% of salaried women worked part-time in 2001). Although a quarter (24.5%) of women in part-time, salaried jobs said they would prefer additional hours of work, this is still significantly (p<.01) less than the proportion of women in hourly part-time jobs (34.6%) who preferred additional work hours. Moreover, although women working full-time were less likely than women working part-time to prefer additional hours of work, regardless of whether they were paid by the hour or a salary, the hourly/salaried disparity holds even among full-time workers; 24.3% of women in full-time hourly jobs versus 15.7% of women in full-time salaried positions preferred to work more hours for more pay (p<.01). These analyses highlight the finding that issues of "opting in" take on added importance among women whose earnings depend directly on the number of hours they work.

Gender roles and work hour preferences

Comparisons of work hour preferences between male and female workers help to distinguish the extent to which women's work hour preferences may be traced to differences in gender roles. Overall, 28.8% of men reported that they would prefer to work more hours for more pay, which is significantly (p<.05) but only modestly higher than the proportion of women who would prefer to work more hours (23.5%). As with women, the majority of men, especially men of color, worked in hourly jobs (54% of white men, 70.1% of African American men, 74.7% of Hispanic men, and 59.2% of men of other races/ethnicities were paid by the hour) in 2001. Also, similar to women, the preference for additional work hours was especially pronounced among men in hourly jobs, especially men of color. Notably, fully 42.8% of African American men and almost half (49.4%) of Hispanic men working in hourly jobs reported that they would prefer to work more hours for more pay. In sum, although work hour preferences are significantly different for men and women when it comes to the proportion preferring fewer and additional hours of work, the overall patterns of work hour preferences are strikingly similar for men and women. A greater proportion of both would prefer to work additional hours for additional pay than to work fewer hours and earn less.

The data thus suggest that rather than women clamoring to reduce their labor force participation as they assume roles traditionally held by men, they instead seek to maintain or increase their work effort. As discussed in other chapters in this volume, the importance of women's labor market participation for families' financial security has increased over the past decades in part due to shifts in the industrial base and declining returns to employment among men with limited education (Boushey 2008). Women are subsuming a greater breadwinner role both in dual-earner households and in households they head on their own. As shown in Tables 3.1 and 3.2, a preference for working additional hours for additional pay is especially pronounced among workers—both men and women—who are the primary wage earners in their families. Notably, among hourly workers, fully 41.4% of men and 35.7% of women who were primary wage earners reported that they would prefer more hours of work for more pay, as compared to 30.8% of men and only 19.7% of women who were not the primary wage earner in their household.

A preference for full-time hours

Perhaps what is most striking in terms of the data on work hour preferences is that—regardless of gender, race, and job status—the majority of workers reported a preference for working the same hours for the same pay: 65.7% of men and 67.6% of women. Given that fully 84.5% of workers (91.5% of men; 77.3% of women) reported working 35 or more hours per week, a preference for working the same number of hours can be interpreted as a preference for full-time employment and full-time pay. As work hours increased, the proportion of workers preferring to work additional hours of work decreased.[3] Specifically, fully 35% of workers working fewer than 35 hours per week reported that they would prefer additional hours of work, whereas 25% of those working between 35 and 40 hours and 22.4 % of those working between 40 and 50 hours per week reported that they would prefer additional hours for additional income. Nonetheless, even in jobs in which workers reported working 50 or more hours, the proportion of workers who preferred additional hours (20.1%) still outweighs the proportion who preferred reduced hours for reduced pay (11.2%). The majority (68.7%) of workers who typically work 50 or more hours per week reported that they would prefer to continue working the same number of hours.

Summary

Only a minority of women in 2001 expressed a preference for "opting out," defined here as preferring fewer hours of work. If the "opting out" thesis holds at all, these data suggest that it holds for a small minority of workers, mostly women who do not have primary responsibility for their family's economic well-being and who are privileged in both the workplace (salaried) and in society (white). Rather than preferring to "opt out," the majority of workers—both men and women—indicate a preference for either full-time employment or at least fuller employment. This preference for fuller labor force participation is especially striking among workers of color and those whose income is directly determined by the number of hours they work week to week. Given that the majority of workers, both men and women, are paid by the hour, these data suggest that a sizable proportion of the workforce faces barriers to "opting in" to full(er) employment.

Barriers to Opting In: Personal Factors

The recent policy literature provides convincing evidence that personal constraints can interfere with labor force participation. Low-income women who face multiple personal barriers, such as personal health problems, domestic violence, and caring for an ill child, are especially at risk of poor employment outcomes (Danziger et al., 2000). Yet, many women continue to labor away in hourly jobs even under difficult personal circumstances, especially now that the receipt of cash assistance is contingent on work effort. For many women, opting out is simply not an option (see Joan Williams and Maureen Perry-Jenkins, this volume). For these women, and others who toil without the additional challenges posed by personal difficulties, the prospects of adequate hours of work, and thus of income, may be shaped as much or more by the realities of the workplace as by the challenges of personal life.

Barriers to Opting In: Labor Flexibility Practices

What then are the workplace realities that serve as barriers to working "enough" in hourly jobs? The answer, in short, is that employers adopt labor flexibility practices that enable them to readily adjust the number of employees and their work hours to match variations in consumer demand. The purpose of these practices is to contain, if not minimize, labor costs. The reasons employers seek to minimize labor costs are debated among scholars who place varying weight on global competition, Wall Street's focus on short-term returns, and business strategies that privilege cost containment over quality enhancement (see Appelbaum, Bernhardt, and Murnane 2003 for a discussion). Regardless of the reason, research indicates that labor flexibility practices have increased since the 1980s, bringing increased volatility in earnings and hours (Dynan, Elmendorf, and Sichel 2008; Gottschalk and Moffitt 2009; Kalleberg 2009).

Below, I highlight a set of labor flexibility practices that frontline managers use to contain labor costs in hourly jobs. These practices include everyday frontline staffing and scheduling strategies that can make it difficult for women to "opt in" to full labor force participation, especially while fulfilling caregiving responsibilities.

Keeping headcount high

Staffing strategies adopted by firms include "headcount," that is, the number of workers hired into particular jobs. For example, is there one administrative assistant or twenty? Fifty sales associates or ten? And are these part-time or full-time positions? The higher the headcount, the larger the pool of workers whose hours can expand or contract depending on business needs and, if part-time, who can be slotted to work short shifts during peak business times. Thus, keeping headcount high, especially in part-time jobs, can provide managers with a great deal of labor flexibility.

Hiring more workers on the payroll does not, however, mean that managers will have more hours to distribute among their staff. Across industries, managers of hourly workers are held accountable for "staying within hours," that is, for running their department, restaurant, or production line using a particular number of worker hours (Lambert 2008). In retail, for example, the number of hours managers can assign when scheduling their staff is usually calculated from a combination of previous year's sales, store traffic, and recent retail trends. In hotels, "hours" are based on a hotel census, and in airline catering, on scheduled flights. Managers are responsible for "scheduling within hours" no matter how many workers they have on their payroll. Thus, the more workers on the payroll, the fewer hours, on average, for each individual employee. There may be three workers for every "real" job.

The responses of store managers in a national retail firm provide insight into the priority frontline managers place on labor flexibility versus the needs of employees for hours of work (Lambert and Henly 2010). When asked about their general hiring strategy, 67 percent of store managers chose the statement "I like to keep my sales associate staff on the large side so that I have several associates I can tap to work when needed," whereas 33 percent chose the statement "I like to keep my sales associate staff on the small side to help ensure that workers get hours." Thus, for the majority of these managers, labor flexibility takes precedence over employees' work-hour needs, although a notable minority seems to have found ways to meet firm accountability requirements while also attending to employees' need for hours of work.

Having workers on the payroll whose labor goes unused is costly to firms when workers come with substantial fixed costs, such as a fixed salary or employer-supported health insurance. One way employers contain labor costs in jobs with high fixed costs is by restricting headcount and instead requiring "over work" during periods of high demand (Lambert and Haley-Lock 2004). Today's hourly jobs, however, come with few fixed costs. For example, rates of employer-provided insurance have dropped since the 1980s (Farber and Levy 2000) and are particularly low in service industries. Analyses of 2006 CPS data indicate that among workers in the retail sector, only 52 percent of full-time workers and 16.4 percent of part-time workers had health insurance coverage through their employer.

Regardless of industry, most employers incur few costs for health insurance for workers in hourly part-time jobs; across industries, in 2006 only 18.6 percent of part-time hourly workers were covered by health insurance through their employer.[4] Moreover, firms have decreased their investments in training for workers in entry-level, hourly jobs (Bernhardt and Marcotte 2000; Bishop 1997). In many firms, the only fixed cost for keeping part-time hourly workers on the payroll is that of maintaining personnel records. The primary costs of hiring part-time hourly workers are, instead, variable costs that are incurred only when workers work hours, that is, wages and the employer share of Unemployment Insurance, Social Security, and Medicare. For firms, then, maintaining a high headcount in hourly jobs, especially part-time jobs, may cost little and may help frontline managers meet firm accountability requirements such as staying within hours. For workers, on the other hand, a high headcount may mean few hours of work and thus, small earnings.

A loose relationship between job status and number of hours worked
Another labor flexibility practice that can help explain why workers in hourly jobs often have a difficult time opting in to full labor market participation is that many firms maintain a tenuous relationship between job status and number of hours worked. Although the U.S. has laws governing minimum wages, we do not have laws governing minimum work hours. Thus managers have a great deal of flexibility when it comes to adjusting workers' schedules to match variations in consumer demand. Hours can fluctuate greatly in part-time jobs, sometimes down to zero for some weeks of the year and above part-time limits for other weeks (Lambert 2008).

Although the overall percentage of jobs that are part-time has remained at about 17 percent over the past decade, this overall average obscures variation in the use of part-time jobs. Not only is there between-firm variation in the use of part-time jobs by employers, but also within-firm variation in the proportion of low-skilled jobs that are part-time (Lambert 2008). For example, in two transportation firms we studied in Chicago, 100 percent of package handling jobs were part-time. In one of these firms, 75 percent of entry-level administrative clerks also worked part-time while in the other firm, only 15 percent of administrate clerks were in part-time positions. In one retail store, 95 percent of the cashiers were part-time whereas in another store 50 percent were part-time. In many of today's firms, there are pockets of highly concentrated part-time employment and many of these jobs—in retail and hospitality particularly—are overwhelmingly held by women.

Although hours in part-time jobs fluctuate enormously, workers in full-time jobs are not immune from hour reductions. For example, in our research in Chicago, workers in full-time positions in airline catering companies were regularly sent home when flights were canceled or delayed. Housekeepers covered by a union contract that required that workers be scheduled (and paid) for a full 8 hours every "work" day were often scheduled for fewer than 5 days a week, even though these jobs were classified as full-time. An emerging practice found in the retail sector is a new job status termed "full-time flex." This status allows managers to schedule workers classified as full-time for as few as 32 or even 26 hours a week, depending on the employers' definition of this job status. Full-time flex thus enhances labor flexibility by enabling managers to distribute staffing hours among a broader set of staff and thus, across shifts and days.

Varying the number of hours in full-time jobs is not necessarily new. Analyses from the Panel Study of Income Dynamics suggest that variation in work hours has increased 23 percent since the 1970s, much of it in full-time jobs (Dynan, Elmendorf, and Sichel 2008). However, creating new job statuses, such as full-time flex, contingent employment, or temporary worker, serves to redefine workplace norms and lower workers' expectations for steady employment and hours. These new statuses effectively shift what were once considered standard jobs into a growing mélange of "nonstandard employment arrangements." In doing so, these new statuses serve as a tool for implementing labor flexibility practices and a means of legitimating employer practices that give priority to employers' preferences for labor flexibility over workers' needs for adequate and stable work hours.

Unstable and unpredictable work schedules

Fluctuating and unpredictable work schedules create barriers to steady employment and full labor force participation. Posting schedules with limited advance notice allows managers to adjust both the number and timing of work hours to recent changes in consumer demand. It is common practice in hourly jobs. For example, in our research in Chicago, all but one of the retailers we studied stated that they posted schedules for sales associates one week in advance. In addition, last-minute adjustments to work schedules—adding or subtracting hours to the posted schedule a day or two in advance—is also common practice, as are real-time adjustments in which workers are sent home or called in as demand changes during the day. These last-minute scheduling practices mean that workers' hours may not only vary week-to-week, but that their work schedules are also largely unpredictable. This is especially troubling since limited advance notice can interfere with women's ability to secure reliable child care, to participate in intimate family routines, and to maintain employment (Henly, Shaefer, and Waxman 2006).

A preference for "open availability"

The task of scheduling workers at the last minute and making changes throughout the workweek is made easier if employees are expected to be flexible in terms of the timing of work hours across shifts and days. "Open availability," that is, being able to work varying and unpredictable work hours, is becoming a valued part of an hourly workers' human capital. Human Resource staff in all retailers we have studied say that when hiring they give priority to applicants who can work varying shifts. Some firms make open availability a requirement for full-time employment (Waxman 2009). In our study of a national retail apparel firm, 94 percent of the store managers surveyed agreed that "they try to hire workers with maximum availability" and 79 percent agreed that "they give more hours to sales associates with greater availability." In contrast, 89 percent disagreed with the statement "I give more hours to sales associates who seem to really need the money." To the extent that caregiving or other personal responsibilities limit women's availability for work, they may not even be hired, and if hired, may not be scheduled for as many hours as their counterparts with greater availability. Because earnings are a function of both hourly wage and number of hours worked, women in hourly jobs who do not have "open availability" may thus incur an earnings penalty.

Informal layoffs

Another labor flexibility practice that can affect the ability of women to opt in fully to the labor market is a practice often referred to as "workloading." Workloading constitutes a type of informal lay-off. Workers are kept on the firm's payroll so they technically have a job, but they are not scheduled for any hours—sometimes for weeks or even months. This practice enables employers to maintain a ready pool of workers to draw on when consumer demand increases. Workloading places workers in the difficult position of deciding whether they might be better off looking for a new job or holding on to their "no-time job" with the hope of eventually securing enough seniority to avoid a reduction in work hours in the future. Just like women in professional and technical jobs, women in low-level hourly jobs face trade-offs. In this case, the trade-off is often between working "enough" hours and working during preferred times.

The Importance of Opting In

Because income in hourly jobs is a function of both wage rate and hours worked, when hourly workers do not get enough hours, they do not earn enough income. Among families with at least one full-time, year-round earner—hourly or salaried—the poverty rate in 2009 was 3.5%. This stands in stark contrast to the 26.1% poverty rate among families in which at least one member held a part-time or part-year job but no member worked full-time, year-round. The protection of stable, full-time employment holds for married-couple families (2.5% poverty rate with at least one full-time worker versus 15.8% poverty rate with no full-time worker but at least one part-time worker) and for female-headed households (8.8% poverty rate with full-time worker versus 45.2% poverty rate with no full-time worker but at least one part-time worker in the household). Full labor force participation is a cornerstone of financial stability for families. Without it, children are at risk of poverty. In 2009, 20.7% of children under 18 lived in poverty. Fully 41.9% of African American children and 35% of Hispanic children under 5 years old lived in a family with an income below the U.S. poverty line. These statistics alone are ample reason to pay attention to both parts of the earnings equation—wage rates and work hours.

Another reason to be concerned about employer practices that can interfere with workers' ability to opt in to full labor force participation is that access to many social benefits is conditioned on number of hours of work. For example, employers make health insurance and time off—including paid sick time—conditional on both job status and number of hours worked. The number of work hours required for benefits varies greatly among today's employers, some requiring both full-time status and full-time (commonly 35 or more) hours, and others requiring more modest work effort (commonly 20 to 25 hours) but higher employee contributions. When jobs do not provide workers with the minimum hours required for benefits, employers effectively deny workers benefits that would otherwise be available to them as a matter of firm policy. Moreover, jobs with fluctuating hours can put employer-sponsored benefits at risk of cancellation. When hours drop below what an employer has established as full time (usually 35 hours) for multiple pay periods (ranging from two pay periods to six months), workers in hourly jobs can lose their eligibility for paid time off and health insurance, even though their employer may continue to classify the job as full time and the employee may prefer to work the qualifying number of hours.

Many social benefits provided by the government are also conditioned on number of hours worked. For example, to qualify for a parental leave under the Family and Medical Leave Act, workers must have worked for their employer for a minimum of 12 months, logging a minimum of 1,250 hours over this time. This breaks down to an average of 24 hours a week for 52 weeks of the year, a requirement that helps account for the fact that, in 2000, only 62 percent of workers met the eligibility requirements for a leave under the Family and Medical Leave Act (Cantor et al. 2001). Many other social benefits are also conditioned on work hours, including public housing, child care subsidies, and Unemployment Insurance. Thus, fluctuating and especially reduced work hours can interfere with the ability of low-income workers to access benefits needed to support themselves and their family.

The role of work-hour requirements is especially pertinent to the ability of women to receive income support through block grants to states under Temporary Assistance to Needy Families (TANF). Currently, federal legislation defines work-hour requirements for single parents in terms of 30 hours of weekly "work activities" of which 20 hours are to be in a job. Half of a state's caseload must meet this requirement in order to be in compliance with federal law. What qualifies as "work activities" varies by state, however, and some states have implemented tougher work requirements (up to 40 hours per week) than first legislated in the 1996 law (Golden 2005).

Twenty or even thirty hours of work in a job may seem like a reasonable requirement, until one considers the labor flexibility practices outlined above. Over-hiring can severely hamper the number of hours available to workers on a firm's payroll and scheduling practices that allow managers to vary workers' hours with demand may mean that workers may meet work requirements one week but not the next. Note that employers are most likely to hire when they have relatively ample hours to spread among staff, that is, when demand is high. When demand slackens, frontline managers have fewer hours to divide up among staff. The common practice is that workers with the least seniority and/or the least availability bear the brunt of work-hour reductions. Thus, recent entrants to the labor force and those with family responsibilities—characteristics of women receiving TANF—are at increased risk of having their work hours reduced or of even being "workloaded." As a result, these women may not meet the work-hour requirements to receive public assistance, through no fault of their own. In sum, conditioning access to social benefits on work hours can place low-income women and their families in double jeopardy. They are at risk of losing important family supports, such as cash assistance and housing, at the same time that their earned income is low.

Conclusion

The rhetoric of "opting out" epitomizes many of the shortcomings of our society: growing inequality in opportunities and in income and a tendency to frame complex social problems as individual failings or "choices." My goal in this chapter is to offer one alternative for understanding why some women "opt out" of full labor force participation, defined here as working less than full-time hours. The census data provide evidence that rather than choosing to work less, many women are kept from working more. The firm data reveal the daily practices that can serve to restrict hourly workers' full labor force participation. By focusing exclusively on the work behaviors of women, the "opting out" discourse obscures the fact that men and women both face barriers to opting in to full labor force participation, especially workers of color and those paid by the hour. A greater proportion of all workers—regardless of gender, race, or job status—reported that they would like to work additional rather than fewer hours.

As argued throughout this volume, issues of work hours constitute a complex economic issue that can be understood only if placed in a broader social context. One part of this context is the changing nature of employment and employers' adoption of labor flexibility practices to contain labor costs in hourly jobs. Keeping headcount high in jobs may make it easier for employers to match labor to demand, but it can make it more difficult for each worker to get the hours needed to earn an adequate income. Last-minute posting of work schedules may help managers contain short-term labor costs, but it may undermine the ability of workers to make long-term gains in the labor market. What may look, then, like voluntary reductions in work hours may in fact be driven by employer practices that structure instability into today's hourly jobs. Today's workers, especially those in hourly jobs, are better characterized as striving to "opt in" rather than choosing to "opt out" of full labor force participation.

NOTES

1. The author would like to thank Lauren Gaudino for her fine analysis of the CPS data and Luke Shaefer for calculating estimates of employer-sponsored health insurance. The author is also grateful for the input of Julia Henly and Lonnie Golden on the ideas developed in this chapter and for the support of the Ford Foundation, Russell Sage Foundation, and the Annie E. Casey Foundation for the research drawn on in this chapter.

2. Questions on work-hour preferences have not been replicated by the U.S. census since 2001. The General Social Survey (GSS) includes this question, but it does not include questions about hourly/salaried pay status.

3. Statistics on work-hour preferences as compared to usual work hours are provided in the text, not in Tables 3.1 or 3.2.

4. Source: H. L. Shaefer analysis of 2006 Current Population Survey (CPS) data. Part-time workers are defined as those who report working less than 35 hours per week at all jobs.

4

The Challenges to and Consequences of "Opting Out" for Low-Wage, New Mothers

MAUREEN PERRY-JENKINS

The idea of women "opting out" of paid employment to stay at home and care for children has been a topic of hot debate in both the public media and among academics who study women's employment patterns (Belkin, 2003). In her provocative book *Opting Out: Why Women Really Quit Careers and Head Home*, Stone (2007) demonstrates the subtle and not so subtle forces that slowly push women off the career track and send them home with the children, leaving us with the faulty assumption that women are making a "choice" to leave their careers. In fact, Stone convincingly argues that high achieving, professional women are often not opting out at all; they are being shut out. In the present chapter, my aim is to consider how issues of choice and constraint, of opting out or being shut out, shape the work and family experiences of a different and unique group of employed women, specifically working-class, low-wage women.

When considering the topic of work and family issues in the United States, a critical question becomes: work and family issues for whom? Much of the work-family literature has documented the experiences of employment for white, middle-class, two-parent households and highlighted the stressors these families face in juggling the demands of work and family (Hochschild, 1989, 1997; Stone, 2007). In addition, a second area of research has focused on families in poverty and movement into and out of marginal employment (Chase-Lansdale et al., 2003; Edin and Lein, 1997). The unique issues of working-class families, however, have received far less attention because they are often subsumed under the broader category of the "middle class." In this chapter I argue that the experiences of dual-career families (e.g., middle- to upper-middle class) are not generalizable to dual-earner, working-class families or single employed mothers due to differences in social class, the nature of the problems confronted by these different types of families, their resources, and the solutions they devise to deal with their problems (Mortimer and London, 1984; Rubin 1976, 1994).

Social class creates different opportunities for women to "opt out." Social class gives different meanings to the experience of opting out and may lead to quite different outcomes for women of different classes who do "opt out." Since 2000 I have been conducting a study that examines how low-income, working-class mothers, both married and single, cope with the challenge of having a baby and maintaining secure employment across the transition to parenthood. These young, working mothers differ from the career women in Stone's book in some key ways. The majority of mothers in my study have high school degrees sometimes coupled with an Associates or technical degree, such as a beautician degree, or Certified Nursing Assistant degree. These working-class mothers earn far less than the career women in Stone's study, making between $23,000 and $30,000 per year. Finally, these women are in jobs that offer little flexibility or supports and they often have little control over their job activities. In the words of Stone, I want to explore the "disjuncture that occurs between the rhetoric of choice and the reality of constraints" (Stone, 2007) for this significant group of employed women at the lower end of the social class hierarchy. To that end, this chapter will explore three questions. The first question is: Who is opting out? Although Stone describes the issues facing career women, low-wage, employed women also opt out of employment, although the consequences for opting out among the working class and working poor are often quite dire. Second, I will examine the question of "Why?" Specifically, why do low-wage, employed women quit their jobs even when it often places them in financially precarious situations? Third, I will explore the psychological implications for working-class and working-poor women of having to "opt in" to paid employment for financial reasons even when they would prefer to be stay-at-home mothers.

Who "Opts Out"?

In her sample of highly educated, professional women Stone argues that these women did not quit their jobs simply because their husbands made enough money However, it is obvious that the financial security of these families gave women the opportunity to consider the possibility of leaving paid work. The ultimate "choice" to leave the workforce is greatly influenced by a family's economic security and, consequently, for those who live from paycheck to paycheck the major constraint of the job is primarily a financial one.

The stories of the families from the Work and Family Transitions Project (WFTP) point to the real constraints of low-wage employment for new mothers and fathers. The WFTP is a longitudinal study, funded by the National Institute of Mental Health, which examines the transition to parenthood for working-class and working-poor parents. A primary aim of this project was to examine how work conditions, work preferences, and workplace policies across the transition to parenthood shape the mental health and relationship quality of new parents and, ultimately, affect their children's development. To document these experiences, five in-home interviews were conducted by trained interviewers over the course of the first year of the baby's life for a sample 360 families. We interviewed both mothers and fathers (if involved with the family) in two-to-three hour, face-to-face interviews in their homes and asked many questions about why they worked, how they felt about their jobs, their work preferences, their beliefs about how their work affected their children, and how their work affected them personally and in their relationships. A key criterion for selection into the study was that mothers were employed prior to the child's birth and that mothers planned to return to employment within six months of their child's birth. Although at the outset of the study all mothers planned to return to work, a small subgroup of new mothers never returned to paid work after the baby's birth, some returned only part-time, and others moved into and out of the workforce multiple times over the course of the year. Thus, we have the unique opportunity to consider what factors played a role in women's decision to step out of the paid labor force.

The WFTP has two unique subsamples. Our first sample of 153 is comprised of two-parent families earning an average family income of close to $50,000 (mothers and fathers combined earnings), with mothers' average income in this group being $21,500. Thus, if mothers were to step out of the workforce, many of these families would be teetering on the edge of poverty. The majority of both mothers and fathers in this sample hold either a high school degree or in some cases a one- or two-year Associates degree. Importantly, none of the parents hold college degrees. The second sample consists of 207 families, 180 of whom are single mothers. Approximately half of these single mothers are cohabiting with the child's biological father while the other half either live alone or with extended family. In this sample the average maternal income is $22,000 a year, a group that has come to be called the "working poor." In this sample, the majority of mothers held a high school degree or General Education Degree (GED). However, a full 18% had less than 12 years of education.

It is important to note at the outset that despite limiting our sample to employed parents, there were clear differences in income, education level, and patterns of employment in our two-parent sample and single-parent sample. Our sample of single mothers worked more hours and made more money than mothers in dual-earner families, but they also had lower levels of education than mothers in the two-parent sample. Single mothers were also more likely to move into and out of the workforce over the first year of parenthood. In the following section we examine a number of reasons why new mothers leave the workforce even though they realize they will face severe financial hardship and the possibility of relying on public aid.

Why Working-Class Mothers "Opt Out" of Jobs: Time and Timing

In Stone's study, many of the women leaving professional careers for home pointed to the stress of heavy work demands, such as extensive travel and expectations of 24/7 availability, that were the final "deal breakers" for workers raising young children. In contrast to professional occupations, low-wage jobs don't typically require much travel away from home; rather it is the issue of time scheduling that presents the real challenge to new mothers in our study. Specifically, the unpredictability of weekly schedules, the lack of notice about when work hours would be cut or increased, shift work schedules requiring evening and night work, and the challenge of mandatory overtime were some of the key issues that created significant problems for new mothers. For example, one young mother in our study, Ceil, was employed as a package delivery worker for a postal service store. Ceil received her work schedule every Thursday for the upcoming week. At that point, she would sit down and work out a child care schedule with the baby's father and other family members for her new baby Joshua. As Ceil described it,

> It gets very tiring to set up a new child care plan each week. To top it off, there are times when my boss will call out of the blue to have me come in earlier or will ask me to stay later than my scheduled shift which can be a real problem. I need the money but if my babysitter has other plans I have to get home.

Although it is clear that the lack of a consistent weekly schedule can create chaos in child care plans, it was also clear that even for mothers with stable and full-time work schedules, if their job requires working the evening (i.e., the 3–11 p.m. shift) or night (11 p.m.–7 a.m.) shifts, they face a different set of problems. Our findings indicate that shift work can hold negative implications for new parents' mental health as well as for the quality of their close relationships (Perry-Jenkins, Goldberg, Pierce, and Sayer, 2007). Specifically, our analyses revealed that working evening or night shifts, as opposed to day shifts, was related to higher levels of depressive symptoms for new mothers and fathers. For mothers only, working rotating shifts predicted more relationship conflict. Finally, increases in role overload were positively related to both depression and conflict for new parents, yet working a non-day shift explained variance in depression and conflict above and beyond role overload.

These results suggest that for new parents, working non–day shifts is a risk factor for depressive symptoms and relationship conflict. Sarah, a mother in our study, is a living example of this problem. She works as a Certified Nursing Assistant (CNA) 3 to 4 nights a week on the 11 to 7 shift and she tries to get at least one extra night a week per diem. Sarah has four children and her partner (father of all four children) is home at night with the children while she is at work. She gets home at 7 a.m., gets her five-, six-, and seven-year-old children off to school and then is home all day with her sixteen-month-old baby. Some days her mother-in-law watches the baby, but most days she is home with the baby and naps when the baby naps. Sarah only had the option of unpaid parental leave, so she was back at work within four weeks of her last child's birth. She would love a full-time, day job with benefits, but for now she is getting by on minimal sleep and lots of coffee. I remember this interview so vividly because although Sarah was exhausted and overwhelmed with her work and family demands, she was optimistic and hopeful about the future. When I asked her what was the most significant challenge she faced in managing her job and parenting, she said:

> It is hard because when I get home I want to rest and there is no time to rest … The hardest part is like when you need a day off, like to get some rest and you know, time for yourself, you never have that time. You always have to secure the household, you always have to be available for the kids and the Dad. You just want to go out and go "AHHH" and scream a little bit to relieve the stress.

When I asked her how she managed this exhausting schedule she did not hesitate, "If they are your kids you always want to do whatever you can for your own blood, you know, that is what keeps me going. Because I will do anything for them."

The strain of coping with opposite shifts schedules was a common problem for many of the couples in our study. Janice and Sean were an opposite shift couple. Janice is a Licensed Practical Nurse (LPN) who works in a nursing home on the 3 to 11 shift and Sean is employed as a maintenance worker on the 7 to 3 shift. When we asked Janice the question, "How has managing a job, parenthood, and a marriage been compared to how you thought it would be?" she responded:

> Well, it's probably different than I thought, probably just because we're on different schedules. You know, and if I was able to put him [the baby] in day care and we could be on the same schedule … that would be different. I see plenty of Hunter [the baby], I mean, I'm with him all day and that's great. I think that's benefited us, because I probably would have taken over at night, and Bill wouldn't have been as good as he is. But so we each have our roles there and it's good, but if we were home at night together we'd have more time, Bill and I, which we don't. So I kind of thought that by this time I would have dropped my hours, I keep thinking "oh next month, let's pay this bill off and I'll do it next month," and I don't. So, I figure when I get pregnant next time I'll have to, because there's no way that I will be able to do all of this, plus 40 hours. We don't spend any time together, you know our weekends are like, so packed with everything we have to do, we're together but you know, it would be nice to have a couple more days together.

Mandatory overtime is another issue that arose as a problem for many of our new parents. Mandatory overtime hours are those above the standard workweek (usually 40) that the employer makes compulsory with the threat of job loss or the threat of other reprisals such as demotions, assignment to unattractive work shifts or task, and loss of a day's or multiple days' pay. Based on the Fair Labor Standards Act of 1938, there are no limits on overtime, but an overtime premium must be paid. While many of our new parents welcomed overtime pay, the random nature and timing of mandatory overtime created problems. Not surprisingly, mandatory overtime occurs most often in highly supervised, low control occupations. Time use data clearly indicate that upper-middle-class workers often put in long hours at their workplace; however, the critical variable in these cases appears to be the level of control. When the worker is his or her "own boss," time crunches can often be planned for and there is often some built-in flexibility. For example, a lawyer might run out to do an errand or run home for a quick meal with the family and return to finish a task later in the evening. Mandatory overtime at lower levels of the occupational hierarchy is most often at the discretion of a supervisor and out of the control of the worker. One mother in our sample worked in a manufacturing plant and would often be told halfway through a shift that she needed to work overtime. This meant she had to arrange alternative arrangements for her child's pickup from day care since the child needed to be picked up before her overtime shift ended.

Why Working-Class Mothers "Opt Out" of Jobs: Work-Family Policies and Benefits

Another key factor in mothers' decisions to leave the workforce has to do with work-family policies, or the lack thereof, that are available to low-wage parents. In 1993, landmark legislation was passed in the form of the Family and Medical Leave Act (FMLA) that allows for twelve weeks of unpaid leave with job protection for employees having or adopting children or for the care of an ill child, spouse, or parent. Of course, the critical piece of this legislation for working-class families is the term "unpaid." Findings show that women, parents, those with little income, and African Americans are particularly likely to perceive a need for job leaves. However, it is married (versus single) women and whites who are most likely to take leaves (Gerstel and McGonagle, 1999). Estes and Glass (1996) argue that this type of legislation represents "an emerging class cleavage" in our work and family legislation.

Researchers estimate that anywhere from 38 to 50% of employees are not eligible for FMLA benefits (Cantor et al., 2001; Ruhm, 2005). Employees are only eligible if they have worked for a covered employer for at least one year, and for 1,250 hours over the previous twelve months, and it applies only to workplaces with fifty or more employees. Consequently, FMLA benefits are of little assistance to part-time, seasonal, or temporary workers. Moreover, although the FMLA guarantees an employee's job back at the same pay and equal position, one's work schedule is not guaranteed. Donna, who was a truck driver, learned about this the hard way. Donna had ten weeks of leave after her son's birth; and she pieced together a paid leave package by using sick, vacation, and personal time. She planned to return to her job on the 6 a.m. to 2 p.m. shift and had organized a child care arrangement based on that work schedule. Two days before she was to return to the job, she got a call from her supervisor informing her that her new shift hours would be from 11 a.m. to 7 p.m., starting the next day: "Well, you can imagine. I burst into tears, it was hard enough going back in the first place, but 11 to 7, how was I going to manage that? I was ready to quit, but what could I do? We needed the job."

Donna did not interpret this change in plans as her supervisor's attempt to punish her. Rather she believed that her supervisor was just completely unaware of the issues surrounding child care because he had a stay-at-home wife. Within a month's time Donna had another "run in" with her supervisor. She requested that during her midday break she be allowed to return to the office to pump her breast milk. He turned down the request. So at 3 p.m. every day, Donna parks her truck on the side of the road, slips into the back cab, and pumps her milk for twenty minutes. She summed up her experience with her boss in these words, "He is a guy … he just doesn't get it."

Parents in our study took an average of twelve weeks of maternity leave, ranging from two weeks to forty weeks. For fathers, 74 percent took no time off from work and 25 percent took off at least one day. For the latter group of men, the average time off was 5.91 days, with a range of 1 to 35 days. We learned some important methodological lessons in our attempts to document how much maternity and paternity leave new parents received and utilized. Initially, we simply (and naively) asked new parents if they had taken parental leave when their child was born, how long the leave was, and whether it was paid or unpaid. It quickly became clear that the issue was much more complex. The data revealed that close to 50 percent of our parents reported having some paid leave. We were both pleased and surprised by this result. However, upon further perusal of the data, we soon realized our interpretation of the finding was incorrect. In an effort to better understand exactly how they were paid, we modified our questionnaire to have parents report, week by week, whether the time was fully paid, partially paid, or not paid, and how it was paid (e.g., sick time, personal time, parental leave time, or disability).

We learned quickly that the parents in our sample reported having paid parental leave even when sick leave, personal time, or other types of leave were used. The distinction between paid parental leave versus leave paid by other means is an important one. Specifically, if parents use up all their sick time and vacation time during their parental leave, they return to work with no safety net to catch them if they or their child become ill or another emergency arises. In fact, our qualitative data suggests that parents began to receive more reprimands and "letters in their files" for taking time off that they could not cover. In fact, only 10 percent of mothers in our sample had legitimate paid parental leave when their infant was born. Fifteen percent of mothers used personal, sick, or vacation time to pay for their leave in full, while 4 percent used these benefits to partially pay for their leave time. Twelve percent of mothers received partial disability benefits and 4 percent received full disability benefits during their leave. Less than 1 percent of women used comp time to cover their leave. The largest percentage, 44 percent of mothers, had unpaid leave. Finally, 11 percent of mothers dealt with the problem of juggling work and new parenthood by quitting their jobs when the baby was born and starting a new one after they had recovered from the birth. No fathers received paid parental leave for the birth of their baby.

Table 4.1 in the appendix highlights the other types of benefits to which low-wage parents had access and it reveals that the only benefit afforded to the majority of mothers and fathers in our study was paid personal or sick time for family needs. Specifically, we asked, "Does your company offer paid personal or sick time for family emergencies, like if your child is ill?" Close to 70 percent of both mothers and fathers report having this benefit; however, only about 34 percent of fathers and 39 percent of mothers report using the benefit. The question of why parents don't use this benefit is an interesting one. Perhaps using sick time is not officially sanctioned by supervisors despite having a formal policy "on the books." As one mother noted:

> It's hard to get a day off. If you want a day off you put a request slip in and nine times out of ten it gets denied because of short staff. And the fact is that if, ya know, if I had to leave somewhere, leave a few hours early to go to the doctor's for Brianna or something, ya know, I'd get docked. Which is expected, I guess. But they would still be like, "Well, could you do this first before you go?" The job does come first.

Of course, the other problem is that it is virtually impossible to predict if a child will be ill more than 24 hours before he or she get sick. Thus, the idea of having to "plan" one's personal or sick time is, quite simply, impossible. Many of the mothers in our sample did not feel comfortable or equipped to make schedule requests of their boss or negotiate a day off when their child was ill. Janessa, a young mother I interviewed, worked as a telemarketer and was in her fifth month of the six-month probation period required of all new employees. Thus, she had not yet accrued leave time or sick time, and not surprisingly, her baby became ill with an ear infection. She made no attempt to call her boss to ask for more time off or to negotiate some way to deal with her problem; she simply stayed home with her baby. The next day when she walked into work she was fired on the spot, and she was completely surprised by this response from her supervisor. Extended probationary periods, where workers must "prove themselves" prior to being hired as a full-time employee, are becoming more popular in many occupations. This practice places parents of young children in precarious situations because often for many months they have no leave benefits (e.g., sick days, personal days, or family leave) on which to rely when a child becomes ill.

A related problem that Janessa faced was accessing high-quality, affordable child care. The lack of child care as well as concerns about the effects of nonparental care on children is a major reason that low-wage women "opted out" of paid employment. In 2007 in Massachusetts, where the majority of families in our study lived, there was a shortage of affordable child care for low-income workers, which had resulted in a two-year waiting list for subsidized care (Kim, 2007). Turning to child care benefits, what is most striking is not only the low percentage of child care benefits offered, but the even lower percentages of those who use the benefits offered. For example, as shown in Table 4.1, close to 20 percent of parents report that their workplace offers child care referral services; however, only between 3 and 5 percent use this benefit. This lack of use is most likely a result of parents' preference for having family members or friends care for their infant. Only one family in our sample used a child care center to provide care for their infant.

It is also interesting to note that 22 percent of fathers and 25 percent of mothers report having a dependent care assistance plan (DCAP) at their workplace; however, only 1.5 percent and 3 percent of fathers and mothers, respectively, report using this resource. A DCAP allows parents to deduct child care expenses from their paycheck before taxes, saving parents between 20 to 25 percent of their child care expenses. Although we did not routinely ask parents why they did not use the DCAP, anecdotal data suggest that the complicated paper work is a challenge to complete, day care providers must also sign and complete forms on a monthly basis, and workers are told that if they overestimate the amount they will spend on child care, they will lose that money. It is ironic that a policy that could literally put more money in the pockets of many families with infants is too complicated and misunderstood to do any real good for the families it is designed to support.

In terms of child care vouchers, contributions to child care slots, on-site child care, or any type of subsidized care, the percentages ranged from a low of 2 percent to a high of 8 percent. Clearly, supportive workplace policies around child care are almost nonexistent for low-wage new parents, and often the care that is available is extremely costly. As the comments below indicate, a consistent theme in the challenges of maintaining work was the problem of finding and keeping satisfactory child care.

My boss seems to care, but his hands are tied. The company that owns us doesn't really care. They don't offer day care or anything. They offer one more week of leave than they have to by FMLA … that is it. You can make informal arrangements with your supervisor. As a whole, no child care, no subsidized care. Overall organization doesn't offer a lot. They're been good to me, because they've allowed me to take time off, rearrange my breaks, and now they're allowing me to work part time, but we lose money. So for me they've been great, but if I need child care they'd be no help.

A number of mothers indicated that their workplace or supervisor were receptive and supportive, but it appears that child care policies were often at the discretion of the supervisor.

I think they're very receptive. Both owners have a 4-year-old son so they know how I feel about daycare. The baby goes to work with me. They don't have a problem with her being there. One of the owners is like a big brother to me. It's all informal. She's pretty good if I can't make it in, or if I need my schedule changed, otherwise there's not really anything she can do.

The question of how to support parents in both their choice of child care and in making it affordable is an important one. The majority of parents with infants have a strong preference for parental or relative care during the first year. After the first year, more parents are open to using child care centers and family day cares as child care options. However, often the cost is formidable. The concerns and needs of parents are usually based on the child's developmental stage. Thus, longer and paid parental leaves would support parents' desires to be primary caregivers for their infants; however, for toddlers and preschoolers we need more subsidized, affordable, and quality-care settings. As children grow, parents need access to quality after school programs, before school programs, and affordable summer camp options so that they can maintain full-time employment.

Why Working-Class Mothers "Opt Out" of Jobs: Identities as Mother and Worker

Many of the women in Stone's sample mentioned that leaving their careers often left them with a loss of identity. However, this was not a theme we heard often among our working-class mothers. Although many women were satisfied with their jobs, felt valued, and enjoyed the adult contact, few worried about a loss of identity if they were to leave their job. As Charlene, a hair stylist in our study, stated during an interview, "I would quit in a minute, why do I want someone else taking care of my baby while I take care of people's hair? Bottom line is we need the money, we just need the money."

A significant group of mothers in our sample, although employed full-time, held firm beliefs about their primary role and identity as a mother. In fact, we found that a distinct discrepancy often exists between attitudes about mothers' and fathers' "rightful" roles and the behaviors that new parents engage in. For example, in one study we examined the relationship between the division of household and child care tasks and new mothers' mental health (Goldberg and Perry-Jenkins, 2004). It was hypothesized that as fathers performed more child care tasks, mothers would see the division of labor as more fair and report feeling less depressed. In fact, analyses revealed that the more child care tasks fathers performed, the more depressed new mothers became. Further scrutiny of this counterintuitive finding revealed a significant interaction indicating that mothers with traditionalist mind-sets whose husbands performed higher proportions of child care were significantly more depressed than their egalitarian counterparts.

Thus, a significant subgroup of our sample, although working full-time, held traditional notions of their role as new mothers. They expected to be performing more child care than they actually were and their husbands were highly involved; for these new mothers things were not as they should be. An interview with Melissa brought this issue to light. Melissa worked in shipping at a candle factory and her hours were 8 a.m. to 4 p.m. Monday through Friday. Her husband, Josh, worked the 3 to 11 shift as a bus driver and thus had primary care for their son Ryan during the day. Melissa's younger cousin provided coverage for Ryan between the couples' shift overlap between 2:30 and 4:00. As Melissa began to fill out the child care questionnaire at the phase 3 interview, when she had been back at work for over a month, she dropped her head into her hands and started to quietly sob. I asked her what was wrong and through her tears she told me:

> Don't get me wrong, Josh is a great Dad. He is home all day and takes care of Ryan really well. Then I get home at 4:00 and the baby is tired and whiney and almost ready for bed. Then last night he woke up, I think he is beginning to get his first tooth and all he wanted was Daddy, not me. That hurt. That is not how it should be.

Baca Zinn and Eitzen (1990) contend that certain classes may come to embrace particular values as a way to cope with the opportunity structure in our society. If this is the case, then what values are unique to particular class statuses? Do these values change as families "move up or down" the social class hierarchy? Finally, do these values affect work and family challenges and opportunities in different ways for workers and their family members? The question of whether there are cultural norms within class levels that shape the ways in which work and family life are experienced is an intriguing one and deserving of further inquiry.

Work Preferences: What Happens When You Must "Opt In" to Low-Wage Work

Perhaps the more pressing question for working-class mothers is not who "opts out" but rather what happens when you must "opt in" to a low-wage job? Work preferences have consistently emerged as an important variable linking paid employment to maternal mental health. Specifically, working mothers who prefer to be employed report significantly higher well-being than those who would prefer not to work (Steil, 1997). Little research has documented whether work preferences differ across social class status. In the few studies that have addressed this issue, women in higher status jobs emphasize the greater centrality of paid employment in their lives than women in lower status occupations (Steil, 1997). In a recent study of 300 career women, ages 35 to 49, although 87% reported that they were considering job changes to accommodate their family life, the vast majority did not want to relinquish their careers, only modify them (Morris, 1995).

Women in blue-collar occupations are more likely to work because of economic necessity and usually contribute a more significant proportion of the family income than their white-collar counterparts (Steil, 1997). Nevertheless, these results should not suggest that women in working-class occupations are not committed to their jobs. In fact, one study found a stronger, positive relationship between paid work and well-being for blue-collar than white-collar female workers (Warr and Parry, 1982). In addition, a number of studies indicate that working-class mothers would work even if they didn't need the money (Ferree, 1987; Malson, 1983).

Missing from this more general discussion of work preferences, however, is the question of how a family's life course stage may affect how workers feel about their jobs. Specifically, in our sample of working-class new parents, prior to the baby's birth 88.9% of women and 81% of men preferred that the women be employed. We asked mothers in both samples about their work preferences once their baby was born. Over half (64%) of mothers in two-parent families and 42% of single mothers indicated that they would prefer NOT to work after their child is born. However, 84% of mothers in two-parent families and 90% of mothers in single-parent families were sure they would be returning to work once the baby was born, with 76% and 83%, respectively, reporting that finances were the primary reason for staying in the workforce. Thus, the issue of choice is complicated in this group and it is unclear if these mothers would actually quit their jobs if finances were not an issue.

For many mothers, across race and class divides, opting out is seen as a way to save one's sanity and/or as a way to provide the best possible care for their child. The question of how both mothers and children fare when working-class mothers would prefer to "opt out" of work but are unable to do so is an important one. Results suggest that mothers most at risk for poor mental health are those who work full-time but would prefer to be at home with their babies. Specifically, results from our study indicate that mothers in this group report significantly higher levels of depressive symptoms, higher role overload, and lower self-esteem than mothers who prefer to be working and are employed. Since a large literature documents the detrimental effects of mothers' well-being, particularly depression, on children's well-being, these findings point to a significant problem area for working-class families.

Final Thoughts on Opting Out

The goal of this chapter was to demonstrate that the historical and social context of behavior, in this case women moving into and out of the workforce, gives different meanings to what, from the outside, looks like the same behavior. New mothers leave the workforce to become full-time mothers across all levels of the social class system. However, the meaning of that behavior, to both society at large and to the actual mothers, can be quite different and hold quite different consequences. For low-wage working women, where employment is quite often a means to an end (i.e., supporting the family), stepping out of the workforce to be a full-time, stay-at-home mother may be the dream, but the financial reality does not allow it.

At the same time, many of the mothers in our study working in unskilled, low-wage jobs love their work, would not quit even if they had enough money, and gain much personal satisfaction from their jobs. The point here is that there exists great variability among the working class, as well as among women of the working-poor, and middle and upper classes. Our research and theorizing must consider the different constraints, be they financial, ideological, or relational, that serve to shut women out of certain jobs or shut them out from being stay-at-home mothers as well as considering the opportunities and policies that would give women and men choice about their work and family roles.

Appendix

TABLE 4.1

Summary of Workplace Benefits and Policies
Offered to and Used by Mothers and Fathers

Benefit	% of sample reporting their organization offers benefit*		% of sample reporting they actually use benefit*	
	Fathers	Mothers	Fathers	Mothers
Schedule Benefits				
Paid personal/sick leave for family	69.1	68.7	33.8	38.8
Option to work at home	7.5	16.4	3.8	12.5
PT work with FT benefits	11.8	22.4	2.2	9.0
Receive one or more of the above scheduling benefits	69.9	75.4	38.2	50.0
Child care benefits				
Child care info/referral	20.6	18.0	2.9	5.3
DCAP	22.1	24.6	1.5	3.0
Child care vouchers	5.1	4.5	0.0	0.0
Contributors to child care center	2.2	2.6	0.0	0.7
On-site child care center	8.1	8.3	0.7	1.5
Infant care @ on-site child care center	5.1	5.3	0.0	1.5
Subsidized child care center	4.4	0.8	0.0	0.0
Receive one or more of the above child care benefits	33.8	35.1	5.1	8.2

*Ns for individual variables varied from 133 to 136 for fathers and from 128 to 134 for mothers

Reprinted from "Work-Family Challenges for Blue-Collar Parents," by Maureen Perry-Jenkins, Heather Bourne, and Karen Metever, in The Future of Work in Massachusetts, Tom Juravich, ed. Copyright 2007 by the University of Massachusetts Press and published by the University of Massachusetts Press.

5

The Future of Family Caregiving

The Value of Work-Family Strategies That Benefit
Both Care Consumers and Paid Care Workers

——————— PEGGIE R. SMITH ———————

Introduction

When higher-income women "opt in" for full-time employment, they are in a position to contract out some share of their responsibilities in the home to lower-income women who then provide these services. This traditional model of redistributing care work frequently presumes that only child care responsibilities are at stake. However, the aging of the population has increasingly focused attention on workers' needs for help caring for elderly family members. Indeed, care giving for the elderly may equal, if not surpass, child care as the work-family concern of the twenty-first century. Because elder care, similar to child care, is heavily gendered, its workplace consequences will fall disproportionately on working women. As with child care, working women who can afford to outsource the cost of elder care will turn to other women to help in the struggle to manage family responsibilities with workplace obligations. Because home is the preferred setting of most elderly Americans who require long-term care,[1] outsourcing will commonly result in the hiring of home care workers to assist in the care of aging family members.

Briefly defined, home care refers to the range of in-home services provided to individuals with long-term care needs to enable them to function as independently as possible for as long as possible. These services primarily consist of personal and household duties but may also encompass low-level medical tasks such as administering medications and checking temperatures.[2] The majority of all home-care consumers are elderly.[3] The demand for home care is so strong that jobs in the field rank among the top five areas where experts project employment to grow the fastest.[4] However, similar to child care, the demand for quality home care outstrips supply, an imbalance caused not only by an aging generation but also by unfavorable working conditions. Home care is characterized by low pay, extreme physical and emotional demands, and limited opportunities for occupational advancement.[5] As a group, workers in the industry are poor women who do not have the luxury of rejecting the workplace even as they have been repeatedly failed by the workplace. Home-care workers rarely receive job-related benefits such as health insurance, sick leave, vacation time, or retirement plans.

This essay argues that a comprehensive long-term care policy must represent not only the interests of elderly individuals who need care, and their families, but also the interests of home-care workers, as workers, who should be fairly compensated and provided workplace benefits. Against the backdrop of limited funding for long-term care of the elderly,[6] home-care policies in the United States tend to privilege consumers of home care while ignoring the economic interests of women who labor as home-care workers. This unfortunate dynamic most recently took center stage in the 2007 Supreme Court decision of *Long Island Care at Home, Ltd. v. Coke.*[7] The *Coke* decision addressed the rights of home-care workers under the Fair Labor Standards Act (FLSA), which guarantees most employees a right to a federal minimum wage and overtime compensation.[8] In a unanimous decision, the U. S. Supreme Court ruled that hundreds of thousands of home-care workers are not entitled to the most basic of federal labor protections.[9] As this essay discusses, the *Coke* decision threatens to further erode the precarious economic status of home-care workers and undermine the quality of care that they provide to clients.

Faced with low-wage work and a legal system that reinforces their marginal job position, many home-care workers welcome union efforts to help them secure collective bargaining rights. Unions are well positioned to advocate for the type of government policies that can help ensure that home-care workers do not continue to subsidize America's poorly funded long-term care system by working for substandard wages and few benefits. Importantly, home-care unionization stands to benefit the home-care workforce and home-care consumers. By marshaling the shared interests of both groups, the labor movement has initiated home-care campaigns that understand the critical relationship between the availability of quality home care on the one hand, and the economic status of the home-care workforce on the other hand.

A Brief Overview of the Home-Care Industry

The substantial growth of America's elderly population is the most significant factor driving the exploding demand for home care.[10] In 1900, the U. S. population included 3.1 million people aged sixty-five and older who accounted for 4 percent of the total population.[11] By 2003, the sixty-five and older population was close to 36 million, a figure that translated into 12 percent of the total population.[12] According to projections, 72 million Americans will be sixty-five and older by 2030, representing 20 percent of the total population.[13] The projected climb from 2003 to 2030 tracks the aging of the baby boom generation which comprises the 76 million people born in the United States from 1946 to 1964.[14] The first wave of boomers will turn sixty-five in 2011 and will reach age eighty-four in 2030.[15]

While many elderly individuals lead healthy lives, for others disability and chronic health problems accompany longevity[16] and create a need for long-term care.[17] Such care involves services that assist the elderly with daily activities such as dressing, bathing, toileting, eating, shopping, cooking, cleaning, taking medications, and visiting health-care providers.[18] Although family members and other informal, unpaid caregivers represent the most critical source of long-term care to the elderly,[19] the need for formal long-term care remains pressing.[20] The pool of informal caregivers has dwindled as more and more women, who constitute the majority of informal caregivers, have entered the workforce.[21] As women juggle the demands of elder-care responsibilities with child care and work, they often require assistance from formal caregivers.

The demand for formal care also stems from elderly individuals with long-term care needs who live alone or who lack family networks to provide assistance.[22] This problem partially reflects the disproportionate number of elderly women who have outlived their spouses and who need long-term care, as well as an increasing number of elderly individuals who never had children.[23] Formal care may also become urgent for those elderly persons who reside a substantial distance apart from family members. According to a 2004 study, 30 percent of informal caregivers for the elderly live at least an hour away from the person for whom they provide care.[24]

Frontline, direct-care workers who deliver hands-on assistance to elderly individuals provide the bulk of formal long-term care.[25] While sometimes employed in residential-care facilities, these workers also care for clients in private homes. According to official statistics, approximately 1.5 million home-care workers were employed in 2006.[26] This number, however, likely underestimates the total size of the workforce as official reports do not capture the many workers who are hired directly by families.[27] A national study of home-care workers serving Medicare recipients suggests the degree of undercounting; the study found that 29 percent of the workers were self-employed.[28]

While precise numbers are elusive, researchers agree that the expanding need for long-term care has transformed home care into one of the fastest growing occupations in the country, with a projected employment growth rate of close to 50 percent between 2006 and 2016.[29] Yet even as the demand for home care will continue to climb for the foreseeable future, the industry picture is bleak when viewed from the perspective of home-care workers. The typical worker is a low-income woman between the ages of 25 and 54.[30] She is unmarried and a mother of children under the age of eighteen.[31] There is a substantial likelihood that she is a woman of color, either African American or Hispanic.[32] There is a 20 percent chance that she is an immigrant and speaks a language other than English at home.[33]

In 2003, the wages of home-care workers, including both personal and home-care aides as well as home health aides, when annualized for full-time employment, were less than $17,000.[34] As home care provides only part-time employment for some workers,[35] these figures, when computed on the basis of a thirty-hour week, fell to less than $13,000 a year.[36] In light of these numbers, many workers must rely on public assistance for additional support. Among workers who are single parents, between 30 and 35 percent receive food stamps.[37] A lack of benefits, including health insurance, medical leave, and pension plans,[38] further exacerbates home-care workers' poor economic position. In addition, because workers are usually paid only for the time they work in a client's home, they must use their meager earnings to pay for time spent traveling between clients' homes.[39]

Job dissatisfaction among home-care workers also hinges on the work's physically demanding and emotionally draining character. Workers experience high rates of workplace injuries[40] and must deal with clients who suffer from cognitive impairments that can result in disruptive, violent behavior.[41] In addition, workers commonly report that, despite their critical role in caring for the elderly, they are often treated with disrespect.[42] As one worker complains: "Nobody'll listen to you . . . you're just the aides. I get so tired of being thought of as incompetent and stupid."[43]

Compensation for Home-Care Employees and the Coke Case

The story of Evelyn Coke vividly illustrates the economic constraints faced by home-care workers and some of the legal challenges that must be confronted in order to transform the job into an economically viable occupation. Ms. Coke worked as a home-care employee for a home-care agency in New York, Long Island Care at Home, for more than twenty years. She often slept in her clients' homes and worked twenty-four-hour shifts.[44] She alleged that Long Island Care at Home failed to pay her minimum wages and overtime wages to which she was entitled, in violation of the FLSA.[45]

Enacted in 1938, the FLSA establishes minimum employment standards including a minimum wage and overtime compensation for hours worked in excess of forty hours a week. As originally adopted, the FLSA did not reach individuals who worked inside private homes performing domestic service type work because of doubt about whether they were engaged in interstate commerce.[46] Congress specifically extended coverage to these workers in 1974, when it amended the FLSA to apply to employees "employed in domestic service in a household."[47]

In passing the 1974 domestic service amendments, Congress simultaneously limited their reach by crafting exemptions from the FLSA's minimum wage and overtime provisions for casual babysitters and for persons who "provide companionship services for individuals who (because of age or infirmity) are unable to care for themselves."[48] The legislative history of the 1974 amendments indicates that Congress, in exempting companions, intended to exclude those individuals who, similar to casual babysitters, worked in a casual, nonprofessional capacity for a private household.[49] The prevailing image of a companion was a neighbor or a friend who would spend time with an elderly person and who, because he or she was not a regular breadwinner, did not require the protection of the FLSA. Thus, as explained by Senator Harrison Williams, the primary sponsor of the amendments, the companionship exemption was intended for "'elder sitters' whose main purpose of employment is to watch over an elderly or infirm person in the same manner that a babysitter watches over children."[50] A companion was also understood as someone who worked directly for the individual household.[51]

This image of a companion stands in stark contrast to most of today's home-care workers. Contrary to the one-on-one employment relationship between an employing household and a companion, many home-care workers are employed by agencies.[52] Also unlike companions who worked on an itinerant basis, home-care workers commonly work on a full-time, regular basis.[53] In short, there is little similarity between the casual labor pattern of a neighbor who intermittently works as a companion and the regular, dedicated service performed by home-care workers who shoulder significant responsibility for the economic well-being of their families.

After the enactment of the 1974 amendments, the Department of Labor (DOL) adopted regulations interpreting the companionship exemption that significantly increased its scope. First, the DOL defined companionship services in broad, sweeping terms to include the performance of a range of household and personal tasks that greatly exceeded the provision of companionship.[54] Second, the DOL provided that the exemption covers not only workers employed by private households but also workers employed by third-party employers, such as home-care agencies.[55] At issue in *Long Island Care at Home, Ltd. v. Coke* was the validity of the DOL regulation that interpreted the "companionship exemption" to exclude both home-care workers employed by an individual homeowner employer and workers employed by a third-party employer as was the case with Evelyn Coke. The Supreme Court ruled against Ms. Coke and held that because Congress did not clearly express its intentions in 1974 regarding the scope of the exemption, the DOL's interpretation of the exemption was reasonable and entitled to judicial deference.[56]

Troubling Fault Lines: Pitting Consumers against Workers

The *Coke* case illuminated a troubling fault line in discussions that focus on the importance of work-family policies that can help employed family members address caregiving. In the context of elder caregiving, such discussions all too frequently relegate the labor rights of home-care workers to the needs of their elderly clients and the clients' families. Thus critics claim that extending FLSA protection to home-care workers will result in clients and/or their families being unable to afford home care. Not only is this claim greatly exaggerated since Medicare and Medicaid fund much of the services provided by home-care workers,[57] but more importantly the claim disregards the interests of workers to the most basic of federal labor protections. To be sure, granting home-care workers FLSA protection may require state and federal governments to shoulder greater responsibility for the cost of publicly funded home care. However, in a caring society, collective responsibility for long-term care should be vastly preferred to placing the responsibility on the weary shoulders of poor and low-income home-care workers by excluding them from minimum labor protections extended to the majority of employees in the United States.

The *Coke* case also underscored the repeated failure of policymakers and others to appreciate the high degree to which the availability of quality home care is inextricably linked to the economic status of the home-care workforce. Critics, for example, argue that extending FLSA protection to home-care workers will reduce the availability of care for the elderly and, in turn, compromise the quality of care.[58] Ironically, the current reality suggests that the exact opposite is true. Home-care workers are exiting the job—and, as a result, the quality of care is suffering—because of the job's poor working conditions, including low compensation levels. As the American Association of Retired Persons argued in its brief to the Supreme Court on behalf of Ms. Coke, the exemption of home-care workers employed by third-party employers from the FLSA operates not to protect the interests of clients but to compromise their interests.[59]

Clients are disadvantaged by the severe labor imbalance that characterizes the home-care industry. Despite the projected growth of employment in home-care jobs and the increased demand for workers, a labor shortage exists in the home-care industry. Organizations that provide long-term care invoke the term "crisis" to describe the problems they face in attracting and retaining home-care workers.[60] Significantly, turnover rates among workers are extremely high. Estimates indicate that as many as 50 percent of all workers quit their jobs every year.[61] Low wages and oppressive job conditions greatly exacerbate the shortage of home-care workers. Faced with low-wage and low-status work, it is no surprise that many workers leave the job in search of more sustainable employment opportunities.[62]

Poor compensation not only contributes to a shortage of workers but also endangers the quality of care provided to elderly and disabled persons. A worker's departure can have devastating consequences for a client who must adjust to a new worker and who may experience service disruptions that can lead to hospitalization.[63] For other clients, turnover may culminate in their relocation to an institutional setting such as a nursing home.[64] Thus, far from undermining access to quality services, extending home-care workers FLSA protection "will strengthen the home-care workforce and result in higher quality of care and continuity of care for America's older and disabled persons."[65]

Against this backdrop, it is imperative that steps are taken to protect the rights of home-care workers to fair compensation. In the absence of legislative protection, however, many home-care workers are turning to unions to achieve and sustain improvements in their labor conditions. As the next section demonstrates, unions can play an instrumental role in alleviating the vulnerability of workers, redefining home care as skilled, valuable labor that merits respect, and linking home-care quality with improved working conditions.

The Value of Unionization

The labor movement has become an active force in organizing home-care workers, especially those workers who provide publicly subsidized home care. The campaign to unionize home-care workers first achieved national attention in California under the leadership of the Service Employees International Union (SEIU). To most observers, it seemed impossible for SEIU to unify a group of workers who labor in isolation from each other, and within the private sphere of individual clients' homes. To further complicate matters, home-care workers often provide services for more than one client.[66] In light of this reality, prevailing wisdom held that such workers were unorganizable.

However, in the face of naysayers, SEIU mounted a labor-intensive campaign in the 1980s to identify and contact the thousands of home-care workers who were scattered throughout the County of Los Angeles. Whereas in manufacturing jobs, organizers can usually contact workers by leafleting outside the factory gates,[67] SEIU mobilized the home-care workforce by engaging in a form of grassroots activism that relied on media outlets, public rallies, the distribution of leaflets and pamphlets in various languages, canvassing malls and shopping centers, and contacts with community-based organizations such as churches.[68] With time and patience, the workers came together.

Along with figuring out how to reach the workers, SEIU confronted the task of identifying an employer on their behalf with which the union could bargain. In California, government-funded, home-care services are administered by the state's In Home Support Services Program, which in turn is implemented by each county.[69] Under the program, county officials decide whether a client qualifies for a home-care worker and assess the type of assistance required.[70] Given the level of public involvement in the delivery of home-care services, SEIU tried to convince the California courts that the county of Los Angeles employed the workers. The court disagreed and held that the workers' relationship with the county was that of an independent contractor.[71]

This ruling was potentially devastating, since federal antitrust law treats unionizing on the part of independent contractors as impermissible anti-competitive behavior.[72] It thus was critical for the union to create an employment relationship on behalf of the workers that would survive antitrust scrutiny. To do so, SEIU pursued a political campaign in coalition with a range of interest groups (including senior citizen groups, consumer advocacy groups, and disability activists). The campaign ultimately resulted in the California State Legislature enacting legislation in 1992 that authorized, and later required, each county in the state to create "public authorities," agencies that would serve as the legal employer for home-care workers for purposes of local collective bargaining laws.[73] The County of Los Angeles established a public authority in 1997,[74] and two years later SEIU won the right to represent the County's 74,000 home-care workers.[75] The victory marked the largest increase since 1941 in new union membership resulting from a single union election.[76] Since 1999, the labor movement has successfully pursued a comparable organizing approach to extend labor law protections to publicly subsidized home-care workers who provide publicly subsidized care in several additional states,[77] and has won the right to represent over 300,000 home-care workers.[78] The achievement has had a notable and positive effect on the economic status of unionized workers, leading to increase pay rates, health insurance benefits, and workers' compensation coverage.[79]

Lessons for the Future of Family Caregiving

The unionization of home-care workers offers several instructive lessons for the future of family caregiving, both paid care for the elderly as well as paid child care. First, it highlights the point that those who most need care, including children and the elderly, are often least able to pay for it.[80] As a result, many care recipients lack the financial resources to improve the wages of paid care workers.[81] Absent family members providing informal care or paying for formal care, individuals in need of care routinely rely on the government for assistance. Consequently, strategies to improve the economic well-being of care workers must be accompanied by parallel strategies to increase public support for family caregiving.

Second, and related, home-care unionization illuminates the value of forging a strong coalition that can mobilize for increased public support of caregiving. For example, SEIU built a coalition for its California home-care campaign that represented a partnership, first and foremost, between workers and consumers, but which also attracted the backing of community organizations and advocacy groups.[82] The coalition succeeded in demonstrating to consumers that they shared common interests with workers and convincing them that unionization was not a "'zero sum' proposition in which increased wages for workers could only come at the expense of fewer hours of care for consumers."[83] Because the coalition recognized the financial constraints on consumers, the group made it a priority to mobilize public support to pressure state and local governments to provide greater funding for home-care services.[84] Third, the successful unionization of home-care workers hinged on demonstrating that poor wages in the industry were undermining the level of care provided to clients.[85] Working as part of a coalition, labor effectively made the case that problems which had long plagued home-care services, including high turnover rates and poorly trained workers, could be ameliorated by restructuring home-care work into a decent job.[86]

Conclusion

All indicators suggest that the need for formal home care will remain strong for the foreseeable future, especially as working families, and employed women in particular, struggle to find an acceptable balance between their work obligations and caregiving responsibilities. Yet, despite the growing demand for home care, a labor shortage persists. Turnover rates among home-care workers are extremely high and attracting new and qualified workers to the field is an uphill battle. Home-care consumers pay a price for the job's instability in the form of inconsistent care, poor quality care, and a lack of available care. This essay has maintained that sustainable, long-term improvement on this front requires a multifaceted approach that connects the availability of quality home care with policies that can help develop and support the home-care workforce.[87] As long as workers earn poverty-level wages and lack the resources to afford benefits such as health insurance, the problems of poor quality of care and high turnover rates will persist.

While determining how to best resolve this problem is a complicated task, this essay has argued that the labor movement can help assure that the solution reflects the interests and perspectives of home-care workers as well as the interests of elderly consumers and their families. As a growing body of research demonstrates, the current home-care crisis is not only a problem of affordability and availability for consumers but, as importantly, a labor problem for workers. Aware of this reality, unions are increasingly at the forefront of campaigns to lobby government officials for additional funding for home care. When funds are used to support a stabilized home-care labor market—characterized by improved wages, decent working conditions, and low turnover rates—the end result benefits not only workers but elderly consumers as well.

NOTES

1. Evelinn A. Borrayo et al., "Who Is Being Served? Program Eligibility and Home- and Community-Based Services Use," 23 *J. Applied Gerontology* 120, 120 (2004) ("The majority of older adults in the United States reside in the community, and when faced with deteriorating health status and functional ability, they overwhelmingly prefer to avoid institutionalization and remain at home."); Robyn I. Stone, "The Direct Care Worker: The Third Rail of Home Care Policy," 25 *Ann. Rev. Pub. Health* 521, 521 (2004) ("National polls indicate that older adults and younger people with disabilities want to remain in their own homes in their own communities for as long as possible."); *see also* Vera Prosper, "Aging in Place in Multifamily Housing," 7 *Cityscape:J. of Pol'y Dev. Res.* 81, 82 (2004) (commenting that "most older people prefer to remain living where they are and to age in place").

2. *See* Anna Loengard and Jeremy Boal, "Home Care of the Frail Elderly," 20 *Clinics in Geriatric Med.* 795, 796 (2004); Jane Aronson and Sheila Neysmith, "'You're Not Just in There to Do the Work': Depersonalising Policies and the Exploitation of Home Care Workers' Labour," 10 *Gender & Soc'y* 59, 60 (1996).

3. A. E. Benjamin, "Consumer-Directed Services at Home: A New Model for Persons with Disabilities," 20 *Health Aff.* 80, 80 (2001) (reporting that a majority of long-term care recipients are elderly individuals who receive care primarily in their homes); U. S. Gen. Accounting Office, *Long-Term Care: Some States Apply Criminal Background Checks to Home Care Workers* 4 (1996) [hereinafter *Long-Term Care*], *available at* http://www.gao.gov/archive/1996/pe96005.pdf (noting that the typical home care recipient is "a woman with functional limitations who is very elderly, has a low income, and lives alone"); Nat'l Ass'n for Home Care & Hospice, *Basic Statistics about Home Care* 8 (2004), *available at* http://www.nahc.org/04HC_Stats.pdf (reporting that in 2000, 69.1 percent of home-care recipients were over age 65). Although this essay focuses on home care as it relates to the elderly, home-care consumers are more diverse, and also include "children and young adults with disabilities" and "people with a wide range of conditions such as birth defects, developmental disabilities, mental illness, AIDS, Alzheimer's disease, spinal cord injury, stroke, muscular degeneration, broken bones, surgical recovery, or accident victims." Dep't of Labor, Report of the Working Group on Long-Term Care (2000), *available at* http://www.dol.gov/ebsa/publications/report2.htm.

4. Bureau of Labor Statistics, U.S. Dep't of Labor, *Occupational Outlook Handbook* 5, chart 7 (2008–09 ed.) [hereinafter *BLS Outlook Handbook*] (listing "personal and home care aides" as the occupation that is expected to grow the second fastest between 2006 and 2016, and "home health aides" as the occupation that is expected to grow the third fastest during the same time period).

5. *Id.* at 441.

6. *See* Judith Feder, "Paying for Home Care: The Limits of Current Programs," *in Financing Home Care: Improving Protection for Disabled Elderly People* 27, 44 (Diane Rowland and Barbara Lyons, eds. 1991) (overviews of public and private expenditures on home care and noting their limitations); Richard Kaplan, "Cracking the Conundrum: Toward a Rational Financing of Long-Term Care," 2004 U. Ill. L. Rev. 47, 62–64 (highlighting the limitations of Medicare to address the long-term care needs of older Americans); *id.* at 69–72 (noting structural features in Medicaid that limits its ability to fund long-term care); *see also Long-Term Care Financing: Growing Demand and Cost of Services Are Straining Federal and State Budgets: Hearings before the H. Subcomm. on Health, Committee on Energy and Commerce*, 109th Cong. 11 (2005) (Statement of Kathryn G. Allen Director, Health Care—Medicaid and Private Health Insurance Issues) [hereinafter *Long-Term Care Financing*], *available at* http://www.gao.gov/new.items/d05564t.pdf (highlighting the consequences of inadequate funding for long-term care on elderly individuals).

7. Long Island Care at Home, Ltd. et al. v. Coke, 551 U.S. 158 (2007).

8. Fair Labor Standards Act of 1938, 29 U.S.C. §§ 201–219 (2007).

9. Long Island Care at Home, 551 U.S. at 174.

10. *See* Office of the Assistant Sec'y for Planning & Evaluation, U.S. Dep't of Health & Human Servs., *The Future Supply of Long-Term Care Workers in Relation to the Aging Baby Boom Generation: Report to Congress* 4 (2003) [hereinafter *Future Supply*], *available at* http://aspe.hhs.gov/daltcp/reports/ltcwork.pdf.

11. Wan He et al., U.S. Census Bureau, P23 209, *Current Population Report Special Studies 65+ in the United States: 2005*, at 1, *available at* http://www.census.gov/prod/2006pubs/p23-209.pdf.

12. *Id.*

13. *Id.*

14. James T. Patterson, *Grand Expectations: The United States, 1945–1974*, at 77 (1997) (describing the increase in birth rates that started in 1946 and leveled off in 1964); *Future Supply*, at 7–8 (discussing the effect that aging baby boomers will have on the demand for caregiving).

15. He et al., at 4. The population growth of elderly Americans has been the most pronounced among individuals 85 and older. This segment of the elderly population, which is the fastest growing, included 4.7 million people in 2003. It is expected to double to 9.6 million in 2030, and to double yet again to 20.9 million in 2050, the point at which all the remaining boomers will be 85 and older. *Id.* at 6.

16. *See Long-Term Care: Aging Baby Boom Generation Will Increase Demand and Burden on Federal and State Budgets: Hearings before the S. Special Comm. on Aging*, 107th Cong. 3 (2002) (statement of David M. Walker, Comptroller General of the United States), *available at* http://www.gao.gov/new.items/d02544t.pdf (highlighting medical conditions among the elderly that have led to an increase in demand for long-term care services).

17. H. Stephen Kaye et al., "The Personal Assistance Workforce: Trends in Supply and Demand," 25 Health Aff. 1113, 1115 (2006); Peggie R. Smith, "Elder Care, Gender, and Work: The Work-Family Issue of the 21st Century," 25 *Berkeley J. Emp. & Lab. L.*351, 356–57 (2004) *Future Supply*, at 3–5.

18. He et al., at 58 (distinguishing between activities of daily living which include personal care tasks such as bathing, eating, toileting, and dressing, and instrumental activities which include "household management tasks like preparing one's own meals, doing light housework, managing one's own money, using the telephone, and shopping for personal items").

19. *See* Kaye et al., at 1113; Robyn I. Stone, *Long-Term Care for the Elderly with Disabilities: Current Policy, Emerging Trends, and Implications for the Twenty-First Century* 8 (Milbank Memorial Fund, 2000), *available at* http://www.milbank.org/reports/0008stone/LongTermCare_Mech5.pdf.

20. NGA Ctr. for Best Practices, Nat'l Governors Ass'n, Issue Brief: *State Support for Family Caregivers and Paid Home-Care Workers* 5 (June 25, 2004), *available at* http://www.nga.org/Files/pdf/0406AgingCaregivers.pdf ("Twenty-eight percent of community-based elders receive assistance from both family and paid in-home workers, and 8 percent of elders receive care solely from paid in-home workers.").

21. *See Long-Term Care*, at 4 (connecting the increased reliance on home care with projections "indicat[ing] that labor force participation will continue to increase among women, who have traditionally provided much of the informal care for the elderly").

22. *See* Steven Katz et al., "Gender Disparities in the Receipt of Home Care for Elderly People with Disability in the United States," 284 *J. Am. Med. Ass'n* 3022, 3022 (2000) ("[C]hanges in the pattern of living arrangements will increase the number of elderly people living alone and thus reduce the availability of informal care."); Diane Rowland, "Measuring the Elderly's Need for Home Care," 8 *Health Aff.* 39, 48 (1989) ("[M]ore than one in four elderly people with multiple impairments live alone. For this group, the absence of a resident caregiver is likely to result in a greater need for formal home care services.").

23. *Long-Term Care*, at 4 ("Among those in need of home care, reliance on paid home-care workers is also expected to rise, partly because adults in the baby boom generation have had smaller numbers of children and will therefore have fewer available to provide or supervise their care in old age."); Smith, at 360–61 (discussing the gendered dimension of elder care as it relates to elderly women who have outlived their husbands).

24. Smith, at 367–68 (referencing a study by the National Council on Aging).

25. *Future Supply*, at 22 ("Home health, personal care and home care aides represent the majority, approximately 67 percent (548,000 of 816,000), of the long-term care direct care workers in [residential care and home health care settings].").

26. The 1.5 million figure reflects the approximate combined totals for home-health aides, and personal- and home-care aides. *BLS Outlook Handbook*, at 442 (documenting 787,000 home health aides in 2006); *id.* at 505 (documenting 767,000 personal and home aides in 2006).

27. *See* Steve Dawson and Rick Surpin, *Direct-Care Health Workers: The Unnecessary Crisis* 12 (2001), *available at* http://www.directcareclearinghouse.org/download/Aspen.pdf ("[B]eneath the formal sector lies a gray-market workforce of paid caregivers who are hired directly by consumers, but whose income is not reported. The size of this unreported workforce is significant but unquantifiable."); Robyn I. Stone, *Long-Term Care Workforce Shortages: Impact on Families* 2 (2001) [hereinafter Stone, Workforce Shortages], *available at* http://www.bjbc.org/content/docs/LTC_Workforce_Shortages.pdf (noting that "many home care workers are hired privately and official federal statistics may not include them); *see also* Dep't of Health & Human Servs., *Nursing Aides, Home Health Aides, and Related Health Care Occupations—National and Local Workforce Shortages and Associated Data Needs* 9 (2004) [hereinafter Home Health Aides], *available at* http://www.directcare-clearinghouse.org/download/RNandHomeAides.pdf (observing that there is "a sizable gray market of direct care workforce who consumers hire directly").

28. *See* Stone, *Workforce Shortages*, at 2; *Home Health Aides*, at 9.

29. *BLS, Outlook Handbook*, at 443 (reporting projections which indicate that employment of home health aides will grow by 49 percent during the same time period); *id.* at 505 (reporting projections which indicate that employment of personal and home care aides will grow by 51 percent from 2006 to 2016).

30. James Cooper and Diane Cooper, "Crisis in Workforce Supply—Read All about It!" *Annals of Long-Term Care*, Feb. 2005, at 23, 24 (adding that relative to workers in other jobs, the typical paid direct-care worker is "more likely to be nonwhite. Only 10–20% of direct care workers are male. Home-care aides tend to be older than aides in other settings, and less likely to be native-born U.S. citizens."); Dawson and Surpin, at 12 (commenting that the "typical direct-care worker is a low-income woman, between the ages of 25 and 54, who is a single mother"); Rhonda Montgomery et al., "A Profile of Home Care Workers from the 2000 Census: How It Changes What We Know," 45 *Gerontologist* 593, 595 (2005) (explaining that typically direct-care workers are women who are: "much less likely to be under the age of 25 and more likely to be 65 years or older").

31. Stone, *Workforce Shortages*, at 2 ("Compared to the workforce in general, nursing home and home health care aides are more likely to be non-white, unmarried and with children under age 18 at home."); *Nursing Workforce: Recruitment and Retention of Nurses and Nurse Aides Is a Growing Concern: Hearings before the S. Comm. on Health, Education, Labor and Pensions*, 107th Cong. 22 (statement of William J. Scanlon Director, Health Care

Issues) (2001) [hereinafter *Nursing Workforce*], *available at* http://www.gao.gov/new.items/d01750t.pdf ("Nursing home and home health care aides are also two to three times more likely as other workers to be unmarried and have children at home.").

32. Dawson and Surpin, at 12 (observing that "86 percent of [direct-care workers] . . . are women, 30 percent are women of color"); Montgomery et al., at 595 (commenting that "the home care industry tends to have somewhat fewer African American workers and proportionally more Hispanic or Latino workers").

33. Montgomery et al., at 595.

34. Bernadette Wright, AARP Pub. Policy Inst, *Direct Care Workers in Long-Term Care* 2 (2005), *available at* http://www.hcbs.org/files/75/3748/directcare.pdf (reporting annualized full-time employment earnings of $16,750 for personal and home care aides, and $18,200 for home health aides).

35. *Id.* at 1 ("30.5% of home-care aides . . . work part time.").

36. *Id.* at 2 (reporting annual earnings, based on a thirty-hour week, of $12,558 for personal and home-care aides, and $13,650 for home-health aides).

37. *Home Health Aides*, at 10 (stating that in addition to the number of single parents receiving food stamps, "less than half of [direct-care workers] . . . receive health insurance through their employers[;]" more than 10 percent receive Medicaid; and others receive Medicare or aide from other government programs); *see also Nursing Workforce*, at 13 (reporting that "aides working in nursing homes and home health care are more than twice as likely as other workers to be receiving food stamps and Medicaid, and they are much more likely to lack health insurance"); Susan Harmuth, "The Direct Care Workforce Crisis in Long-Term Care," 63 *N.C. Med. J.* 87, 89–90 (2002) (highlighting a government report indicating that "nurse aides working in home care and nursing homes are twice as likely as workers in other occupations to receive public benefits, particularly food stamps and/or Medicaid covered health benefits").

38. Dawson and Surpin, at 6 (commenting that the "quality of direct-care jobs tends to be extremely poor. Wages are low and benefits few; ironically, most direct-care staff do not receive employer-paid health insurance"); Rebecca Donovan, "We Care for the Most Important People in Your Life": Home Care Workers in New York City, 17 *Women's Stud. Q.* Spring/Summer 1989, at 56, 62 (reporting on the lack of benefits available to home-care workers).

39. *BLS Outlook Handbook*, at 444, 506.

40. *See* Brian Taylor and Michael Donnelly, "Risks to Home Care Workers: Professional Perspectives," 8 *Health, Risk & Soc'y* 239, 245 (2006) (observing that home-care workers face "many and varied hazards ranging across access issues, hygiene and infection, manual handling, aggression and harassment, domestic and farm animals, fleas and safety of home equipment").

41. *BLS Outlook Handbook*, at 504 (commenting that some home-care clients "are pleasant and cooperative; others are angry, abusive, depressed, or otherwise difficult"); *see also* Ella Hunter, "Violence Prevention in the Home Health Setting," 15 *Home Healthcare Nurse* 403, 404–08 (1997) (evaluating strategies to reduce workplace violence against home-care workers); Jacqueline A. Naduiairski, "Inner-City Safety for Home Care Providers" *J. Nursing Admin.*, Sept. 1992, at 42, 42 (observing that "one of the biggest issues in the delivery of home care in the inner cities is safety of employees. . . . [Home care employees] encounter weapons and drugs in the homes of patients they serve every day.").

42. Donovan, at 63 (observing that workers resent their "second-class position" and feel undervalued); WI Council on Long Term Care Reform, *Strengthening Wisconsin's Long-Term Care Workforce* 4 (2005), *available at* http://www.directcareclearinghouse.org/download/Strengthening%20WI%20long%20term%20care%20workforce.pdf. ("A growing body of research is concluding that the reasons for workers quitting add up to a failure of employers, supervisors, society as a whole, and sometimes even consumers, to adequately respect and value them and the work that they do.").

43. Clare L. Stacey, "Finding Dignity in Dirty Work: The Constraints and Rewards of Low-Wage Home Care Labour," 27 *Soc. Health & Illness* 837, 839 (2005); *see also* Sheila Neysmith and Jane Aronson, "Home Care Workers Discuss Their Work: The Skills Required to 'Use Your Common Sense,'" 10 *J. Aging Stud.* 1, 3 (1996) ("Home care workers . . . provide the hands on daily care yet they have no voice in the home-care drama. Their relatively powerless position is reflected in their low pay rates and low occupational status."); *id.* at 8 (observing that many clients and their families "diminished the home care worker's job by referring to her as a 'cleaning lady'"); Stone, at 522 ("The negative public image of the home care worker (e.g., a poorly trained woman with few skills receiving low pay for unpleasant work and with little hope for advancement) discourages individuals from seeking or remaining in this occupation.").

44. *H.R. 3582, The Fair Home Health Care Act: Hearing before the Subcomm. on Workforce Protections H. Comm. on Education and Labor*, 110th Cong. 3 (2007) (Prepared Statement of Hon. Lynn C. Woolsey, Chairwoman, Subcommittee on Workforce Protections).

45. Long Island Care at Home, Ltd. et al. v. Coke, 551 U.S. 158, 164 (2007).

46. Patricia Mulkeen, Note, "*Private Household Workers and the Fair Labor Standards Act,*" 5 *Conn. L. Rev.* 623, 626 (1973).

47. 29 U.S.C. § 206(f) (1) (including domestic service workers in the minimum wage provision); 29 U.S.C. § 207(l) (including domestic service workers in the overtime provision).

48. 29 U.S.C. § 213(a) (15).

49. *Brief for Law Professors and Historians as Amici Curiae Supporting Respondents,* Long Island Care at Home, Ltd. v. Coke, 551 U.S. 158 (2007) (No. 06-593), at 12–13.

50. Application of the Fair Labor Standards Act to Domestic Service, 66 Fed. Reg. 5481, 5482 (proposed Jan. 19, 2001) [hereinafter *FLSA Application*] (quoting Sen. Williams during the 1974 FLSA Amendments).

51. *Brief for Law Professors and Historians, supra* note 49, at 4–11.

52. *Brief for the Urban Justice Center et al.* as Amici Curiae Supporting Respondent, Long Island Care at Home, 551 U.S. 158(No. 06-593) at 7 (referencing Montgomery et al.,"A Profile of Home Care Workers from the 2000 Census: How It Changes What We Know," 45 *Gerontologist* 593 (2005).

53. Wright, at 1.

54. 29 C.F.R. § 552.6.

55. 29 C.F.R. § 552.109(a).

56. Long Island Care at Home, 551 U.S. 158, at 174.

57. Loengard and Boal, "Home Care of the Frail Elderly," 20 *Clin. Geriatric Med.* 795, 797 (2004) (reporting that in "2000, home health agencies derived their payments from Medicare (28%), Medicaid (18%), private insurance (18.5%), out-of-pocket (24.4%), and other sources (5.2%)"); Long-Term Care, at 3 (observing that "the broadest federal programs for supporting [home-care] services" are Medicare and Medicaid).

58. *See Brief for the United States as Amicus Curiae*, Coke v. Long Island Care at Home, Ltd., 376 F.3d 118 (2004) (No. 04-1315) at 16 (highlighting various groups that submitted amicus briefs in *Coke* which indicated that the decision would increase the cost of home care and disrupt services for the elderly and disabled); Jonathan D. Colburn, "Home Health Firms Watch Developments in Overtime Case," *San Fernando Valley Bus. J.*, Jan. 30, 2006.

59. *Brief for AARP and Older Women's League as Amici Curiae Supporting Respondents*, Long Island Care at Home, 551 U.S. 158 (No. 06-593), at 4.

60. "Long-Term Care Workforce Shortages: Impact on Families," 1 (*Family Caregiver Alliance* 2001), *available at* http://www.bjbc.org/content/docs/LTC_Workforce_Shortages. pdf; Cooper and Cooper, at 23; Harmuth, at 93.

61. Paraprofessional Healthcare Institute, *Training Quality Home Care Workers* 3 (2003), *available at* http://www.directcareclearinghouse.org/download/PHI_Training_Overview. pdf.While researchers agree that turnover in home care is a major problem, estimates of the problem vary. *See, e.g.*, Dawson and Surpin, at 1 (reporting turnover rates among direct-care workers ranges between 40 and 100 percent annually); Carol Raphael, "Long-Term Care: Confronting Today's Challenges," 1 (*Academy Health* 2003), *available at* http:// www.academyhealth.org/files/publications/ltcchallenges.pdf (reporting a 28 percent turnover rate for home health aides).

62. Harmuth, at 89.

63. *See, e.g.*, Dorie Seavey, "The Cost of Frontline Turnover in Long-Term Care," 15 (*Better Jobs, Better Care* 2004), *available* at http://www.bjbc.org/content/docs/TOCostReport.pdf ("Strong arguments can be made that turnover adversely affects continuity of care and care recipient relationships, causing disruptions that prevent or interfere with the development of relationships critical to both client and caregiver."); *Home Health Aides*, at v ("In areas where levels of service have been reduced, elderly or chronically ill persons deprived of access to care must either remain in more restrictive, more costly environments . . . or seek care from family or friends. Both quality of care and quality of life suffer as people are denied services, or services are provided by persons less qualified or experienced.").

64. Ron Osterhout and Rick Zawadski, "On Homecare Workforce," 64 *Pol'y & Prac. Pub. Hum. Services* 30, 30 (2006).

65. *Brief of AARP and Older Women's League Supporting Respondent*, Long Island Care at Home Ltd. v. Coke, 551 U.S. 158 (2007) (No. 06-593), at 15.

66. *See* Jessica Toledano, "Health Workers for Home-Bound to Vote on Union," *Los Angeles Bus. J.*, Feb. 8, 1999.

67. James Green and Chris Tilly, "Service Unionism: Directions for Organizing," 38 *Lab. Law J.* 486, 487 (1987) (observing that union organizers tend to depend on the existence of a large, centralized workplace, which often does not exist in the service industry). *See also* Immanuel Ness, "Organizing Home Health-Care Workers: A New York City Case Study," 3 *Working USA* 59, 73 (1999) (discussing the grassroots strategies that labor used to organize home health care workers in New York).

68. Stu Schneider, "Victories for Home Health Care Workers," *Dollars & Sense*, Sept.–Oct. 2003, at 25.

69. *See* Serv. Employees Int'l Union, Local 434 v. County of Los Angeles, 225 Cal. App. 3d 761, 765 (1990).

70. *Id.*

71. *Id.*

72. The Sherman Act prohibits "[e]very contract, combination . . . or conspiracy" that unreasonably restrains competition. 15 U.S.C. § 1 (Supp. IV 2006). Although antitrust law exempts labor organizations, the exemption extends only to the organization of employees, not independent contractors. *See* Clayton Act, ch. 323, § 6, 38 Stat. 730, 731 (1914) (current version at 15 U.S.C. § 17 (2006)) (immunizing labor organization activities designed to carry out the "legitimate" purposes of labor unions from liability under antitrust laws); 29 U.S.C. § 152(3) ("[The] term 'employee' . . . shall not include . . . any individual having the status of an independent contractor.").

73. Cal. Welf. & Inst. Code § 12302.25(a) (West Supp. 2007). *See generally* Janet Heinritz-Canterbury, Paraprofessional Healthcare Institute, *Collaborating to Improve In-Home Supportive Services: Stakeholder Perspectives on Implementing California's Public Authorities* 4–6 (2002), *available at* http://www.sfihsspa.org/documents/6454889.pdf (discussing the formation of the public authority model in California).

74. Linda Delp and Katie Quan, "Homecare Worker Organizing in California: An Analysis of a Successful Strategy," 27 *Lab. Stud. J.* 1, 11 (2002).

75. *See* Schneider, at 26.

76. *Id.*

77. *See* Peggie R. Smith, "The Publicization of Home-Based Care Work in State Labor Law," 92 *Minn. L. Rev.* 1390, 1403–04 (2008) (listing states).

78. Schneider, at 27.

79. *See* Smith, at 1413 (highlighting the benefits of unionization).

80. *See, e.g.,* Paula England et al., "Wages of Virtue: The Relative Pay of Care Work," 49 *Soc. Probs.* 455, 456 (2002).

81. *See* Delp and Quan, at 4–5 (noting that many home-care consumers do not have the ability to increase the wages of workers).

82. *Id.* at 11–12; *see also* Ness, at 64 (noting the importance of "political coalitions" and "movements" in gaining political power for workers).

83. Delp and Quan, at 12.

84. *See id.* at 11–14 (explaining that consumers already had established lobbying groups).

85. Dorothy Sue Cobble, "The Prospects for Unionism in a Service Society," *in Working in the Service Society* 333, 349 (Cameron Macdonald and Carmen Sirianni, eds., 1996) (observing that "home health-care groups reached out to the clients . . ., making the case that raising wages for aides would help clients maintain quality services").

86. Heinritz-Canterbury, at 20.

87. *See* Stone, at 526–31 (discussing various policies that may empower workers including career ladders, the provision of health insurance, educational incentives, and wage increases).

6

Care Work and
Women's Employment

A Comparative Perspective

JOYA MISRA

This chapter examines the similarities among industrialized nations in the demand for care work (child care, elder care, care for the disabled, etc.) as the result of women's rising employment rates, and the differences international policy impose upon outcomes: who provides care, where, and how they are compensated. While most wealthy countries encourage women's employment outside the home, many European countries have shifted from supporting high-quality public sector care to a greater reliance on market-based solutions. New social care legislation has focused on creating low-paying service jobs in order to lower unemployment rates, while also meeting care needs outside the more costly public sector.

This chapter also examines where care work is most highly paid, showing that where care work is carried out within the public sector (for example, state-provided child care and elder care services), care work is more highly valued, better paid, and carries more social benefits. This suggests that while increasing women's employment rates may shift *who* does care work, with proper state support those who do care work can receive appropriate pay and benefits for carrying out work that is crucial to both society and the economy. Therefore, higher employment rates for middle- and upper-class women need not lead to greater inequality among women, but can instead lead to lower levels of inequality both among women and between men and women.

Care Work and Women's Employment: A Comparative Perspective

In this chapter, I consider how the "opt-out" revolution might be understood outside the United States, and how care providers—who make it possible for many middle- and upper-class men and women to work outside the home—

should be adequately rewarded and valued for the important work that they do. As Smith (this volume) points out, care workers in the United States often have limited legal rights and receive very low wages and few benefits. Yet, both legal and political solutions exist to these problematic inequalities. By placing what we know about women's employment and care work into a comparative perspective, I suggest a number of solutions to existing inequalities.

Across wealthy countries, there has been a remarkable rise in women's employment and, along with this, changes in who provides care for children, the elderly, and the disabled. Figure 6.1 summarizes employment patterns and trends for childless women and mothers between 25 and 45 years of age in a number of wealthy countries around the year 2000 (Misra, Budig, and Böckmann 2009, Table 2). The dark bars represent the percentage of childless women who are employed, while the lighter bars represent the percentage of mothers who are employed. In most countries, more than 80 percent of childless women in this age range are employed. Although Italy and Spain stand out for their lower levels of childless women's employment, there is otherwise relatively little cross-national variation in employment for childless women. However, these patterns are quite different for mothers—arguably the women most likely to face care demands from children. Among

Figure 6.1. Employment Patterns for Childless Women and Mothers between 25 and 45 Years of Age (Excluding Self-employed and Military) circa 2000

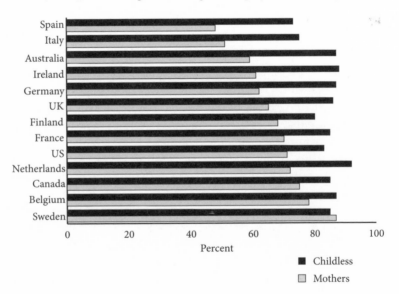

Figure 6.2. Full-time Employment Patterns for Childless Women and Mothers between 25 and 45 Years of Age (Excluding Self-employed and Military) circa 2000

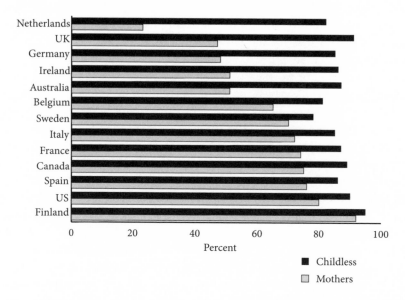

mothers, employment rates vary from 87% of all mothers in Sweden to 48% of all mothers in Spain.

Taken together, these data suggest that differences in caregiving responsibilities help explain much of the cross-national variation in women's employment rates. Childless women, who for the most part have fewer care responsibilities for children, though many may be involved in elder care, are employed at similar levels across these nations. Yet, mothers' employment varies far more, and may suggest that in some countries mothers are more likely to be *pushed* (via jobs that do not allow for work-family balance, or wages too low to replace caring labor in the home) or *pulled* (via a lack of other options regarding the provision of care for their families) out of the labor market. Indeed, in this figure, it appears that American mothers are not exceptional in their "opt-out" behavior and, in fact, are more likely than mothers in other countries to maintain an attachment to the labor force, perhaps because of the availability of low-cost market-based child care (Morgan 2005).

Figure 6.2 examines full-time employment patterns for employed women between 25 and 45 years of age cross-nationally (Misra, Budig, and Böckmann 2009, Table 2). Among childless women between 25 and 45 who are employed, more than 80% (except in Sweden) work full-time, here defined as 30 hours of work or more a week. Yet, for mothers between 25 and 45, there is much more variation. Indeed, while over 90% of employed Finnish mothers work full-time, less than a quarter (23%) of Dutch employed mothers work full-time.

Again, these findings suggest that the caregiving responsibilities of mothers shape their access to, and engagement with, employment. These differ cross-nationally. There is not one simple explanation for why mothers either leave employment or work part-time. Instead, these data suggest that social and cultural contexts may shape the opportunities for mothers as workers. For example, in some countries we find work hours influencing women's choices. In Sweden, mothers (and childless women) tend to work part-time rather than full-time in order to balance caregiving with employment, but men also are less likely to work very long hours. In the Netherlands, on the other hand, childless women have relatively high levels of full-time employment, but mothers have very low levels of full-time employment. Men here also tend to avoid working very long hours, and caregiving time is valued (although certainly still gendered!). Yet, in countries like Spain and Italy, mothers are much less likely to be employed, but when they are employed they have moderate levels of full-time employment. In the United States and France, although mothers have only moderate levels of employment (clearly, some mothers do leave the labor force), those that remain tend to work full-time. These differences in employment patterns reflect differences in cultural contexts regarding maternal employment, differences in work-family policies that help mothers (and fathers) reconcile care and employment, and differences in other structural factors (Misra, Budig, and Böckmann 2009).

Across these contexts, employed parents often rely on others to provide care for children. These caregivers may vary, from highly educated and well-compensated workers, to educated but less well-compensated workers, to less educated and poorly compensated workers. Among these caregivers, immigrant women workers play important roles in many countries. Yet, immigrant women workers tend to be among the most disadvantaged of care workers, even though they play an integral role in many economies. In the next two sections, I contextualize what we know about immigrant caregivers in Europe, and how the United States reflects larger patterns regarding these workers.

Migration and Transnational Caregiving

Care work is distributed in an international system where poor immigrant women workers provide care work for more affluent families in wealthier regions or countries (Glenn 1992; Heyzer and Wee 1994; Momsen 1999;

Anderson 1997, 1999; Hondagneu-Sotelo 2000, 2001; Lutz 2000, 2002; Parreñas 2001, 2005, 2008; Misra and Merz 2006; Lan 2006). Immigrant caregivers do not simply relieve individual middle-class women of care burdens. They enable middle-class men and women to focus on employment, and *subsidize* the reproduction of labor, making crucial contributions to the economies of many countries (Misra, Woodring, and Merz 2006). States and policies have played a key role in creating and reinforcing the redistribution and internationalization of care work.

Given higher levels of women's employment, wealthy countries need greater numbers of care providers. A corresponding shift has occurred in migration; more migrants work in service sector and care jobs, and women make up more than half of all migrant flows, strongly predominating in some countries (such as Indonesia, the Philippines, and Sri Lanka) (OECD 2001; Lutz 2002; Sassen 2003). Immigrant women workers are responsible for significant amounts of care work in North America, Europe, East Asia, Australia, the Middle East, and other regions (Pyle 2001; Pyle and Ward 2003). Care workers are also more likely to emigrate only temporarily in order to support their families at home, sending their earnings home, helping to guarantee a smooth flow of currency for their home country (Bakan and Stasiulis 1996; Lutz 2002; Parreñas 2001; Pyle and Ward 2003). These workers are often considered guest workers, with only temporary work permits, but many more work underground and are not recognized as legal workers (Heyzer and Wee 1994; Pyle and Ward 2003).

In wealthy countries, welfare state restructuring has led to a decline in both social spending and social care services (Daly and Lewis 1998; Jenson and Sineau 2001). States have moved from providing services and care to encouraging the development of low-wage private sector services (Pierson 2001; Jenson and Sineau 2001). Despite the rollback in state provision, however, low-paid immigrant women caregivers maintain social reproduction in these countries (Momsen 1999). Indeed, Milkman, Reese, and Roth (1998) show that countries with higher levels of income inequality and lower levels of state provision of care, such as the United States, also have much higher levels of foreign domestic workers.

At the same time, migration flows are not simply based on immigrants' individual choices, but are embedded in and patterned by social and economic processes, such as networks of migrants, while being regulated by migration policies and historical relationships between countries (Heisler 1985; Mitchell 1989; Rystad 1992; Massey et al. 1998; Massey 1999; Sassen 1998). Bilateral immigration policies, as well as multilateral agreements with organizations like the International Labour Organization, play a central role in shaping how workers move around the globe. Migration choices are then shaped by their institutional context (Rystad 1992).

Immigration policies also shape the conditions of employment for immigrant workers. For example, if countries do not give work visas or permits for care work, even when many immigrants illegally take such positions, migration policy then may support a flow of undocumented and vulnerable workers (Heyzer and Wee 1994; Anderson 1997; Hess 2002; Kofman 2003). On the other hand, care workers with work visas are more likely to be protected by labor laws, including minimum wage laws, protection of hours worked, and rights to privacy (Anderson 1997; Sassen 2003). Therefore, migration flows are shaped by economic conditions, but are also shaped by historical factors and migration policies.

Rather than states taking responsibility for aiding families, political economic strategies have encouraged the development of an international division of care work that places the burden for care on the least powerful (immigrant women workers). At the same time, migration policies have not always recognized the importance of immigrant caregivers' jobs, leaving many immigrant care workers in undocumented and particularly unprotected jobs. As Heyzer and Wee powerfully argue:

> The shifting division of responsibility between the State and the family for the social reproduction of everyday life has, thereby, been transformed into a trans-national division of labour between middle class women and working class women. . . . [T]his results in hidden savings for the governments of the receiving countries, because the need for adequate state investments in child care, care of the handicapped, care of the elderly and other social services is instead provided for by the income subsidy of middle class professional women and by the labour subsidy of relatively low-paid female migrant workers (1994, 44–45).

Care Work Inequalities in France and Germany

Policies play a role in shaping these labor flows (Misra and Merz 2006; Misra, Woodring, and Merz 2006). For example, in France and Germany, neoliberal policies of the last two decades have exacerbated inequalities between care workers and the families for whom they provide care. As in the United States, demographic trends in both countries have led to a greater demand for care workers, including rising elderly populations, changing family structures, and higher levels of women's employment.

In these wealthy countries, welfare state restructuring has led to greater reliance on market-based solutions. Rather than providing care, the state has encouraged the development of low-wage market-based care services, such as those that exist in the United States. Differences in institutional contexts—including migration policy, labor market policy, and welfare state policy—mean that these processes play out differently in particular contexts.

In Germany, restructuring appears to have actually *expanded* care provision (Seeleib-Kaiser 2004). Legislation now provides for long-term care insurance, as well as a caregivers' allowance, and an expansion of child-care. However, rather than defining professional standards of care, the new social care legislation creates low-skill and low-paying care jobs (Ostner 1998). Immigrant workers carry out much of the needed elder care in private homes, yet they are relatively poorly compensated. While the German government allows tax rebates for families employing domestic workers for more than ten hours a week, very few people have used this system, in part because it requires employers to make contributions to the social insurance program (Smet 2000). German care workers prefer to work in higher-paying and regulated public sector jobs, but this care is more expensive. Therefore, immigrant workers, many of whom are not legal immigrants, have become more responsible for covering home-based care work.

German immigration policy limits long-term residency to highly skilled workers. However, bilateral agreements with various Eastern European countries have set up temporary visas for care workers (Okolski 2004). Until 2001, care workers were not given work permits for their work in Germany. Due to the widespread use of undocumented immigrants for elder care, immigration policy now allows for three-year work permits for "household help" for those receiving long-term care insurance benefits (Meier-Braun 2002; OECD 2004). Yet these work permits are limited to low-paid "household helpers," even though many immigrant care workers have nursing certifications. As a United Nations (2005: 121) report notes, "Though legally employed and paid at German rates, the state stipulates that these carers cannot compete against German-trained homecare employees and that their permit must be for 'household assistant'. . . they have in effect sanctioned deskilling." In addition, despite the permit system, thousands of care workers continue to enter Germany illegally, often on three-month tourist visas. While employers are legally bound to pay German-level wages, many care workers, particularly the undocumented, earn significantly less (Kofman 2003).

In France, we see a slightly different dynamic in action. French welfare state restructuring has focused on pursuing active labor market policies, primarily centering on creating new employment through welfare policy (Mandin and Palier 2002). Care for both children and the elderly has been increasingly privatized, not simply to cut government costs but also to create jobs. The French state shifted from providing institutional care for the elderly and young children to more of a mix between formal and informal care, with direct payments for those caring for children and the elderly at home. As a result, France has also seen a strong increase in private care, with annual expenditures devoted to these arrangements increasing significantly (Letablier 2001). This care is subsidized through a tax rebate (since 1993), and facilitated through a voucher system that allows families to pay care workers without having to calculate contributions to the social security system (Morgan 2002; Smet 2000).

Upper-middle-class families who can use private, flexible, individualized care have benefited from this arrangement. While the state has some control over wages and employment conditions for registered workers, most employers do not register their care workers. And the consequences of restructuring have been quite problematic for poor, working-class, and lower-middle-class families. For example, the French crèche system has provided excellent high-quality care for children under the age of three through a sliding scale system; with wealthier families instead hiring private caregivers, crucial economic and political support for the crèche has been weakened. Poor, working-class, and lower-middle-class families have found it much more difficult to place their children in crèche. As Jenson and Sineau (2001) point out, as care is privatized, class distinctions, once mitigated through state care provisions, have become increasingly visible.

At the same time, care workers themselves receive lower wages and benefits. While the French state has not reduced welfare spending, it has shifted its role from a provider to a financer of care, in part as a means of creating more care jobs, but with serious repercussions for both care workers and families with fewer resources. Immigrant women caregivers fill a significant portion of these newly created positions.

French policy limits immigration by restricting work permits and making it difficult for immigrants to attain citizenship. Temporary work permits tend to go to highly educated workers; however, less well-educated workers can receive seasonal work permits for agricultural labor. Women are less likely to receive work permits, and often enter illegally on tourist visas. While France does not issue work permits for care workers, researchers estimate that perhaps more than 50 % of immigrant women in France work as care workers (Weinert 1991; RESPECT 2000). Little incentive exists for employers to register and legalize workers, which can be a difficult and arduous process, and almost always means that employers must pay higher wages and taxes, reduce their employees' work hours, and provide vacation leave (average wages for legal workers are still lower than average wages in other sectors) (Weinert 1991; Blackett 1998; Mozère et al. 2001).

Welfare state restructuring in these contexts has stimulated employment, while also limiting welfare state provision of care. Both countries address the demand for care in ways that limit the state's responsibility for providing care. In both cases, restructuring has only increased the demand for immigrant care workers. Both governments are also quite ambivalent about immigration, aware of the need for immigrant caregivers, but unwilling to fully recognize this need through supportive immigration policies. Yet restructuring in Germany and France has taken somewhat different forms. In Germany, support for care has increased; yet the quality of care has decreased. While German restructuring has meant an expansion of care through long-term care insurance as well as a caregivers' allowance, these policies do not provide adequate support for care. In France, public care provision has been replaced by more privatized forms that promote inequalities between families. While French subsidies are more generous than German subsidies, the French system remains inadequate, due in part to lack of enforcement.

The differences between these cases should provide evidence for the importance of taking context into account in considering how the international division of caring labor is created and reinforced by state policies. There are tremendous inequalities—by gender, class, race, ethnicity, and nationality—in how care work is done. Yet these inequalities are not due simply to the exploitation of workers by employers. Complicit in this system are domestic political institutions that benefit from the labor subsidies of immigrant women care workers. By exploring the relationship between welfare state restructuring and immigration in this integrated fashion, I am trying to draw attention to both the contradictions and consistencies in state policies, and the ways that policies may be working to support a redistribution of care that relies upon the economic exploitation of immigrant women workers.

Care Work Protections and the Public Sector

Although this research on immigrant caregivers is relatively sobering, as it suggests that policy changes in recent decades have primarily reinforced inequalities by nationality, race/ethnicity, gender, and citizenship, more broadly comparative research also suggests somewhat better news. By examining the earnings of care workers cross-nationally, it appears that low wages for care work are not universal (Budig and Misra 2010), and that policies can reinforce greater equality regarding care work employment. Research based in the United States (England, Budig, and Folbre 2002) shows that care workers are paid less than one would expect (5–6% less), taking into account their skills, education, experience, and other characteristics (England 1992; Cancian 2000; Folbre 2001a, 2001b). England et al. (2002) argue that care work is devalued in part because it is associated with women, but also due to the tension between the expense of high-quality care provision versus the resources of those needing care. This might explain why care employment would pay less well than other occupations, controlling for other factors that might explain variations in wages.

Yet there are reasons to believe that wages for care work may vary based on context. For example, in a context where there is greater government support and regulation of care work or unionization of care work, we might expect that wages for care work are higher (Morgan 2005; Budig and Misra 2008). If the government subsidizes—or, even better—provides care through the public sector, care work may be better compensated, since governments are less likely to pay low wages due to greater regulation and public scrutiny (Gornick and Jacobs 1998; Kearney and Carnevale 2001). In addition, there may be a relationship between the overall level of income inequality and wages for care work; just as gender wage gaps are smaller in countries with lower levels of income inequality (Blau and Kahn 1992, 2003), wage penalties to care may lessen in such contexts.

Indeed, research that examines wages for care work across twelve different countries, including Belgium, France, Germany, the Netherlands, Russia, Hungary, the U.S., Canada, Mexico, and Taiwan, indicates that care work is not always penalized (Budig and Misra 2010). Overall, care workers are more highly educated than other workers, and are more likely to be in professional jobs and in jobs in the public sector. Care employment does often mean penalties, or lower wages than we would expect, controlling for other factors. The fact that care employment is more likely to be carried out by women accounts for some but not all of the penalties incurred by care workers (Budig and Misra 2010).

Yet in a number of countries there are *no* penalties for engaging in care work, and in some countries there are bonuses—workers employed in care make *more* than similar workers who are not employed in care. Where income inequality is greater and where the public sector is smaller, higher wage penalties are incurred for performing care work. However, in countries that have policies aimed at limiting income inequality, and in countries where the public sector is large, engaging in care work does not lower wages (Budig and Misra 2008). Given that welfare state restructuring has moved some care provision out of the public sector and into more individualized family-based settings, this might mean that care occupations will begin to see greater penalties in some of these countries.

But with the current shift in some countries away from free-market neo-liberal policies and, hopefully, a corresponding movement away from privatization, there is potential for greater opportunities regarding care work. Unionizing care workers is an excellent step, and may help increase the pay and prestige of these occupations. Yet public sector expansion—such as through early education and care programs, expanded federal programs to support elder care, and care of the sick and disabled through community programs, with workers in these sectors provided with opportunities for career development and better wages—may also be an effective strategy. By taking these approaches, as well as measures such as living wage policies that would strengthen wages for low-end workers, we could also deeply reduce the inequalities faced by care workers.

Although in almost every context, the increased labor market participation of middle-class and upper-middle-class women has required *other* women—often immigrants and/or racial/ethnic minority women—to step in and provide care, this change should not necessarily lead to greater exploitation and intensifying inequalities. Notwithstanding that there are many examples of the intensification of these inequalities, I would also argue that there are political and economic measures we can take that can mediate these inequalities, rather than intensify them. While there has been a remarkable increase in women's labor market participation across many countries, and these changes require corresponding increases in care employment, there are ways of structuring care employment so that it is valued and rewarded rather than devalued and exploited. Through a comparative lens, it is possible to identify mechanisms—such as migration policy that allows work permits for care workers and welfare state policies that emphasize public rather than private caregiving—that will lead to more equitable outcomes. Through such approaches, we can create the conditions for greater equality and more effective care.

IV

Conclusion

7

The Opt-Out
Revolution Revisited

JOAN C. WILLIAMS AND JAMIE DOLKAS

The media tends to cover work/family conflict as the story of highly educated professional mothers "opting out" of fast-track careers in the face of
inflexible career paths and very long workweeks, ignoring the experiences of
working- and middle-class women.[1] Given that less than 8% of U.S. women
hold high-level white collar and other traditionally masculine jobs,[2] while
27% of U.S. women hold low-wage or blue-collar jobs,[3] this paints an inaccurate picture of the issues surrounding women's workforce participation.
Further, the media's narrow focus on professional mothers of young children
suggests that work/family conflict is a trivial issue that impacts only a small
portion of the workforce.

Based on WorkLife Law's database of union arbitrations, this chapter con-
cludes this book with a discussion of the unexplored territory of work/family
conflict among the Missing Middle—a term we use to describe Americans
who are neither poor nor privileged.[4] Part I discusses how these families
experience work/family conflict differently from professional families. The
arbitrations paint a vivid picture of inflexible workplaces and a shortage of
financial resources that makes child care difficult—and retaining a job of par-
amount importance. Part II discusses how outdated workplace ideals place
Americans at all class levels in impossible situations, where their responsibilities to their employers conflict with their responsibilities to their families.
As a consequence, employers often fail to come to terms with the realities
of workers' lives. In addition, some employers actively discriminate against
adults with family responsibilities. Work/family conflict among the Missing
Middle is thus a new frontier that academics and policymakers should consider as a central component of the Opt-Out debate—both because of the
ways that work/family conflict uniquely impacts Americans who are neither
poor nor privileged, and because of the valuable insights these people's lives
provide into the larger Opt-Out debate.

I. How Working-Class Families Experience Work/ Family Conflict Differently from Professional Families

A. What Inflexibility Looks Like among the Missing Middle

Media coverage of the Opt-Out debate typically focuses on professional women and uses the rhetoric of individual choice, depicting women who cheerfully opt out as they discover they were more traditional than they ever imagined.[5] In fact, many women don't cheerfully opt out—they are pushed out by workplace inflexibility.[6] For professional workers, "inflexibility" usually refers to long hours, a lack of part-time options, and relegation to the "mommy track" for workers who take time off or reduce their hours.

Unlike professional workers, who have the ability to work from home, leave work to take family members to the doctor, or make a phone call to check on a sick child, blue-collar workers typically lack the kind of flexibility and control professionals take for granted. Nonprofessionals often have highly supervised jobs where they clock in and out, adhere to rigid schedules, must take lunch and breaks at designated times, can be fired for arriving even a few minutes late, and have limited ability to take leave to handle family emergencies. One study found that flexible scheduling is available for nearly two-thirds of workers with incomes of more than $71,000 a year but to less than one-third of working parents with incomes less than $28,000.[7] Another found that one-third of working-class employees cannot decide when to take breaks, nearly 60% cannot choose starting or quitting times, and 53% cannot take time off for sick children. In addition, 68% of working-class families have two weeks or less of vacation and sick leave combined.[8] For these workers, workplace inflexibility is the main source of work/family conflict.

Union arbitrations vividly illustrate how workers in the Missing Middle lack basic flexibility and control. For example, a bus driver was fired when she arrived three minutes late because her severely asthmatic son had had an asthma attack.[9] A packer was fired when she found out that her daughter was in the emergency room with a head injury and left work early.[10] An employer implemented a new schedule requiring workers to start work at 8:00 a.m. for the first four days of the week and at 8:30 a.m. on the fifth day.[11] The employer refused to accommodate workers who complained that this schedule made it extremely difficult to arrange child care. A press operator at the *Chicago Tribune*, who was the primary caregiver for her mother, came to work 20 minutes late because she was up until midnight monitoring her mother's dangerously high blood pressure.[12] When she arrived home, her one-year-old was having trouble sleeping. She fell asleep while rocking her child to sleep and overslept the next morning. In another case, a worker called in sick 17 minutes late and was suspended 5 days without pay.[13] He was busy getting his four kids ready for school; he then had to drive them to school because they missed the bus, so he did not have time to call. He tried calling his employer before he left for school, but his employer did not have an answering machine. In another case, a service technician was suspended 1 week for taking three and a half hours for lunch (instead of an hour).[14] He went home during lunch to check on his recently hospitalized father and stayed because his father was unattended and needed care. He was later fired pursuant to his employer's progressive discipline policy for an additional infraction—taking his lunch 15 *minutes* outside of the designated lunch period (he took lunch from 12:15 to 1:15 instead of 12:00 to 1:00).

In some cases in which workers discussed their family obligations with their supervisors and requested more flexible arrangements, employers still refused very minor schedule adjustments. In *AT&T Information Systems, Inc. and Communications Workers of America*,[15] a packing and dismantling worker went home every day during his lunch break to administer vital medication to his 85-year-old father. He needed to get home as quickly as possible, but was often delayed by long lines of workers who were also waiting to clock out. He explained to his supervisor that he needed to clock out immediately each day because a few minutes could mean the difference between life and death for his father. He asked if he could leave a few minutes early or if he could move the time card rack near his desk, but his supervisor refused. In *AT&T Corp. and Communications Workers of America*,[16] a corporate financial organization clerk who had worked for his employer for 30 years asked his manager for an earlier start time so he could spend more time caring for his seriously ill father after work. His manager repeatedly denied his request. In *Simpson v. District of Columbia Office of Human Rights*,[17] a secretary challenged her employer's insistence that she start work one hour and a half earlier, thereby making it impossible for her to care for her elderly and ailing father before she arrived at work. These cases illustrate examples of employers that refuse to allow flexibility, even where they could allow flexibility without jeopardizing their business needs.

Nonprofessional workers lack other basic rights afforded to most professionals, such as the ability to call home to check on family members during the day. This is especially important during the summer, when one in ten children aged 6 to 12 is home alone or with a sibling under age 13.[18] In *AT&T Communications and Communications Workers of America*,[19] a phone operator with 11 years of service and a good performance record was discharged for making a personal call from her work phone. Her employer prohibited workers from using their work phones for personal use, but allowed them to use a designated phone for personal calls if they asked for permission. Her 12-year-old daughter with emotional and mental problems ran away the night before her shift. Her employer refused to give her the day off, so she went to work and, with her supervisor's permission, repeatedly called home to check on the situation. She used her work phone once without permission to call home and was terminated.

Several common workplace policies cause particular difficulties: "no fault" progressive discipline systems that fail to provide leniency for absences caused by genuine family emergencies, mandatory overtime systems, and lack of paid sick leave for care of sick family members. No fault attendance policies give workers points for absenteeism regardless of the cause, unless the situation is covered by work rules or union contract. A worker who garners enough points is first disciplined and then fired, regardless of the reasons for the absences in question. Because no fault policies operate without consideration for the cause of the absence, they fail to give proper leeway to workers who are absent because of legitimate family emergencies. For example, in *Communications Workers of America, Local 13500 and Verizon*,[20] a collection center consultant was placed on probation pursuant to her employer's "no fault" attendance policy for absences related to her own medical problems, then terminated for missing one day of work when her daughter injured her ankle and needed immediate medical attention. However, in light of the worker's legitimate family emergency, the arbitrator ordered her reinstatement, stating that she "[did] not believe that the grievant should have been expected to abdicate her parental responsibility to her daughter as the price for keeping her job. . . . No-fault attendance programs such as [the employer's policy at issue] have to be administered with some degree of flexibility to take account of situations, such as the personal emergency with which the grievant was confronted."[21] Though employers clearly have a right to count on employees to show up, employees should not be fired when a family emergency triggers the final attendance point.[22]

Another form of workplace inflexibility that shows up again and again in the arbitrations is mandatory overtime. Unions and policymakers need to recognize that the design of mandatory overtime systems can make or break workers' ability to avoid discipline or discharge when work and family conflict. The overtime issue is important, in part, because Americans work longer hours than workers in virtually any other developed economy.[23] Long hours are largely the province of men: while managerial and professional men are more likely to work 50 plus hours per week, *one in five male hourly workers do so, too.*[24]*Many more work overtime*: working-class men average 42 to 43 hours per week, far longer than their European counterparts. [25] As discussed further below, the increasing demand for mandatory overtime is especially difficult for single parents, divorced parents, and tag-team families.

Additionally, many employers do not provide sick leave that workers can use to care for sick family members, so family illness may lead to discipline or discharge for blue-collar workers. A recent online survey revealed that 58% of respondents (and 69% of workers who earned less than $40,000 a year) said they did not have paid sick leave to care for sick family members.[26] In today's workplace, in 70% of families all adults in the household are employed.[27] When a child gets sick in one of these families, one working parent needs to stay home. (Studies have shown that children stay sick longer when parents cannot stay home to care for them.)[28] This poses major problems for the 58% of workers who do not have paid sick leave for family care. Without paid sick leave, even routine childhood illness is a major concern. Families with infants visit the doctor an average of 4 to 6 times a year (or an average of 11 times a year for families with infants with special needs).[29] Families with children aged 2 to 4 visit the doctor an average of 4 times a year (or 7 times a year for special needs 2- to 4-year olds).[30] For example, *Naval Air Rework Facility* involved a child with chickenpox.[31] Since the child care facility would not accept the child within his contagious period, the mother had no choice but to stay home with her ill child. She was denied sick leave upon returning to work, and as a result, discharged.[32]

In some workplaces where unions have secured a contractual right to paid sick leave for workers to care for sick family members, employers add additional qualifications to narrowly restrict the right to sick leave. In *Detroit Lakes Education Association and Independent School Dist. No. 22*,[33] the labor contract granted paid sick leave for workers who care for a family member's "serious illness." The employer added an additional requirement, with a policy that family members did not have a "serious illness" unless they were hospitalized. A teacher whose newborn was repeatedly hospitalized with respiratory problems struggled with the unfairness of this policy when her doctor said that, although her baby was still very sick, she could check her child out of the hospital if she was able to provide constant care and monitoring at home. The teacher requested sick leave and, even though her child was seriously ill, her employer denied her request because of its hospitalization requirement. The arbitrator held that because the employer had failed to notify workers about the hospitalization requirement, the teacher was entitled to paid sick leave for her child's serious illness.

Workers caring for an immediate family member (spouse, child, or parent) with a serious health condition are entitled to up to 12 weeks of unpaid leave each year, so long as they have worked for at least one year (and 1,250 hours in the year prior to the leave) for an employer with 50 or more employees, under the Family and Medical Leave Act (FMLA).[34] Workers can take leave for serious health conditions in an intermittent pattern, which is particularly useful for workers who need to bring family members to doctors' appointments or who have family members with chronic diseases.[35] Yet many workers are not covered.[36] Others fail to request FMLA leave in a manner the employer recognizes[37] or to obtain the necessary medical documentation;[38] sometimes it is unclear whether the FMLA was ever considered.[39] For example, in *Bellsouth Communications, Inc. and Communications Workers of America*,[40] a sales associate with positive performance evaluations throughout her first six years of employment used all her FMLA leave for the year when she took maternity leave for her child's birth. After she returned from leave, her child underwent emergency surgery and her husband had a stroke. These family emergencies caused her to accumulate numerous absences and she was fired for excessive absenteeism. The arbitrator held that although all the worker's absences were caused by serious family health situations beyond her control, she was not protected by the FMLA and therefore her discharge was lawful.

B. Economic Factors: Heavy Reliance on Family Members for Child Care

For nonprofessional families, inflexible work schedules combined with an unusually heavy reliance on family members for child care create a volatile situation. Child care in the U.S. is both expensive and of highly variable quality. In 2002, the OECD estimated that the cost of center-based care for two children in the U.S. could amount to as much as 37% of a single parent's income.[41] Consequently, working-class families typically patch together a crazy quilt of family-delivered care, with parents working different shifts and/or drafting grandparents and other family members to help with child care. Working-class families are more likely to rely on relatives for family care than more affluent families.[42] One-third of low-income families must rely on a relative to care for their children while they are at work.[43] Heavy reliance on family-delivered care continues in families with older children. Nearly one-fifth of children aged 6 through 12 are cared for by relatives outside of school hours.[44]

These informal child care arrangements break down more often than more formal ones because if any relative in the chain of custody is forbidden to leave or is ordered to work overtime, the care arrangements quickly fall apart.[45] A study of child care in Massachusetts found that four out of ten low-income parents were forced to miss work because of problems with child care; nearly three-fourths lost pay due to work/family conflicts.[46] One study found that 30% of workers surveyed had to cut back on work for at least one day during the week surveyed in order to care for family members: nearly one-quarter of men as well as over one-third of women.[47] Cutbacks were more frequent among lower-income workers with the most inflexible schedules, presumably because they were only half as likely to rely on child care centers.[48]

Working-class families are affected by child care breakdowns, in significant part because of "tag teaming," where parents work different shifts so that each parent can care for the children while the other is at work. About one in three working families with children under 6, and one in four with children, handle child care by tag teaming.[49] Tag teaming is especially common in nonprofessional families, in part for simple economic reasons: the average price for child care for a 1-year-old is higher in every state than the average cost of college tuition at the state's university.[50] Several arbitrations involving phone operators illustrate the lack of child care options plaguing working-class families. In these cases, workers without viable child care options were forced to leave their children home alone and were disciplined or discharged for monitoring the phone lines to check on their children. One arbitration involved more than 30 phone company workers who were fired for tapping into customer phone lines.[51] A worker reported having a mentally unstable son who had threatened to kill her, her family, and himself. Three other workers had children who they said threatened and/or attempted suicide. Two workers monitored the phones of parents; one had a mother who was "suffering from confusion;" the other's father was ill and, according to the worker, had been threatened with harm from other tenants in her building.

Parents of young children are not the only workers who find their jobs at risk due to the lack of suitable child care. Because the average age at which Americans become grandparents for the first time is now 47, three-fourths of grandmothers and almost nine out of ten grandfathers are in the labor force.[52] Thus, more than one-third of grandmothers who provide care for preschool-aged children are otherwise employed.[53] In *Department of Veterans Affairs Medical Center*,[54] a grandmother was suspended from her job as a nursing assistant when she was unable to work her scheduled shift (3:30 p.m.

to midnight) because she was unable to find child care. *Mercer County*[55] also involves a grandmother who needed time off to care for her grandchildren. She happened to have custody, but grandparents frequently provide regular child care: over one-fifth of preschool-aged children are primarily cared for by grandparents when their parents are at work,[56] and a new study reports that 2.4 million grandparents have primary responsibility for the care of their grandchildren.[57] Over one-fourth had cared for their grandchildren for five or more years.[58] In another case, a grandmother working as a bus driver lost her chance at promotion because she had been absent for a significant period caring for her injured son.[59] These older family caregivers are vulnerable to the same work/family conflicts faced by their grown children, even if a grandparent does not provide routine child care. One arbitration involved a school isolation monitor who was suspended from work for 20 days (reduced by the arbitrator to 10) when she took more leave than had been authorized to care for her pregnant daughter and granddaughter.[60] Another involved a base assembler in a steel plant who was fired when she stayed home to care for her adult daughter, who had been injured in a car accident.[61]

Elder care creates similar problems for working-class families due to their inability to afford professional care and their reliance on informal family arrangements. One in four American families take care of elderly relatives.[62] Among people aged 50 to 64 needing support for their health and emotional needs, 84% rely on informal care networks.[63] Almost one in five caregivers say they provide 40 plus hours of care per week,[64] and the average length of care is 4.3 years.[65] Fully 57% of working caregivers say that they have had to go to work late, leave early, or take time off during the day to provide care.[66] One arbitration involving an elderly parent is *Sprint/Central Telephone Co. of Texas*,[67] in which a phone customer service representative failed to meet her sales quota because of the stress caused by caring for her mother, who had died by the time of the arbitration.

Beyond luxury goods and shopping sprees—
Working-class families need their incomes as a matter of survival
The Opt-Out debate, as framed by the media, ignores the serious economic consequences for women who are pushed out of the workforce. WorkLife Law's 2006 report, *Opt Out or Pushed Out? How the Press Covers Work-Family Conflict,* found that many articles discussing the Opt-Out debate completely ignored the economic consequences for women who opt out.[68] The articles that actually mentioned women's economic consequences tended to frame the issue in terms of short-term belt tightening, focusing on opt-

outers' inability to buy luxuries rather than discussing the serious long-term consequences of women's economic vulnerability.[69] These articles told the stories of former "shop-a-holic[s]"[70] who traded fancy cars, first-class vacations,[71] and shopping sprees for more modest spending habits.[72]

In reality, many families face serious financial consequences when mothers are pushed out of the workforce. Employed women, on average, bring home 28% of the family income.[73] Twenty-one percent of women in dual-income households earn more than their husbands.[74] Sixty-two percent (and 58% of working women with children) earn about half or more of their families' incomes.[75]A recent online survey of approximately 20,000 working women by the AFL-CIO found that, although working women have virtually no time for themselves, 50% said they would work another job if they had free time.[76] After work and family responsibilities, nearly half of the respondents (and 72% of respondents who are parents) said they only have an hour or less to themselves each day.[77] Further, more than half (53%) of the respondents said that the thing they needed most—more than better health care, child care, or pension contributions—was a 10% raise.[78] In contrast with the media image of professional women who work not for money but to find "stimulating and personally fulfilling" careers,[79] 72% of survey respondents said that if given the choice between a job that paid better or one that was more fun, they would choose the one with higher pay.[80]

Union arbitrations further demonstrate that working mothers' incomes are necessary for their families' survival. Several arbitrations involved workers who went to *extreme* lengths to keep their jobs in the face of pressing family obligations. In *AT&T and Communications Workers of America*,[81] a customer contract associate managed to work over ten hours of overtime each week while caring for her seven children and her husband who had a seizure and related heath problems. Because she was on probation for earlier absences (related to her husband's care) and could not afford to lose her job, she juggled all of this without a single absence for six months. In another case, a divorced mother was frequently absent to care for her daughter after she was sexually abused and developed psychological problems, including suicidal tendencies.[82] The worker was placed on probation for her attendance, but needed her job so badly that she tried to return to work after a horse stepped on her and seriously injured her foot. She tried to convince the company physician that she could work despite the injury, but the doctor would not allow it and she was fired pursuant to her employer's rule designating absences for off-the-job injuries as unexcused. In *BellSouth Telecommunications*,[83] a service representative commuted 200 miles each day while caring for her two sick and elderly parents. In numerous cases involving flight attendants, working mothers whose babysitters canceled at the last minute decided to bring their children (even infants as young as 16 months) on their flights because they could not risk losing their jobs due to an unexcused absence.[84] These stories send a clear message: working-class women face serious economic consequences if they lose their jobs and they are willing to go to great lengths to keep them. In contrast with the Opt-Out imagery that women's incomes constitute pin money that pays for shopping sprees, new cars, and luxury items, many families need women's incomes to pay for the basics: food, rent, car payments.

II. A Workplace Perfectly Designed for the Workforce of 1960
A. The Outdated Definition of the Ideal Worker

In 1960, only 10% of mothers worked, and only 10% were unmarried. So it made sense for employers to shape jobs around the ideal worker of a breadwinner who was available for work anytime, anywhere, for as long as the employer needed him.[85] Today 70% of American children live in households where all adults are employed.[86] One in four Americans—more every year—are caring for elders.[87] Hospitals let patients out "quicker and sicker." Yet employers still enshrine as ideal the breadwinner who takes care of business while his wife takes care of family. For most Americans, that's not real life.

Employers have not caught up. They still enshrine the Ideal Worker who starts to work in early adulthood and works, full time and full force, for forty years straight. This ideal only worked in a world of breadwinner-housewife families. Most families no longer follow this pattern, but workplaces still are designed around those that do. As a result, having a wife at home greatly enhances men's earning power: men with stay-at-home wives earn an average 30% "wage premium,"[88] presumably because their wives' work at home allows them to fulfill employers' expectations that any worker who is truly committed will always be available for work.

Outdated workplace ideals have different effects on different classes of families. Escalating hours of professional-managerial workers push professional/managerial men into overwork and their families into neotraditional patterns, where the husband's career takes precedence, while the wife works fewer hours off the fast track.[89] Families who are neither poor nor rich cannot live up to the old-fashioned definition of the ideal worker because both parents typically are employed: roughly three-fourths of married women are employed at every income level below $120,000.[90] A simple point: workplaces designed around the Ideal Worker of 1960 do not fit the realities of twenty-first-century life.

The penalty against real, as opposed to ideal, workers:
Single parents, divorced parents, tag-team families, and male caregivers
In the union context, the penalty for workers who fail to live up to out-dated workplace ideals becomes vividly clear in arbitrations involving single parents, divorced parents, tag-team families, and workers who lose their domestic support when a spouse is sick or disabled. These workers often face discipline or discharge when the realities of life intrude upon outdated ideals. Two cases provide particularly vivid examples of situations where workers face an acute and sudden loss of domestic support and immediately struggle with workplace demands. In *Suprenant Cable Corp.*,[91] an extruder operator in vinyl extrusion who worked ten years without any attendance infractions developed a sudden attendance problem when his full-time stay-at-home wife left him alone to care for their four-year-old son. Shortly thereafter, social services notified him that they were investigating him for child neglect. They found none, but he accumulated many absences in the interim due to his lack of child care and his preparation for the abuse complaint. He tried to find day care, but all he could find during the summer were high school babysitters who were inconsistent and unreliable. He was placed on final warning for attendance. The worker called his supervisor to request one week of leave because he did not have a babysitter for the following week and could not afford additional absences. He explained that his attendance would subsequently improve because his son was starting a day care program and he would have consistent, reliable care. His supervisor refused and the worker was terminated. The arbitrator ordered the worker's reinstatement, criticizing the employer for failing to consider his entire work history, his special family circumstances causing the absences, and the fact that he resolved his child care situation so he was unlikely to have ongoing attendance problems.

In *AT&T and Communications Workers of America*[92] (mentioned above), a customer contract associate with 5 years of "more than satisfactory" ratings developed attendance problems when her husband had seizure and related health problems. She struggled to meet the competing demands of her employer's mandatory overtime system and her need to care for her husband and their seven children. She was placed on probation for excessive absences, then took leave without pay. She returned to work and went 6 months without a single absence while working over 10 hours of overtime each week and continuing to care for husband and children. However, her employer's mandatory overtime system caused severe emotional distress, and the worker ultimately took leave because of a nervous breakdown and related hospitalization.

Like their professional counterparts, nonprofessionals similarly struggle with long hours. Employers expect workers to be available for long hours of overtime work, which is especially difficult for single parents. In *State of New York, Rochester Psychiatric Center*,[93] a health center fired a mental health aide[94] who had worked for the employer for nine years because of attendance problems, almost all of which stemmed from her status as a single parent and her employer's demand for mandatory overtime.[95] She was ordered to work an additional eight-hour tour after her shift ended (at 11:20 p.m.). Her sitter could not stay.[96] Then the aide said she could stay if she could bring her children to work, but refused to leave her children alone.[97] The arbitrator overturned the worker's discharge, opining that the situation was

> shocking to one's sense of fairness. . . . [The worker] does not hold a high-paying job. She would probably be better off financially if she chose to stay home, watch her kids, and go on the dole. However, instead of becoming a public charge, she has chosen to make a public contribution. . . . Her recent performance evaluation indicates "she can function well on any ward she is assigned." As the parties are aware, I take a very dim view of time and attendance infractions and insubordination. . . . However, [she] deserves every conceivable "break". . . . Her children were well-groomed, neatly dressed, and well-behaved. It is her efforts to be a good parent that have created her problems at work.[98]

The arbitrator took a proactive role, directing the aide to identify, 30 days in advance, 3 days a month when she could work overtime. This is an example of how to design an overtime system that does not have a punitive impact on adults with family responsibilities—particularly if it is combined, to the maximum extent possible, with a system that relies on voluntary overtime.

In two other arbitrations, nurses' aides were fired, and were not reinstated, when they refused mandatory overtime because they had no one to care for their children.[99] *Tenneco Packaging Burlington Container Plant*[100] involved a janitor who was the divorced mother of a 17-year-old son with the mentality of an 18-month-old child. She was fired, despite her 27 years of service with her employer, for attendance problems caused by her employer's continuous demand for overtime (she worked 60-hour weeks, including most Saturdays). The arbitrator reinstated her, and noted the particularly difficult impact mandatory overtime policies have on single parents.[101]

In tag-team families, nonprofessional parents try to approximate the breadwinner/homemaker dichotomy by working opposite shifts so each parent can care for the children while the other is at work. However, if one parent gets stuck working overtime when the other is scheduled to start work, one of the parents might find his or her job in jeopardy. When employers expect men to be Ideal Workers with around-the-clock availability, men in tag-team families, who act as primary caregivers while their wives are at work, suffer. In one case, the father of a toddler was the primary caregiver while his wife was at work. He started his warehouse job at 7:00 a.m. in order to pick up his daughter from preschool at 3:00 p.m. The father won a grievance challenging his employer's attempt to change him entirely to a 9 to 5 schedule, on the grounds that the union contract did not allow the company to unilaterally change start times.[102] In another case, the arbitrator reduced a father's discharge to a one-month suspension for refusing to take an assignment because he had to pick up his daughter.[103] The simple fact is that in tag-team families, both parents' schedules cannot simultaneously have priority.

Men, particularly single or divorced fathers, are frequently sanctioned for refusing overtime. In *Bryant v. Bell Atlantic Maryland*[104] (reported in a court case), an African American construction lineman who was the single father of two minor children was fired for refusing overtime. The arbitrator held that the employer lacked just cause to terminate, and strongly suggested that Bryant be placed in a position that did not require overtime, or, in the alternative, that "Bryant be scheduled for overtime in a manner that would allow him to meet his workplace and child care obligations."[105] In *Marion Composites*,[106] a factory worker who regularly worked overtime whenever his employer asked was suspended three days for insubordination when he left after 8 hours of a 12-hour overtime shift because he had to get home to care for his two children.

Working-class men may be reluctant to admit that they need to leave work for care for children. Numerous arbitrations involve situations where workers had valid reasons for leaving work early or arriving late but were nonetheless disciplined because they failed to admit that they had caregiving responsibilities. For example, in *Tractor Supply Co.* (mentioned above), a grandfather was fired for insubordination when he refused to stay at work past his regular shift because he had to get home to care for his grandchild.[107] When his supervisor asked why he would not stay, the worker repeatedly said it was none of his business, even after his supervisor explained that accommodations could be made for reasonable excuses.[108] The arbitrator ordered his reinstatement. In *Midwest Body, Inc.*,[109] the arbitrator upheld the dismissal of an industrial worker who failed to report for overtime work on Saturday or for work on Monday. When asked why, "he replied he had family problems and declined to be more specific,"[110] again refusing to explain at a meeting with two supervisors and a union representative. "Reluctance to give specific information with respect to 'family problems' may be understandable," said the arbitrator, "but an employee who is unwilling to give [it] should refrain from using that sort of excuse."[111] Another worker who needed to leave to pick up his son said only that he needed to leave for personal reasons.[112]

Men's reluctance to discuss their family obligations magnifies their work/family conflict because employers often have rules that allow workers to refuse overtime for legitimate reasons. Even where these rules are lacking, supervisors are more likely to allow a worker to attend to pressing family needs than to accommodate a worker who refuses to disclose his reason for wanting to leave. And when employers remain staunchly inflexible, arbitrators are more likely to find in favor of a worker who explained why he needed to leave than a worker who remained silent. Recent studies of working-class men suggest that men's reluctance to discuss their caregiving obligations with employers may reflect insecurities about their inability to fulfill the traditional breadwinner role. The current generation of men has seen high school educated men's wages fall sharply: Their real wages have fallen by 25% since 1973.[113]

While their fathers and grandfathers could supply the "good life"—a house, a car, a washing machine—on their salaries alone, or with only intermittent part-time work from their wives, they often cannot. To quote a white 30-year-old forklift operator, "I know she doesn't mind working, but it shouldn't have to be that way. A guy should be able to support his wife and kids."[114] A 1994 study reported that working-class men feel badly when they "can't support their wives."[115] A 1996 study found that older working-class men did not like the fact that their wives needed jobs.[116] One man explained, "As far as I was brought up, Pop did the work, Mom stayed home with the kids."[117] These studies provide important context for understanding working-class men's reluctance to admit that they need to leave to attend to child care.

Reality check: If arbitrators recognize that workers' family responsibilities sometimes trump employers' needs, so should employers
Union arbitrations highlight the growing gap between what employers expect of workers and the realities of workers' everyday lives. In many decisions, arbitrators refused to enforce full discipline although workers clearly broke work rules because workers' family care responsibilities were mitigating factors.[118] In some cases, arbitrators refused to enforce *any* discipline because

workers' family care obligations were so compelling.[119] This illustrates the disconnect between what employers ask of their workers and universally accepted principles about family obligations.

In several arbitrations, arbitrators treated it as an obvious and well-accepted fact that, in the face of family emergencies, workers have no choice but to stay with their families. In *Local Union 1345, United Mine Workers of America and Old Ben Coal Co.*,[120] a mineworker challenged his employer's refusal to excuse him from work when a severe storm damaged his home and continued to threaten his family's safety. The arbitrator explained that it was unreasonable for the employer to expect him to go to work and leave his family in an unsafe situation, thus he had no choice but to keep his family safe, stating, "[H]is decision to stay home can be clearly viewed as an appropriate response to an [*sic*] *compelling moral obligation to look after the welfare of his family*."[121] In *U.S. Air and Association of Flight Attendants*,[122] a flight attendant was fired for refusing to work an extended shift when she called home and learned that her son had become ill with chicken pox and her babysitter could not stay to watch him. Finding that the worker did nothing wrong, the arbitrator stated, "In my opinion, an Attendant who learns that her child is ill and may not be attended should be considered in the same category as being ill [herself] and properly relieved of completing her sequence." The arbitrator ordered the employee's reinstatement. In another case, the arbitrator refused to uphold the worker's discipline, despite her "unacceptable attendance record" when the final absence resulting in termination was caused by a family emergency (her husband threw out his back and needed to see a doctor).[123] The arbitrator explained that the worker should not be fired because she responded reasonably to a legitimate family emergency and properly notified her supervisors about the situation.

In another case, the arbitrator held that, although the worker repeatedly violated his employer's rules by spending his allotted lunch and break time at home without permission, the penalty should be reduced because of the mitigating circumstances, which included his length of service (17 years), his good record, and his need to check on his 10-year-old son who was home alone for the summer while his wife was away on business.[124] The arbitrator stated that the employee "unquestionably had a valid reason for concern about the welfare of his son." These opinions acknowledge the importance of family care and dramatize the gap between employer expectations and workforce realities.

B. Discrimination against Caregivers

New research documents that motherhood is one of the key triggers of gender bias.[125] Many women, far from cheerfully opting out, are suing their employers when they are pushed out by "maternal wall" bias, typically triggered when a woman gets pregnant, returns from maternity leave, or seeks a part-time schedule. The result is a sharp rise in lawsuits challenging discrimination based on family responsibilities.[126] In a recent survey of approximately 20,000 working women, the AFL-CIO found that 80% of respondents said, "having children hurts their career and prospects in the job market" (27% said it hurts strongly).[127] The best-known study found that that mothers were 79% less likely to be hired, 100% less likely to be promoted, offered an average of $11,000 less in salary, and held to higher performance and punctuality standards than women without children.[128]

The arbitrations provide unique insight into caregiver bias because of the "just cause" provisions contained in most collective bargaining agreements. Just cause provisions prohibit employers from treating some workers less favorably than others, such as punishing one worker for violating a rule that it allows most workers to break. When workers challenge employer discipline, arbitrators typically examine whether the employer held the disciplined worker (the "grievant") to higher standards than other workers as part of the just cause analysis. Such situations provide unique insight into the ways bias affects caregivers across class lines.

For example, "two consecutive absence" rules (and other similar policies) repeatedly trigger unfair discipline and discharge against caregivers. "Two consecutive absence" rules are intended to penalize workers who are absent several days without calling. In some instances, employers ignore most workers' violations of two consecutive absence rules but strictly enforce the rules against caregivers. In one case, a repair clerk who had taken intermittent leave to care for her sick child requested an additional 30-day leave when her child was hospitalized.[129] She told her employer that she was not coming to work that week while her leave request was pending, but was fired pursuant to her employer's rarely enforced rule prohibiting three days of consecutive absence "without notice." The arbitrator found that the worker gave her employer plenty of notice by repeatedly stating that she would be absent while waiting for approval of her leave request, and by asking both her husband and her union to contact the employer on her behalf. The case revealed other facts suggesting caregiver discrimination. Although the employer granted the worker's past leave requests without asking for medical documentation and did not apply strict leave policies toward other employees in the past—suddenly and without explanation—the employer required a doctor's note. Furthermore, other workers missed more than five days of work without providing any notice and the employer gave them verbal warnings only.[130] In light of these findings, the arbitrator held that the worker was discharged without just cause and ordered her reinstatement.

In *Monterey Coal Co. and United Mine Workers of America*,[131] a worker took extended maternity leave, and then used up all her sick days to care for her very ill premature baby. She returned to work, but then was absent two days without calling her supervisor. Her supervisor knew about her baby's poor health and the worker returned with a doctor's note confirming that she was absent due to her baby's medical emergency. Nonetheless, the worker was fired for violating the rule against two consecutive absences without consent or proven sickness. Several facts suggested caregiver discrimination. The employer narrowly interpreted the rule against the worker, stating that her doctor's note was ineffective because the exemption for "proven sickness" covered only an employee's sickness, not that of a family member. Again, the employer applied an objective rule rigidly to a mother but leniently to others: other employees had been excused for two consecutive absences in the past.[132] Although the arbitrator did not address these claims, the union alleged that the employer was using the rule as a pretext to "get rid of" the worker because she had too many family-care related absences.[133]

Similarly, in *Communications Workers of America, Local 13500 and Verizon*[134] (discussed above), the employer applied its rules in an unusually harsh way against a single mother. In that case, the arbitrator criticized the employer for applying "a very rigid standard" against the worker when it refused to excuse her for being absent for one day in order to take her daughter to the doctor for an emergency. The employer ignored contract language obligating it to grant leniency to workers who are absent due to emergencies, stating that it was not an emergency unless the employee or their family member actually went to the emergency room. The employer also ignored contract language obligating it to grant leniency toward workers who significantly improved their attendance for a period of time. The worker had gone five months without a single absence or being tardy, but the employer argued that she needed six months without an infraction to qualify. The arbitrator held that the employer applied its policy unfairly and ordered the worker's reinstatement.

CWA and ITT World Communications, Inc.,[135] is a final example where an employer used a rarely enforced rule to terminate a caregiver. The case involved a field service engineer who shared childcare responsibilities with his wife. His family responsibilities occasionally clashed with his employer's demands. For example, his employer called late one night and asked him to drive to the office; the employee refused because he was caring for his two young children. He also took a few hours off here and there to take his wife to the doctor when she was pregnant with their third child. The worker ultimately was fired for violating a policy requiring authorization to drive company vans home after work, even though the employer never put this policy in writing, rarely enforced it, and regularly permitted workers to drive company vans to and from work as long as they returned the vans by the morning shift. The worker took the company van home the night before and planned to return it the following morning. However, he was at the hospital all night due to his wife's pregnancy complications and took the next day off. His employer did not need the van the entire day and made no attempt to retrieve it, but fired the worker anyway. Because the policy was rarely enforced and never put in writing, the arbitrator held that the employer did not have just cause to dismiss, and ordered the worker's reinstatement.

One benefit of the arbitration database corrects the overemphasis in the work-family literature on the conflicts faced by women. As the arbitrations show, many men face serious work-family conflicts that jeopardize their jobs. One recent study found that men reported significantly higher levels of work-family conflict than similarly situated women.[136] In addition, nonprofessional men—like professional ones—often encounter severe stigma when they request time to care for family members.[137] A 2004 survey of 500 plus employees found that, when compared to mothers, fathers who took a parental leave were recommended for fewer rewards and viewed as less committed, and that fathers with even a short work absence due to a family conflict were recommended for fewer rewards and had lower performance ratings.[138] Unlike women, men who experienced a work/family conflict encountered lower overall performance ratings and lower reward recommendations.[139]

Discrimination against male caregivers follows several patterns. In one type, male workers are penalized for taking caregiving leave, as when a worker who takes leave receives negative performance evaluations even though he received positive evaluations in the past, and his performance has changed significantly. One such case involved an employer that implemented a new attendance policy in which it placed workers with "suspicious absenteeism" on a list and subjected them to stricter attendance rules. A cable splicing technician who received an "exceeds expectations" in his annual evaluation, was never disciplined for absences, and only had two absences for the entire year, was placed on the list of employees with "suspicious absenteeism." The worker asked why he was on the list and his supervisor said it was because he took FMLA child bonding time.[140]

Men also may face double standards from employers who allow flexibility for female caregivers but refuse it for male caregivers. In *Independent Association of Publisher's Employees and Dow Jones, Inc.*,[141] a worker was repeatedly tardy because he was up late with his newborn child and was fired as a result. The arbitrator found that the employer had failed to establish a clear tardiness policy and had allowed flexibility for other employees (mostly female) who were tardy due to sick children, and the like, and reduced the worker's termination to a disciplinary suspension. A third common scenario occurs when employers or supervisors discriminate against men on the grounds that men's proper role is as breadwinners, not caregivers.[142]

In *Communications Workers of America and General Telephone Co. of the Southwest*,[143] an installer-repairman was 15 minutes late because he had to take his very sick child to the doctor. He thought he should be excused because he had a doctor's note, but his supervisors said that he was not excused and that his job was more important than his family. The worker got angry and was later terminated for insubordination. The arbitrator found that, although there was some evidence that the worker was "hotheaded," his supervisors were the real source of the problem. The arbitrator criticized the employer for hiring supervisors who assigned unexcused absences when workers took their children to the doctor. The arbitrator stated that if supervisors "really believe a man's job is more important than his family, it seems to me incumbent upon [the employer] to question their faculties and/or see if this logic is applied anywhere else." The arbitrator held that the employer lacked just cause for his discharge.

A troubling aspect of these cases is that no one—neither the unions nor the arbitrators—acknowledged that these workers faced workplace discrimination. Not only are employers failing to recognize discrimination against male caregivers; so are workers and their advocates. This is particularly troubling because the arbitrations surveyed are only the tip of the iceberg. The workers discussed in this chapter have far more protection than their nonunionized counterparts, and were fortunate enough to have the help of their union to grieve their discipline. For every arbitration discussed in this chapter, many other disputes are settled informally, are inaccessible because most arbitrations are not published, or are never grieved because the union has other priorities. All this suggests that academics and policymakers need to take a closer look at this piece of the Opt-Out puzzle.

Conclusion

Once the experiences of "ordinary Joe and Jane" are placed at center stage, one sees how misleading is the message that work-family conflict is a story about privileged women leaving fast-track careers. An unknown face of work-family conflict is the story of workers struggling to make ends meet while trying to reconcile extremely inflexible workplaces with their conviction that "family comes first." Work/family conflict is not just a professional women's issue, and in fact it is not just a women's issue. As the arbitrations throughout this chapter illustrate, work/family conflict spans all classes, and impacts men as well as women, grandparents as well as parents, spouses, sons, and daughters. Work/family conflict is a serious issue that affects a very broad range of Americans. The press, academics, and policymakers need to start treating it as such.

NOTES

1. Joan C. Williams, Stephanie Bornstein, and Jessica Manvell, *Opt Out or Pushed Out? A New Perspective on Work/Family Conflict* (San Francisco: University of California Hastings College of the Law, Center for WorkLife Law, 2006), 4–6 (analyzing the content of 119 print news stories that discuss women leaving the workplace, published between 1980 and 2006).

2. S. J. Rose and H. I. Hartmann, *Still a Man's Labor Market: The Long-Term Earnings Gap* (Washington, D.C.: Institute for Women's Policy Research, 2004), http:// www.iwpr. org/pdf/C355.pdf.

3. U.S. Department of Labor, Women's Bureau, (2005).

4. Theda Skocpol and Richard C. Leone, *The Missing Middle* (Washington, D.C.: Century Foundation, 2001). *See*, as well, Joan C. Williams, *Reshaping the Work-Family Debate: Why Men and Class Matter* (Cambridge: Harvard University Press, 2010).

5. Williams, Bornstein, and Manvell, *"Opt Out or Pushed Out?"* 10–19.

6. Ibid., 7–8, 10–11.

7. AFL-CIO, "Family Friendly Work Schedules," http://www.aflcio.org/issues/workfamily/workscheduls.cfm (62% and 31%, respectively).

8. Jody Heymann, *The Widening Gap: Why America's Working Families Are in Jeopardy and What Can Be Done about It* (New York: Basic Books, 2000), 231.

9. *Chicago Transit Authority,* case no. 97-0166 (Hayes, 1999) (arbitrator reinstated the bus driver).

10. *Knauf Fiber Glass,* 81 Lab. Arb. Rep. (BNA) 333 (Abrams, 1983).

11. *Communications Workers of America and Pacific Bell Co.,* case no. 9-94-15 (Kelly, 1996).

12. *Chicago Tribune Co.,* 119 Lab. Arb. Rep. (BNA) 1007 (Nathan, 2003) (reinstating grievant and holding that her oversleeping, which led to her tardiness, was an FMLA-qualified event because it resulted from exhaustion from her responsibilities as primary caregiver for her mother).

13. *Burlington County and Communications Workers of America, Local 1044,* case no. AR-95-685 (Brent, 1995).

14. *Bell Telephone Co. of Pennsylvania and Federation of Telephone Workers of Pennsylvania*, case nos. 13-81-14, 14-30-1319-81J (Kasher, 1982). *See also Consolidation Coal and UMWA Local 1545*, case no. 88-12-93-3205 (Judah, 1992) (A worker's fiancée was knocked unconscious while horseback riding. He was preoccupied by the emergency and forgot to call his employer, and his employer refused to excuse the absence because he did not call beforehand).

15. *AT&T Information Systems and CWA*, case no. WES-85-3 (Fisher, 1987).

16. *AT&T Corp. and CWA*, case no. 1J-2001-119 (Waltin, 2002).

17. Simpson v. D.C. Office of Human Rights, 597 A.2d 392 (D.C. Cir. 1991).

18. Netsy Firestein, "A Job and a Life: Organizing and Bargaining for Work Family Issues: A Union Guide," *Labor Project for Working Families* (2005), 15, http://www.working-families.org/organize/guide.html.

19. *AT&T Communications and CWA*, case no. ATT-87-6 (Teple, 1988).

20. *CWA Local 13500 and Verizon*, case nos. 14-300-0063-01, V01006-13500-01009B, 13-2001-005V (Cooper, 2002).

21. *Id.* at 18.

22. A second issue is whether absences covered by the Family and Medical Leave Act can be legitimately treated as garnering points under a "no fault" system. Some influential commentators have argued they cannot. *See* Jeanne M. Vonhoff and Martin H. Malin, "What a Mess! The FMLA, Collective Bargaining and Attendance Control Plans," *Ill. Pub. Employee Rel. Rep.* 21 (2004): 1.

23. J. C. Gornick and M. K. Meyers, *Families That Work: Policies for Reconciling Parenthood and Employment* (New York: Russell Sage Foundation, 2003), 59.

24. Ibid., 46.

25. Ibid., 156–163.

26. AFL-CIO, "2004 Ask a Working Woman Survey Report" (2004), http://www.aflcio.org/issues/jobseconomy/women/speakout/upload/aawwreport.pdf.

27. Karen Kornbluh, "The Parent Trap," *The Atlantic Monthly* 291 (2003): 111–114.

28. Heymann, *The Widening Gap*, 57.

29. Ibid., 73.

30. Ibid.

31. *Naval Air Rework Facility*, 86 Lab. Arb. Rep. (BNA) 1129 (Hewitt, 1986).

32. *Id.*

33. *Detroit Lakes and Independent School Dist.*, case no. 84-PP-772-A (Gallagher, 1984).

34. Family and Medical Leave Act of 1993, Pub. L. No. 103-3, § 107 Stat. 6 (codified at 29.U.S.C. § 2601-2654 (1994)).

35. 29 U.S.C. § 2612(b)(1) (1994); 29 C.F.R. § 25.203(a) (2009).

36. *Miami Valley Regional Transit Authority*, case no. 52-390-484-00 (Campbell, 2001).

37. *Chicago Transit Authority*, case no. 97-0166 (Hayes, 1999).

38. *Budget Rent-A-Car Systems*, 115 Lab. Arb. Rep. (BNA) 1745 (Suardi, 2001) (arbitrator upheld rental car shuttle driver's discipline after he failed to obtain necessary FMLA medical documentation).

39. *Boise Cascade Corp., Insulite Div. Int'l,* 77 Lab. Arb. Rep. (BNA) 28 (Fogelberg, 1981) (The arbitrator reinstated, on probation and without back pay, the father of a handicapped son who was fired after ten years of employment. His absenteeism stemmed from his need to take his son to specialists' appointments and his own on-the-job injury.).

40. *Bellsouth Communications and CWA*, case nos. B3-07-021, B-07-001-3706 (LaPorte, 2007).

41. Organization for Economic Co-Operation and Development, "Can Parents Afford to Work? Childcare Costs, Tax-Benefit Policies and Work Incentives" (January 2006), http://www.oecd.org/dataoecd/35/43/35969537.pdf.

42. Jeffery Capizzano, Gina Adams, and Freya L. Sonenstein, "Child Care Arrangements for Children under Five," *The Urban Institute* (2000), http://urban.org/url.cfm?ID=309438.

43. Heather Boushey, "Who Cares? The Child Care Choices of Working Mothers," *Center for Economic and Policy Research*, no. 1 (2003), http://www.cepr.net/publications/child_care_2003.htm.

44. Capizzano, Tout, and Adams, "Child Care Patterns."

45. Lisa Dodson, Tiffany Manuel, and Ellen Bravo, "Keeping Jobs and Raising Families in Low-Income America: It Just Doesn't Work," *Radcliffe Public Policy Center* (2002), 10 http://www.radcliffe.edu/research/pubpol/boundaries.pdf#search='dodson%20bravo%20keeping.

46. Capizzano, Tout, and Adams, "Child Care Patterns."

47. Heymann, *The Widening Gap*, 24–25.

48. Ibid., 36, 126.

49. Harriet B. Presser, "Toward a 24-Hour Economy," *Science* 284 (June 1999): 1778.

50. Heymann, *The Widening Gap*, 50.

51. *U.S. West Communications*, case no. 7-95-93 (Rinaldo, 1999). *See also Bell Telephone Co. and CWA*, case nos. 13-92-43B, 14-300-0936-92-J (Das, 1993) (worker with 18 years of service was terminated for monitoring phone lines to check on her children, ages 11 and 13, who were home alone); *Ameritech,* case no. 4-99-39 (Bellman, 2001) (worker was fired for monitoring her phone to check on her young children).

52. Heymann, *The Widening Gap*, 97.

53. Presser, "Toward a 24-Hour Economy," 1779.

54. *Dept. of Veterans Affairs*, 100 Lab. Arb. Rep. (BNA) 233 (Nicholas, 1992) (reducing worker's 14-day suspension to 5 days).

55. *Mercer County*, 1996 WL 492101 (Hewitt, 1996).

56. U.S. Census Bureau, "Who's Minding the Kids?" (Fall 1995, issued October 2000), http://www.census.gov/prod/2000pubs/p70-70.pdf.

57. U.S. Census Bureau, "Grandparents Living with Grandchildren: 2000" (2000, issued October 2003): 3, http://www.census.gov/prod/2003pubs/c2kbr-31.pdf.

58. Ibid.

59. *Columbiana County Bd. of Mental Retardation and Disabilities*, 117 Lab. Arb. Rep. (BNA) 13 (Skulina, 2002).

60. *Board of Education of Margaretta Local School District*, 114 Lab. Arb. Rep. (BNA) 1057 (Franckiewicz, 2000).

61. *Federal Mogul Corp.*, 2003 WL 23531172 (Cohen, 2003).

62. Heymann, *The Widening Gap*, 2.

63. Mary Jo Gibson, "Beyond 50.03: A Report to the Nation on Independent Living and Disability," *American Association of Retired Persons* (2003): 59, http://research.aarp.org/il/beyond_50_il.html.

64. Firestein, "A Job and a Life," 16.

65. Ibid., 14.

66. Ibid.

67. *Sprint/Central Telephone Co.*, 117 Lab. Arb. Rep. (BNA) 1321 (Baroni, 2002) (upholding the workers' discharge).

68. Williams, Bornstein, and Manvell, *Opt Out or Pushed Out?* 16–17.

69. Ibid.

70. A. Nakao, "More Mothers Staying at Home; Rate of Working Moms Drops for First Time since Data Collection Began," *San Francisco Chronicle*, October 18, 2001, p. A1.

71. P. B. Librach, "For Kids' Sake: Women Weigh Payoffs." *St. Louis Post-Dispatch*, July 31, 1989, News, p. 1.

72. A. Veciana-Suarez, "Bringing Up Baby on One Paycheck; Compromise, Reducing Lifestyle Crucial," *The Times Union*, June 17, 1994, p. C4.

73. Gornick and Meyers, *Families That Work*, 68–69.

74. R. Freeman, "The Feminization of Work in the U.S.: A New Era for (Man)kind?" in *Gender and the Labor Market: Econometric Evidence on Obstacles in Achieving Gender Equality*, ed. S. Gustaffson and D. Meulders (New York: Macmillan, 2000), 33–54.

75. AFL-CIO, "2004 Ask a Working Woman Survey" (*see supra* note 26).

76. AFL-CIO, "2008 Ask a Working Woman Survey Report" (2008), http://www.aflcio.org/issues/jobseconomy/upload/aaww_2008.pdf.

77. Ibid.

78. Ibid.

79. Lisa Belkin, "The Opt-Out Revolution," *New York Times Magazine,* October 26, 2003, 42.

80. AFL-CIO, "2008 Ask a Working Woman Survey."

81. *AT&T and CWA*, case nos. 6ATT-00-036, 6ATT-00-035 (Angelo, 2002).

82. *AT&T and Communications Workers of America*, case nos. WEM-91-2, 90MFG-40 (Allen, 1991).

83. *BellSouth Telecommunications*, case nos. B00038-3514, B3-2002-063 (Ferguson, 2002).

84. *Airlines Pilots' Ass'n and United Air Lines*, case nos. 64-12-1-063-71, 71-63 (McKelvey, 1971); *U.S. Air Shuttle and Ass'n of Flight Attendants*, case nos. 34-94, 28-94, 66-94, 14-95 (Edelman, 1997); *Association of Flight Attendants (AFA) and American Eagle*, case nos. 52-1-10-95 (Wittenberg, 1996); *Association of Flight Attendants and United Airlines*, case nos. 64-21-1-050-78, DCA 19-78 (Kagel, 1979).

85. Sara McLanahan and Christine Percheski, "Family Structure and the Reproduction of Inequalities," 34 *Annual Review of Sociology* 257–276 (2008).

86. Heymann, *The Widening Gap*, 4.

87. National Alliance for Caregiving and AARP, *Family Caregiving in the U.S., Findings from a National Survey* (1997) (one out of four); *Katherine Mack, Lee Thompson, and Robert Friedland, The Center on an Aging Society, Georgetown University, at Profiles, Family Caregivers of Older Persons: Adult Children 2 (May 2001) (more every year)*.

88. B. Torpy, "Paths to Power: Women Today; Full-Time Mothers Trade Careers for Kids," *The Atlanta Journal-Constitution*, April 8, 2003, p. F1.

89. Phyllis Moen, *It's about Time: Couples and Careers* (Ithaca, N.Y.: Cornell University Press, 2003), 152.

90. Williams, Bornstein, and Manvell, *"Opt Out or Pushed Out?"* 25 (Figure 9).

91. *Suprenant Cable Corp.*, case no. 1-95-85 (Bornstein, 1995).

92. *AT&T and CWA*, case nos. 6ATT-00-036, 6ATT-00-035 (Angelo, 2002).

93. *Rochester Psychiatric*, 87 Lab. Arb. Rep. (BNA) 725 (Babiskin, 1986) (reinstating grievant).

94. Rochester Psychiatric Center website, http://www.omh.state.ny.us/omhweb/ facili-ties/ropc/facility.htm.

95. *Rochester Psychiatric, supra* note 93, at 726.

96. *Id.*

97. *Id.*

98. *Id.* at 727.

99. *Rock County, Wisconsin*, 1993 WL 835474 (McAlpin, 1993); *Fairmont General Hospital, Inc.*, 2004 WL 3422192 (Miles, 2004).

100. *Tenneco Packaging*, 112 Lab. Arb. Rep. (BNA) 761 (Kessler, 1999).

101. *Id.* at 765–766.

102. *Central Beverage*, 110 Lab. Arb. Rep. (BNA) 104 (Brunner, 1998) (holding that uni-lateral change of grievant's working hours violated the contract).

103. *Jefferson Partners*, 109 Lab. Arb. Rep. (BNA) 335 (Bailey, 1997).

104. *Bryant v. Bell Atlantic*, 288 F.3d 124 (4th Cir. 2002).

105. *Id.* at 129 (noting Bryant's claim that the employer accommodated white workers' child care difficulties, but not his).

106. *Marion Composites*, 115 Lab. Arb. Rep. (BNA) 95 (Wren, 2001).

107. *Tractor Supply*, 2001 WL 1301335 (Dichter, 2001).

108. Arbitrator Dichter emphasized the worker's failure to explain why he could not stay, but he found that the discharge was unreasonable in the face of the worker's need to care for the child.

109. *Midwest Body*, 73 Lab. Arb. Rep. (BNA) 651 (Guenther, 1979).

110. *Id.* at 652.

111. *Id.* at 653.

112. *Id.*

113. Gregory DeFreitas and Niev Duffy, "Young Workers, Economic Inequality, and Collective Action," in *What's Class Got to Do with It? American Society in the Twenty-First Century*, ed. Michael Zweig (Ithaca, N.Y.: Cornell University Press, 2004), 145.

114. Joan C. Williams, *Unbending Gender: Why Family and Work Conflict and What to Do about It* (New York: Oxford University Press, 2000), 153.

115. Lillian Rubin, *Families on the Fault Line* (New York: HarperCollins, 1994), 78.

116. Roberta Sigel, *Ambition and Accommodation: How Women View Gender Relations* (Chicago: University of Chicago Press, 1996), 159.

117. Ibid.

118. In fact, nearly one-fourth (around 23%) of the arbitrations involving family care produced split decisions.

119. Nearly a third (33%) of the arbitrations involving family care were considered "union wins" because the arbitrators reversed workers' discipline completely.

120. *Local Union 1345, UMWA and Old Ben*, case nos. 84-12-88-1386, 84-12-88-3096 (Redwood, 1988).

121. *Id.* (emphasis added).

122. *U.S. Air and AFA*, case no. 44-82-01-20-94 (Rubin, 1995).

123. *American Telephone & Telegraph Co. and Communications Workers of America*, case no. ATT-13-92-22A (Caraway, 1993).

124. *Communications Workers of America and Pacific Bell Company*, case nos. 88-04164, 6-87-63 (Marcus, 1988).

125. Mary Still, *Litigating the Maternal Wall: U.S Lawsuits Charging Discrimination against Workers with Family Responsibilities* (San Francisco: University of California Hastings College of the Law, Center for WorkLife Law, 2006), http://www.uchastings.edu/site_files/WLL/FRDreport.pdf.

126. Ibid.

127. AFL-CIO, "2008 Ask a Working Woman Survey" (*see supra* note 76).

128. S. Correll and S. Benard, "Getting a Job: Is There a Motherhood Penalty?" (report presented at the meeting of the American Sociological Association, Philadelphia, Pa., August 2005).

129. *United Telephone Co. of Ohio and Communications Workers of America Local 4473*, case no. 4-80-609 (Ipavec, 1981).

130. *Id.* at 8, 16.

131. *Monterey Coal and UMWA, Local 2295*, case nos. 88-12-91-1341, 88-12-91-2056 (Pratte, 1991).

132. *Id.* at 12.

133. *Id.* at 16, 19–20.

134. *CWA, Local 13500 and Verizon*, case nos. 14-300-0063-01, V01006-13500-01009B, 13-2001-005V (Cooper, 2002).

135. *CWA and ITT*, case no. 1-87-133 (Nicolau, 1988).

136. James T. Bond et al., "Highlights of the National Study of the Changing Workforce," *Families and Work Institute*, no. 3 (2002, Released 2003), 30, http://www.familiesandwork.org/summary/nscw2002.pdf.

137. T. D. Allen, J. E. Russell, and M. C. Rush, "Effects of Gender and Leave of Absence on Attributions for High Performance, Perceived Organizational Commitment, and Allocation of Rewards," *Sex Roles* 31 (1994): 443–464; Michael K. Judiesch and Karen S. Lyness, "Left Behind? The Impact of Leaves of Absence on Managers' Career Success," *Academy of Management Journal* 42 (1999): 641–651.

138. C. Dickson, "The Impact of Family Supportive Policies and Practices on Perceived Family Discrimination" (unpublished dissertation, California School of Organizational Studies, Alliant International University, 2003).

139. A. B. Butler and A. L. Skattebo, "What Is Acceptable for Women May Not Be for Men: The Effect of Family Conflicts with Work on Job Performance Ratings," *Journal of Organizational Psychology* 77 (2004): 553–564.

140. *Communications Workers of America, Local 2105 and Verizon*, case no. 2-2006-009 (Chattman, 2007).

141. *Independent Ass'n of Publisher's Employees and Dow Jones, Inc.*, case no. 71-300-00603-02 (Williams, 2003).

142. *Communications Workers of America and General Telephone Co. of the Southwest*, case nos. 71-300-0055-85, 12-85-17 (Nelson, 1986). *See also AT&T Corp. and CWA*, case no. 1J-2001-119 (Waltin, 2002).

143. *CWA and General Telephone*, case nos. 71-300-0055-85, 12-85-17 (Nelson, 1986).

Bibliography

Academy Health. *Long-Term Care: Confronting Today's Problems.* 2003. http://www.acad-emyhealth.org/files/publications/ltcchallenges.pdf.

Adkins, C. L., E. C. Ravlin, and B. M. Meglino. 1996. Value Congruence between Cowork-ers and Its Relationship to Work Outcomes. *Group and Organization Management,* 21, 439–460.

AFL-CIO, "Family Friendly Work Schedules," http://www.aflcio.org/issues/workfamily/workscheduls.cfm.

———. 2004. Ask a Working Woman Survey Report. http://www.aflcio.org/issues/jobseconomy/women/speakout/upload/aawwreport.pdf.

———. 2008. Ask a Working Woman Survey Report. http://www.aflcio.org/issues/jobsec-onomy/upload/aaww_2008.pdf.

Albelda, R., and A. Clayton-Matthews. 2007. Love's Labor Lost? Costs and Benefits of Paid Family and Medical Leave. In *The Future of Work in Massachusetts.* T. Juravich, ed. Amherst: University of Massachusetts Press.

Allen, T. D., J. E. Russell, and M. C. Rush. 1994. Effects of Gender and Leave of Absence on Attributions for High Performance, Perceived Organizational Commitment, and Allocation of Rewards. *Sex Roles,* 31, 443–464.

Amott, Teresa, and Julie Matthaei. 1996. *Race, Gender, and Work: A Multi-Cultural Eco-nomic History of Women in the United States.* Boston: South End Press.

Anderson, B. 1997. Servants and Slaves: Europe's Domestic Workers. *Race and Class,* 39, 37–49.

———. 1999. Overseas Domestic Workers in the European Union: Invisible Women. In *Gender, Migration, and Domestic Service.* J. H. Henshall, ed. New York: Routledge.

Appelbaum, Eileen, Annette Bernhardt, and Richard Murnane. 2003. Low-Wage America: An Overview. In *Low-Wage America.* Eileen Appelbaum, Annette Bernhardt, and Rich-ard Murnane, eds. New York: Russell Sage Foundation.

Aronson, Jane, and Sheila Neysmith. 1996. You're Not Just in There to Do the Work: Depersonalising Policies and the Exploitation of Home Care Workers' Labour. *Gender & Society,* 10, 59–77.

Aumann, K., and E. Galinsky. 2009. *The State of Health in the American Workforce: Does Having an Effective Workplace Matter?* New York: Families and Work Institute.

Baca Zinn, M. and D. S. Eitzen, 1990. *Diversity in Families.* New York: Harper and Row.

Bakan, A., and D. K. Stasiulis. 1996. Structural Adjustment, Citizenship, and Foreign Domestic Labour: The Canadian Case. In *Rethinking Restructuring: Gender and Change in Canada.* I. Bakker, ed. Toronto: University of Toronto Press.

Bandura, A. 1986. *Social Foundations of Thought and Action: A Social Cognitive Theory.* Englewood Cliffs, N.J.: Prentice-Hall.

Barnes, Riché Jeneen Daniel. 2008. Black Women Have Always Worked: Is There a Work-Family Conflict among the Black Middle Class? In *The Changing Landscape of Work and Family in the American Middle Class: Reports from the Field.* Elizabeth Rudd and Lara Descartes, eds. Lanham, Md.: Lexington Books.

Barnett, Rosalind C., and Caryl Rivers. 1996. *She Works/He Works.* New York: HarperCollins.

Belkin, Lisa. 2003. The Opt-Out Revolution. *New York Times Magazine,* October 26.

Benjamin, A. E. 2001. Consumer-Directed Services at Home: A New Model for Persons with Disabilities. *Health Affairs,* 20, 80–95.

Benko, C. and M. Anderson. 2010. *The Corporate Lattice: Achieving High Performance in the Changing World of Work.* Boston: Harvard Business Review Press.

Benko, C., and A. Weisberg. 2007. Implementing a Corporate Career Lattice: The Mass Career Customization Model. *Strategy & Leadership,* 35, 29–36.

Bennetts, Leslie. 2008. *The Feminine Mistake: Are We Giving Up Too Much?* New York: Hyperion.

Bernhardt, Annette, and Dave Marcotte. 2000. Is Standard Employment Still What It Used to Be? In *Nonstandard Work: The Nature and Challenges of Changing Employment Arrangements.* Francoise Carre, Marianne Ferber, Lonnie Golden, and Stephen Herzenberg, eds. Champaign, Ill.: Industrial Relations Research Association.

Bishop, John. 1997. What We Know about Employer-Provided Training: A Review of the Literature. *Research on Labor Economics,* 16, 19–87.

Blackett, A. 1998. Making Domestic Work Visible: The Case for Specific Regulation. *Labour Law and Labour Relations Programme.* Geneva: ILO.

Blau, Francine D., and Lawrence M. Kahn. 1992. The Gender Earnings Gap: Learning from International Comparisons. *American Economic Review,* 82, 533–558.

———. 2003. Understanding International Differences in the Gender Wage Gap. *Journal of Labor Economics,* 21, 106–144.

Bond, J. T., and E. Galinsky. 2006. *How Can Employers Increase the Productivity and Retention of Entry-Level, Hourly Employees?* New York: Families and Work Institute.

Bond, J. T, E. Galinsky, and E. J. Hill. 2004. *Flexibility: A Critical Ingredient of an Effective Workplace.* New York: Families and Work Institute.

Bond, J. T., E. Galinsky, and J. E. Swanberg. 1998. *The 1997 National Study of the Changing Workforce.* New York: Families and Work Institute.

Bond, J. T., C. Thompson, E. Galinsky, and D. Prottas. 2003. *Highlights of the National Study of the Changing Workforce.* New York: Families and Work Institute.

Borrayo, Evelinn A. 2004. Who Is Being Served? Program Eligibility and Home- and Community-Based Services Use. *Journal of Applied Gerontology* 23/2 (June 1), 120–140.

Boushey, Heather. 2003. Who Cares? The Child Care Choices of Working Mothers. *Center for Economic and Policy Research,* no. 1, http://www.cepr.net/publications/child_care_2003.htm.

———. 2005. *Are Women Opting Out? Debunking the Myth.* Washington, D.C.: Center for Economic and Policy Research.

———. 2008. "Opting Out?" The Effect of Children on Women's Employment in the United States. *Feminist Economics,* 14/1, 1–36.

Bretz, R. D., and T. A. Judge. 1994. Person-Organization Fit and the Theory of Work Adjustment: Implications for Satisfaction, Tenure and Career Success. *Journal of Vocational Behavior,* 44, 32–54.

Brief for Law Professors and Historians as Amici Curiae Supporting Respondents, *Long Island Care at Home, Ltd. v. Coke*, 551 U.S. 158 (2007) (No. 06-593).

Brief for the United States as Amicus Curiae, Coke v. Long Island Care at Home, Ltd., 376 F.3d 118 (2004) (No. 04-1315).

Brief for the Urban Justice Center et al. as Amici Curiae Supporting Respondent, Long Island Care at Home, Ltd. v. Coke, 551 U.S. 158 (2007) (No. 06-593).

Budig, Michelle J., and Paula England. 2001. The Wage Penalty for Motherhood. *American Sociological Review*, 66, 204–225.

Budig, Michelle, and Joya Misra. 2010. How Carework Employment Shapes Earnings in a Cross-National Perspective. *International Labour Review*, 149, 441–460.

Butler, A. B., and A. L. Skattebo. 2004. What Is Acceptable for Women May Not Be for Men: The Effect of Family Conflicts with Work on Job Performance Ratings. *Journal of Organizational Psychology*, 77, 553–564.

Cancian, Francesca M. 2000. Paid Emotional Care. In *Care Work: Gender, Labor, and the Welfare State*. Madonna Harrington Meyer, ed. New York: Routledge.

Cantor, David, et al. 2001. *Balancing the Needs of Families and Employers: Family and Medical Leave Surveys, 2000 Update*. Rockville, Md.: Westat.

Capizzano, Jeffery, Gina Adams, and Freya L. Sonenstein. 2000. Child Care Arrangements for Children under Five. *The Urban Institute*, http://urban.org/url.cfm?ID=309438.

Cardozo, Arlene Rossen. 1986. *Sequencing*. New York: Atheneum.

Chan, D. 1998. Functional Relations among Constructs in the Same Domain at Different Levels of Analysis: A Typology of Compositional Models. *Journal of Applied Psychology*, 88, 605–619.

Chase-Lansdale, P. L., et al. 2003. Mothers' Transition from Welfare to Work and the Well-Being of Preschoolers and Adolescents. *Science*, 299, 1548–1552.

Chatman, J. A. 1989. Improving Interactional Organizational Research: A Model of Person-Organization Fit. *Academy of Management Review*, 14, 333–349.

Cobble, Dorothy Sue. 1996. The Prospects for Unionism in a Service Society. In *Working in the Service Society*. Cameron Macdonald and Carmen Sirianni, eds. Philadelphia: Temple University Press.

Cohany, Sharon R., and Emy Sok. 2007. Trends in Labor Force Participation of Married Mothers of Infants. *Monthly Labor Review* (February), 9–16.

Colburn, Jonathan D. 2006. Home Health Firms Watch Developments in Overtime Case. *San Fernado Valley Business Journal*, January 30.

Collins, Patricia Hill. 1991. *Black Feminist Thought: Knowledge, Consciousness, and the Politics of Empowerment*. New York: Routledge.

Coltrane, Scott. 2004. Elite Careers and Family Commitment: It's (Still) about Gender. *Annals of the American Academy of Political and Social Science*, 596, 214–220.

Coontz, Stephanie. 1992. *The Way We Never Were: American Families and the Nostalgia Trap*. New York: Basic Books.

———. 2011. *A Strange Stirring: The Feminine Mystique and American Women at the Dawn of the 1960s*. New York: Basic Books.

Cooper, James, and Diane Cooper. 2005. "Crisis in Workforce Supply—Read All About It!" *Annals of Long-Term Care*. February, 23–24.

Correll, Shelley J., Stephen Benard, and In Paik. 2007. Getting a Job: Is There a Motherhood Penalty? *American Journal of Sociology*, 112, 1297–1338.

Crittenden, Ann. 2001. *The Price of Motherhood.* New York: Metropolitan Books.

Daly, M., and J. Lewis. 1998. Introduction: Conceptualizing Social Care in the Context of Welfare State Restructuring. In *Gender, Social Care, and Welfare State Restructuring,* J. Lewis, ed. Aldershot, Vt.: Ashgate.

Danziger, Sandra, et al. 2000. Barriers to the Employment of Welfare Recipients. In *Prosperity for All? The Economic Boom and African Americans.* Robert Cherry and William Rodgers, eds. New York: Russell Sage Foundation.

Dawis, R. V., and L. H. Lofquist. 1984. *A Psychological Theory of Work Adjustment.* Minneapolis, Minn.: University of Minnesota Press.

Dawson, Steve, and Rick Surpin. 2001. *Direct Care Health Workers: The Unnecessary Crisis.* Queenstown, Maryland: Aspen Institute. http://www.directcareclearinghouse.org/download/Aspen.pdf.

DeFreitas, Gregory, and Niev Duffy. 2004. Young Workers, Economic Inequality, and Collective Action. In *What's Class Got to Do with It? American Society in the Twenty-First Century.* Michael Zweig, ed. Ithaca, N.Y.: Cornell University Press.

Delp, Linda, and Katie Quan. 2002. Homecare Worker Organizing in California: An Analysis of a Successful Strategy. *Labor Studies,* 27, 1–23.

Department of Health and Human Services Office of the Assistant Secretary for Planning and Evaluation. 2003. *Report to Congress: The Future Supply of Long-Term Care Workers in Relation to the Aging Baby Boom Generations.* http://aspe.hhs.gov/daltcp/reports/ltcwork.pdf.

Department of Health and Human Services. Bureau of Health Professionals. 2004. *Report: Nursing Aides, Home Health Care Aides, and Related Health Care Occupations—National and Local Workforce Shortages and Associated Data Needs.* http://www.directcareclearinghouse.org/download/RNandHomeAides.pdf.

Dickson, C. 2003. The Impact of Family Supportive Policies and Practices on Perceived Family Discrimination. Unpublished dissertation, California School of Organizational Studies, Alliant International University.

Direct Care Workers Issues Committee, Wisconsin Council on Long Term Care Reform. 2005. *Report: Strengthening Wisconsin's Long-Term Care Workforce.* http://www.directcareclearinghouse.org/download/Strengthening%20WI%20long%20term%20care%20workforce.pdf.

Dodson, Lisa, Tiffany Manuel, and Ellen Bravo. 2002. Keeping Jobs and Raising Families in Low-Income America: It Just Doesn't Work. *Radcliffe Public Policy Center,* 10, http://www.radcliffe.edu/research/pubpol/boundaries.pdf#search='dodson%20bravo%20keeping.

Donovan, Rebecca. 1989. "We Care for the Most Important People in Your Life": Home Care Workers in New York City. *Women's Studies Quarterly,* 1/2 (Spring–Summer), 17, 56–65.

Douglas, Susan, and Meredith Michaels. 2004. *The Mommy Myth: The Idealization of Motherhood and How It Has Undermined All Women.* New York: Free Press.

Drago, Robert W. 2007. *Striking a Balance: Work, Family, Life.* Boston: Dollars & Sense (Economic Affairs Bureau).

Dynan, Karen, Douglas Elmendorf, and Daniel Sichel. 2008. *The Evolution of Household Income Volatility.* Washington, D.C.: Brookings Institution. http://www.brookings.edu/~/media/Files/rc/papers/2008/02_useconomics_elmendorf/02_useconomics_elmendorf.pdf.

Edin, K., and L. Lein, 1997. *Making Ends Meet: How Single Mothers Survive Welfare and Low-Wage Work.* New York: Russell Sage Foundation.

England, Paula. 1992. *Comparable Worth: Theories and Evidence*. Hawthorne, N.Y.: Aldine de Gruyter.

England, Paula, Michelle Budig, and Nancy Folbre. 2002. Wages of Virtue: The Relative Pay of Carework. *Social Problems*, 49, 455–473.

Estes, S. B., and J. L. Glass. 1996. Job Changes following Childbirth: Are Women Trading Compensation for Family-Responsive Work Conditions? *Work and Occupations*, 23/4, 405–436.

Fair Labor Standards Act 1938, 29 U.S.C. §§ 201–219 (2007).

Fair Labor Standards Act: Domestic Service, 66 Fed. Reg. 5481, 5482 (proposed January 19, 2001).

Faludi, Susan. 1991. *Backlash: The Undeclared War against American Women*. New York: Crown.

Farber, Henry, and Helen Levy. 2000. Recent Trends in Employer-Sponsored Health Insurance Coverage: Are Bad Jobs Getting Worse? *Journal of Health Economics*, 19, 92–119.

Feder, Judith. 1991. Paying for Home Care: The Limits of Current Programs. In *Financing Home Care: Improving Protection for Disabled Elderly People*. D. Rowland and B. Lyons, eds. Baltimore: Johns Hopkins University Press.

Ferree, M. M. 1987. Family and Jobs for Working-Class Women: Gender and Class Systems Seen from Below. In *Families and Work*. N. Gerstel and H. E. Gros, eds. Philadelphia: Temple University Press.

Firestein, Netsy. 2005. "A Job and a Life: Organizing and Bargaining for Work Family Issues: A Union Guide." *Labor Project for Working Families*, 15, http://www.working-families.org/organize/guide.html.

Folbre, Nancy. 2001a. *The Invisible Heart: Economics and Family Values*. New York: New Press.

———. 2001b. Accounting for Care in the United States. In *Carework: The Quest for Security*. Mary Daly, ed. Geneva: International Labor Office.

———. 2006. Demanding Quality: Worker/Consumer Coalitions and "High Road" Strategies in the Care Sector. *Politics and Society*, 34, 11–32.

Freeman, R. 2000. The Feminization of Work in the U.S.: A New Era for (Man)kind?" In *Gender and the Labor Market: Econometric Evidence on Obstacles in Achieving Gender Equality*. S. Gustaffson and D. Meulders, eds. New York: Macmillan.

Friedan, Betty. 1963, 2001. *The Feminine Mystique*. New York: W. W. Norton.

Friedan, Betty, and Brigid O'Farrell, eds. 1997. *Beyond Gender: The New Politics of Work and Family*. Washington, D.C.: Woodrow Wilson Center Press.

Galinsky, E., K. Aumann, and T. Bond. 2009a. *Times Are Changing: Gender and Generation at Work and at Home*. New York: Families and Work Institute.

———. 2009b. Work-Life Fit: Aligning Workplace Flexibility to Benefit (and Not Exploit) Employees. Paper presented at the Academy of Management 2009 Annual Meeting, Chicago.

Galinsky, E., N. Carter, and J. T. Bond. 2008. *Leaders in a Global Economy: Finding the Fit for Top Talent*. New York: Families and Work Institute and Catalyst.

Galinsky, E., S. L. Peer, and S. Eby. 2009. *2009 Guide to Bold New Ideas for Making Work Work*. New York: Families and Work Institute.

Gelade, G. A., and M. Ivery. 2003. The Impact of Human Resource Management and Work Climate on Organizational Performance. *Personnel Psychology*, 56, 383–404.

Gerson, Kathleen. 2010. *The Unfinished Revolution: How a New Generation Is Reshaping Family, Work, and Gender in America*. New York: Oxford University Press.

Gerstel, N., and K. McGonagle. 1999. Job Leaves and the Limits of the Family and Medical Leave Act: The Effects of Gender, Race, and Family. *Journal of Work and Occupations*, 510–534.

Gibson, Mary Jo. 2003. Beyond 50.03: A Report to the Nation on Independent Living and Disability. *American Association of Retired Persons*. http://research.aarp.org/il/beyond_50_il.html.

Gilligan, Carol. 1993. *In a Different Voice: Psychological Theory and Women's Development*. Cambridge: Harvard University Press.

Glenn, E. N. 1992. From Servitude to Service Work: Historical Continuities in the Racial Division of Paid Reproductive Labor. *Signs*, 18, 1–43.

Goldberg, A., and M. Perry-Jenkins. 2004. The Division of Labor and Working-Class Women's Well-Being across the Transition to Parenthood. *Journal of Family Psychology*, 18, 225–236.

Golden, Olivia. 2005. *Assessing the New Federalism: Eight Years Later*. Washington, D.C.: Urban Institute.

Goldin, Claudia. 1997. Career and Family: College Women Look to the Past. In *Gender and Family Issues in the Workplace*. F. D. Blau and R. G. Ehrenberg, eds. Cambridge: Harvard University Press.

———. 2006. The "Quiet Revolution" That Transformed Women's Employment, Education, and Family. *American Economic Review*, 96, 1–21.

Gornick, Janet C., and Jerry A. Jacobs. 1998. Gender, the Welfare State, and Public Employment: A Comparative Study of Seven Industrialized Countries. *American Sociological Review*, 63, 688–710.

Gornick, Janet C., and Marcia K. Meyers. 2003. *Families That Work: Policies for Reconciling Parenthood and Employment*. New York: Russell Sage Foundation.

Gottschalk, Peter, and Robert Moffitt. 2009. The Rising Instability of U.S. Earnings. *Journal of Economic Perspectives*, 23/4, 3–24.

Graff, E. J. 2007. The Opt-Out Myth. *Columbia Journalism Review*, 45, 51–54.

Green, James, and Chris Tilly. 1987. Service Unionism: Directions for Organizing. *Labor Law Journal*, 8 (August), 486–495.

Hall, D. T. 2002. *Careers In and Out of Organizations*. Thousand Oaks, Calif.: Sage.

Harmuth, Susan. 2002. The Direct Care Workforce Crisis in Long-Term Care. *North Carolina Medical Journal*, 63/2 (March/April), 87–94.

Hays, Sharon. 1996. *The Cultural Contradictions of Motherhood*. New Haven: Yale University Press.

He, Wan, et al. 2005. *Report: Current Population Reports in the United States*. United States Bureau of Census. http://www.census.gov/prod/2006pubs/p23-209.pdf.

Heinritz-Canterbury, Janet. 2002. *Collaborating to Improve In-Home Supportive Services: Stakeholder Perspectives on Implementing California's Public Authorities*. Bronx, New York: Paraprofessional Health Care Institute. http://www.sfihsspa.org/documents/6454889.pdf

Helfat, C. E., D. Harris, and P. J. Wolfson. 2006. The Pipeline to the Top: Women and Men in the Top Executive Ranks of U.S. Corporations. *The Academy of Management Perspectives*, 20, 42–64.

Henly, Julia R., H. Luke Shaefer, and R. Elaine Waxman. 2006. Nonstandard Work Schedules: Employer- and Employee-Driven Flexibility in Retail Jobs. *Social Service Review,* 80, 609–634.

Heisler, B. S. 1985. Sending Countries and the Politics of Emigration and Destination. *International Migration Review,* 19, 469–484.

Hertz, Rosanna. 2004. The Contemporary Myth of Choice. *Annals of the American Academy of Political and Social Science,* 596, 232–244.

Hess, S. 2002. Au pairs alsinformalisiertehausarbeiterinnen. In *Weltmarktprivathaushalt.* C. Gather, B. Geissler, and M. S. Rerrich, eds. Münster: Westfälisches Dampfboot.

Hewlett, Sylvia Ann. 2007. *Off-Ramps and On-Ramps: Keeping Talented Women on the Road to Success.* Boston: Harvard Business School Press.

Heymann, Jody. 2000. *The Widening Gap: Why America's Working Families Are in Jeopardy and What Can Be Done about It.* New York: Basic Books.

Heyzer, N. and V. Wee. 1994. Domestic Workers in Transient Overseas Employment: Who Benefits, Who Profits. In *The Trade in Domestic Workers: Causes, Mechanisms and Consequences of International Migration.* N. Heyzer et al., eds. London: Zed Books.

Hirshman, Linda. 2006. *Get to Work: A Manifesto for Women of the World.* New York: Penguin Books.

Hochschild, Arlie R. 1989. *The Second Shift: Working Parents and the Revolution at Home.* New York: Viking.

———. 1997. *The Time Bind: When Work Becomes Home and Home Becomes Work.* New York: Henry Holt.

Hoff Sommers, Christina. 1995. *Who Stole Feminism? How Women Have Betrayed Women.* New York: Simon and Schuster.

Holland, J. L. 1985. *Making Vocational Choices: A Psychology of Careers.* Englewood, NJ: Prentice Hall.

Hondagneu-Sotelo, P. 2000. The International Division of Caring and Cleaning Work. In *Care Work: Gender, Labor, and the Welfare State.* M. Harrington Meyer, ed. New York: Routledge.

———. 2001. *Doméstica: Immigrant Workers Cleaning and Caring in the Shadows of Affluence.* Berkeley: University of California Press.

Hunter, Ella. 1997. Violence Prevention in the Home Health Setting. *Home Healthcare Nurse,* 15/ 6 (June), 403–409.

Huselid, M. A. 1995. The Impact of Human Resources Management Practices on Turnover, Productivity, and Corporate Financial Performance. *Academy of Management Journal,* 38, 635–672.

Huselid, M. A., S. E. Jackson, and R. S. Schuler. 1997. Technical and Human Resource Management Effectiveness as Determinants of Firm Performance. *Academy of Management Journal,* 40, 171–188.

Jacob, J., J. T. Bond, E. Galinsky, and E. J. Hill. 2008. Six Critical Ingredients in Creating an Effective Workplace. *Psychologist Manager Journal,* 11, 141–161.

Jacobs, Jerry A., and Kathleen Gerson. 2004. *The Time Divide: Work, Family and Gender Inequality.* Cambridge: Harvard University Press.

James, L. R., and A. P. Jones. 1974. Organizational Climate: A Review of Theory and Research. *Psychological Bulletin,* 81, 1096–1112.

Jenson, J., and M. Sineau. 1995. Family Policy and Women's Citizenship in Mitterand's France. *Social Politics,* 2, 244–269.

———. 2001. France: Reconciling Republican Equality with Freedom of "Choice." In *Who Cares? Women's Work, Childcare, and Welfare State Redesign.* J. Jenson and M. Sineau, eds. Toronto: University of Toronto Press.

Judiesch, Michael, and Karen S. Lyness. 1999. Left Behind? The Impact of Leaves of Absence on Managers' Career Success. *Academy of Management Journal,* 42, 641–651.

Kalleberg, Arne. 2009. Precarious Work, Insecure Workers: Employment Relations in Transition. *American Sociological Review,* 74, 1–22.

Kaminer, Wendy. 1990. *A Fearful Freedom: Women's Flight from Equality.* Reading, Mass.: Addison-Wesley.

Kaplan, Richard. 2004. Cracking the Conundrum: Toward a Rational Financing of Long-Term Care. *University of Illinois Law Review,* 47–89.

Katz, Steven, Mohammed Kabeto, and Kenneth M. Lang. 2000. Gender Disparities in the Receipt of Home Care for Elderly People with Disability in the United States. *J. American Medical Association,* 284/23 (December), 3022–3027.

Kaye, Stephen H., et al. 2006. The Personal Assistance Workforce: Trends in Supply and Demand. *Health Affairs,* 25/4 (July/August), 1113–1120.

Kearney, Richard C., and David G. Carnevale. 2001. *Labor Relations in the Public Sector.* New York: Marcel Dekker.

Kerber, Linda K. 1980. *Women of the Republic: Intellect and Ideology in Revolutionary America.* Chapel Hill: University of North Carolina Press.

Kessler, Laura T. 2005. Is There Agency in Dependency? Expanding the Feminist Justifications for Restructuring Wage Work. In *Feminism Confronts Homo Economicus: Gender, Law and* Society. Martha Albertson Fineman and Terence Dougherty, eds. Ithaca: Cornell University Press.

Kessler-Harris, Alice. 1996. Equal Employment Opportunity Commission v. Sears, Roebuck and Company: A Personal Account. In *Applications of Feminist Legal Theory to Women's Lives: Sex, Violence, Work and Reproduction.* D. Kelly Weisberg, ed. Philadelphia: Temple University Press.

———. 2001. *In Pursuit of Equity: Women, Men and the Quest for Economic Citizenship in 20th Century America.* New York: Oxford University Press.

———. 2003. *Out to Work: A History of Wage-Earning Women in the United States.* New York: Oxford University Press.

Kim, M. 2007. Low-Wage Women Workers. In *The Future of Work in Massachusetts.* T. Juravich, ed. Amherst: University of Massachusetts Press.

Kofman, E. 2003. *Women Migrants and Refugees in the European Union.* Paris: Organization for Economic Cooperation and Development.

Kopelman, R. E., A. P. Brief, and R. A. Guzzo. 1990. The Role of Climate and Culture in Productivity. In *Organizational Climate and Culture.* B. Schneider, ed. San Francisco: Jossey-Bass.

Kornbluh, Karen. 2003. The Parent Trap. *The Atlantic Monthly,* 291, 111–114.

Kozlowski, S. W. J., and K. J. Klein. 2000. A Multi-Level Approach to Theory and Research in Organizations: Contextual, Temporal, and Emergent Processes. In *Multi-Level Theory, Research, and Methods in Organizations.* K. J. Klein and S. W. J. Kozlowski, eds. San Francisco: Jossey-Bass.

Kreider, R. M., and D. B. Elliott. 2009. U.S. Census Bureau: America's Families and Living Arrangements, 2007. *Current Population Reports,* 20–561.

Kristof, A. L. 1996. Person-Organization Fit: An Integrative Review of Its Conceptualizations, Measurements, and Implications. *Personnel Psychology*, 49, 1–49.

Kristof-Brown, A. L., R. D. Zimmerman, and E. C. Johnson. 2005. Consequences of Individual's Fit at Work: A Meta-Analysis of Person-Job, Person-Organization, Person-Group, and Person-Supervisor Fit. *Personnel Psychology*, 58, 281–342.

Kuperberg, Arielle, and Pamela Stone. 2008. The Media Depiction of Women Who Opt Out. *Gender & Society*, 22/4, 497–517.

Lambert, Susan. 2008. Passing the Buck: Labor Flexibility Practices That Transfer Risk onto Hourly Workers. *Human Relations*, 61/9, 1203–1227.

———. 2009. Making a Difference for Hourly Employees. In *Work-Life Polices That Make a Real Difference for Individuals, Families, and Organizations*. A. Booth and A. Crouter, eds. Washington, D.C.: Urban Institute Press.

Lambert, Susan, and Anna Haley-Lock. 2004. The Organizational Stratification of Opportunities for Work-Life Balance: Addressing Issues of Equality and Social Justice in the Workplace. *Community, Work and Family*, 7/2, 181–197.

Lambert, Susan, and Julia R. Henly. 2010. *The Work Scheduling Study: Managers' Strategies for Balancing Business and Employee Needs*. University of Chicago, School of Social Service Administration, Working Paper.

Lan, Pei-Chia. 2006. *Global Cinderellas: Migrant Domestics and Newly Rich Employers in Taiwan*. Durham: Duke University Press.

Lapidus, Lenora M., Emily J. Martin, and Namita Luthra. 2009. *The Rights of Women: The Authoritative ACLU Guide to Women's Rights*. New York: NYU Press.

Lareau, Annette. 2003. *Unequal Childhoods: Class, Race, and Family Life*. Berkeley: University of California Press.

Letablier, Marie-Therese. 2001. Le travail envers autrui et sa conceptualisation en Europe. *Travail, Genre et Société*, 6, 19–42.

Levit, Nancy, and Robert R. M. Verchick. 2006. *Feminist Legal Theory: A Primer*. New York: NYU Press.

Loengard, Anna, and Jeremy Boal. 2004. Home Care of the Frail Elderly. *Clinics in Geriatric Medicine* 20/4 (November), 795–807.

Long Island Care at Home, Ltd. v. Coke, 551 U.S. 158 (2007).

Lukas, Carrie L. 2006. *The Politically Incorrect Guide to Women, Sex and Feminism*. Washington, D.C.: Regnery.

Lutz, H. 2000. *Geschlecht, ethnizität, profession: Die neuedienstmädchenfrageimzeitalter der globalisierung*. IKS-Querformat Nr. 1, WestfälischeWilhelms-Universität Münster.

———. 2002. Transnationalitätimhaushalt. Pp. 86–101, in *Weltmarktprivathaushalt*. C. Gather, B. Geissler, and M. S. Rerrich, eds. Münster: WestfälischesDampfboot.

Magnusson, D., and N. S. Endler. 1977. Interactional Psychology: Present Status and Future Prospects. In *Personality and the Crossroads: Current Issues in Interactional Psychology*. D. Magnusson and N. S. Endler, eds. Hillsdale, N.J.: Erlbaum.

Mahar, Maggie. 1992. A Change of Place: Reversing a Decades-Long Trend, Young Women Are Opting Out of the Job Market and Staying Home, with Major Implications for the Economy. *Barron's*, March 21.

Malson, M. R. 1983. Black Women's Sex Roles: The Social Context for a New Ideology. *Journal of Social Issues*, 39, 101–113.

Mandin, L., and B. Palier. 2002. Welfare Reform in France, 1985–2002. In *Welfare Reform and Management of Societal Change Report* (working paper). http://www.kent.ac.uk/wramsoc/workingpapers/index.htm.

Massey, D. S. 1999. International Migration at the Dawn of the Twenty-First Century: The Role of the State. *Population and Development Review,* 25, 303–322.

Massey, D. S., et al. 1998. *Worlds in Motion: Understanding International Migration at the End of the Millennium.* Oxford: Clarendon.

McGrath, Monica, Marla Driscoll, and Mary Gross. 2005. *Back in the Game: Returning to Business after a Hiatus.* Philadelphia: Wharton Center for Leadership and Change.

McLanahan, Sara, and Christine Percheski. 2008. Family Structure and the Reproduction of Inequalities. *Annual Review of Sociology,* 34, 257–276.

Meier-Braun, K.-H. 2002. *Deutschland, einwanderungsland.* Frankfurt: SuhrkampVerlag.

Meyerowitz, Joanne. 1994. *Not June Cleaver: Women and Gender in Postwar America, 1945–1960.* Philadelphia: Temple University Press.

Milkman, R., E. Reese, and B. Roth. 1998. The Macro-Sociology of Paid Domestic Service. *Work and Occupations,* 25, 483–510.

Misra, Joya, Michelle Budig, and Irene Böckmann. 2009. A Cross-National Perspective on Gender, Parenthood, and Employment. Paper presented at the RC 19 Meetings of the International Sociological Association, Montreal.

Misra, Joya, and Sabine Merz. 2006. Neoliberalism, Globalization, and the International Division of Care. In *Wages of Empire: Women's Poverty, Globalization, and State Transformations.* Amalia Cabezas, Ellen Reese, and Marguerite Waller, eds. Boulder, Colo.: Paradigm Press.

Misra, Joya, Jonathan Woodring, and Sabine Merz. 2006. The Globalization of Carework: Neoliberal Economic Restructuring and Migration Policy. *Globalization,* 3, 317–332.

Mitchell, C. 1989. International Migration, International Relations, and Foreign Policy. *International Migration Review,* 23, 681–708.

Moe, Karine, and Dianna Shandy. 2009. *Glass Ceilings and 100-hour Couples: What the Opt-Out Phenomenon Can Teach Us about Work and Family.* Athens: University of Georgia Press.

Moen, Phyllis. 2003. *It's about Time: Couples and Careers.* Ithaca, N.Y.: Cornell University Press.

Moen, Phyllis, and Patricia Roehling. 2005. *The Career Mystique: Cracks in the American Dream.* Lanham, Md.: Rowman and Littlefield.

Momsen, J. H. 1999. Maids on the Move: Victim or Victor? In *Gender, Migration, and Domestic Service.* J. H. Momsen, ed. New York: Routledge.

Montgomery, Rhonda, et al. 2005. A Profile of Home Care Workers from the 2000 Census: How It Changes What We Know. *Gerontologist,* 45/5 (October), 593–600.

Moos, R. H. 1987. Person-Environment Congruence in Work, School, and Health Care Settings. *Journal of Vocational Behavior,* 31, 231–247.

Morgan, Kimberly J. 2002. Does Anyone Have a "Librechoix"? Subversive Liberalism and the Politics of French Child Care Policy. In *Child Care Policy at the Crossroads: Gender and Welfare State Restructuring.* S. Michel and R. Mahon, eds. New York: Routledge.

———. 2005. The "Production" of Child Care: How Labor Markets Shape Social Policy and Vice Versa. *Social Politics,* 12, 243–263.

Morris, B. 1995. Executive Women Confront Midlife Crisis. *Fortune* (September), 60–86.

Mortimer, J. T., and J. London. 1984. The Varying Linkages of Work and Family. In *Work and Family: Changing Roles of Men and Women.* P. Voydanoff, ed. Palo Alto, Calif.: Mayfield Publishing.

Mosisa, Abraham, and Steven Hipple. 2006. Trends in Labor Force Participation in the United States. *Monthly Labor Review,* 129, 35–57.

Mozère, L., et al. 2001. Petits métiers urbains au feminine ou comment échapper à la précarisation. *Migration et Etudes,* 101, 1–6.

Mulkeen, Patricia. 1973. Private Household Workers and the Fair Labor Standards Act. *Connecticut Law Review,* 5/4 (Spring), 623–638.

Naduiairski, Jacqueline A. 1992. Inner-City Safety for Home Care Providers. *Journal of Nursing Administration* 22/9 (September), 42–47.

National Association for Home Care and Hospice. 2004. *Report: Basic Statistics about Home Care.* http://www.nahc.org/04HC_Stats.pdf.

National Governor's Assocation Center for Best Practices, State Support for Family Caregivers and Paid Home-Care Workers. 2004. *Issue Brief.* http://www.nga.org/Files/pdf/0406AgingCaregivers.pdf

Ness, Immanuel. 1999. Organizing Home Health-Care Workers: A New York City Case Study. *Working U.S.A.,* 3/4 (December), 59–95.

Neysmith, Sheila, and Jane Aronson. 1996. Home Care Workers Discuss Their Work: The Skills Required to "Use Your Common Sense." *Journal of Aging Studies,* 10/1 (Spring), 1–14.

Okolski, M. 2004. Seasonal Labour Migration in the Light of the German-Polish Bilateral Agreement. In *Migration for Employment: Bilateral Agreements at a Crossroads.* Paris: Organization for Economic Cooperation and Development.

O'Reilly, C. A., J. Chatman, and D. F. Caldwell. 1991. People and Organizational Culture: A Profile Comparison Approach to Assessing Person-Organization Fit. *Academy of Management Journal,* 34, 487–516.

Organisation for Economic Co-Operation and Development (OECD). 2001. *OECD Employment Outlook.* Paris: OECD.

———. 2003. *Trends in International Migration.* Paris: OECD.

———. 2004. *Trends in International Migration.* Paris: OECD.

———. 2006. Can Parents Afford to Work? Childcare Costs, Tax-Benefit Policies and Work Incentives (January), http://www.oecd.org/dataoecd/35/43/35969537.pdf.

Osterhout, Ron, and Rick Zawadski. 2006. On Homecare Workforce. *Policy and Practice of Public Human Services,* 64/1 (March), 30.

Ostner, I. 1998. The Politics of Care Policies in Germany. In *Gender, Social Care and Welfare State Restructuring in Europe.* J. Lewis, ed. London: Ashgate.

Ostroff, C., A. J. Kinicki, and M. M. Tamkins. 2003. Organizational Culture and Climate. In *Handbook of Psychology, Industrial/Organizational Psychology,* 12, 565–593. W. C. Borman, D. R. Ilgen, and R. J. Klimoski, eds. New York: Wiley & Sons.

Paraprofessional Health Care Institute. 2003. Training Quality Home Care Workers. http://www.directcareclearinghouse.org/download/PHI_Training_Overview.pdf.

Parreñas, R. 2001. *Servants of Globalization: Women, Migration, and Domestic Work.* Stanford: Stanford University Press.

———. 2005. *Children of Globalization: Transnational Families and Gendered Woes.* Stanford: Stanford University Press.

———. 2008. *The Force of Domesticity: Filipina Migrants and Globalization.* New York: NYU Press.

Patterson, James.1997. *Grand Expectations: The United States, 1945-1974.* New York: Oxford University Press.

Pearson, Allison. 2002. *I Don't Know How She Does It.* New York: Alfred A. Knopf.

Percheski, Christine. 2008. Opting Out? Cohort Differences in Professional Women's Employment Rates from 1960 to 2005. *American Sociological Review,* 73, 497–517.

Perry-Jenkins, Maureen, A. Goldberg, C. Pierce, and A. Sayer. 2007. Shift Work, Role Overload and the Transition to Parenthood. *Journal of Marriage and Family,* 69, 123–138.

Pierson, P. 2001. Post-Industrial Pressures on Mature Welfare States. In *The New Politics of the Welfare State.* P. Pierson, ed. New York: Oxford University Press.

Presser, Harriet B. 2003. *Working in a 24/7 Economy: Challenges for American Families.* New York: Russell Sage Foundation.

Prosper, Vera. 2004. Aging in Place in Multifamily Housing. *Cityscape: Journal of Policy Development and Research,* 7/1, 81–106.

Pyke, Karen. 1996. Class-Based Masculinities: The Interdependence of Gender, Class, and Interpersonal Power. *Gender & Society,* 10, 527–549.

Pyle, J. 2001. Sex, Maids, and Export Processing: Risks and Reasons for Gendered Global Production Networks. *International Journal of Politics, Culture, and Society,* 15, 55–76.

Pyle, J., and K. Ward. 2003. Recasting Our Understanding of Gender and Work during Global Restructuring. *International Sociology,* 18, 461–489.

Reimers, Cordelia, and Pamela Stone. August 2007. "Opting Out" among College-Educated Women, 1982–2005: Trends and Explanations. Paper presented at the Annual Meetings of the American Sociological Association, New York.

RESPECT. 2000. Migrant Domestic Workers in Europe: A Case for Action, http://www.solidar.org/Document.asp?DocID=1994andtod=141847.

Roehling, Patricia V., and Phyllis Moen. March 2003. *Dual-Earner Couples.* Sloan Work and Family Research Network. http://wfnetwork.bc.edu/encyclopedia_entry.php?id=229andarea=All

Rokeach, R. P. 1973. *The Nature of Human Values.* New York: Free Press.

Rose, S. J., and H. I. Hartmann. 2004. *Still a Man's Labor Market: The Long-Term Earnings Gap.* Washington, D.C.: Institute for Women's Policy Research. http:// www.iwpr.org/pdf/C355.pdf.

Rowland, Diane. 1989. Measuring the Elderly's Need for Home Care. *Health Affairs,* 8/4 (Winter), 39–51.

Rubin, L. B. 1976. *Worlds of Pain.* New York: Basic Books.

———. 1994. *Families on the Fault Line.* New York: HarperCollins.

Ruhm, C. J. 2005. How Well Do Government and Employer Policies Support Working Parents? In *Work, Family, Health and Well-Being.* S. M. Bianchi, L. M. Casper, and R. B. King, eds. Mahwah, N.J.: Erlbaum.

Rystad, G. 1992. Immigration History and the Future of International Migration. *International Migration Review,* 26, 1168–1199.

Sassen, S. 1998. The *de facto* Transnationalizing of Immigration Policy. In *Challenge to the Nation-State*. C. Joppke, ed. Oxford: Oxford University Press.

———. 2003. Strategic Instantiations of Gendering in the Global Economy. In *Gender and Immigration: Contemporary Trends*. P. Hondagneu-Sotelo, ed. Berkeley: University of California Press.

Schein, E. 1978. *Career Dynamics: Matching Individual and Organizational Needs*. Reading, Mass.: Addison-Wesley.

Schneider, B. 1987. People Make the Place. *Personnel Psychology*, 40, 437–453.

Schneider, Stu. 2003. Victories for Home Health Care Workers, *Dollars & Sense* (September–October), 25–27.

Seavey, Dorie. 2004. *Report: The Cost of Frontline Turnover in Long-Term Care*. Better Jobs Better Care: Washington, D.C. http://www.bjbc.org/content/docs/TOCostReport.pdf.

Seeleib-Kaiser, M. 2004. Germany: Still a Conservative Welfare State? Paper presented at the Annual Conference of Europeanists, Chicago. www.europanet.org/conference2004/papers/J2_SeeleibKaiser.pdf.

Service Employees Int'l Union, Local 434 v. County of Los Angeles, 225 Cal. App.3d 761 (1990).

Siegel, Reva. 2007. The New Politics of Abortion: An Equality Analysis of Woman-Protective Abortion Restrictions. *University of Illinois Law Review*, 991–1053.

Sigel, Roberta. 1996. *Ambition and Accommodation: How Women View Gender Relations*. Chicago: University of Chicago Press.

Skocpol, Theda, and Richard C. Leone. 2001. *The Missing Middle*. Washington, D.C.: Century Foundation.

Smet, M. 2000. *Report on Regulating Domestic Help in the Informal Sector*. European Parliament Session.

Smith, Peggie R. 2004. Elder Care, Gender, and Work: The Work-Family Issue of the 21st Century. *Berkeley Journal of Employment and Labor Law*, 25, 351–398.

———. 2008. The Publicization of Home-Based Care Work in State Labor. *Minnesota Law Review*, 92 (May), 1390–1423.

St. George, Donna. 2009. Most Stay-at-Home Moms Start That Way, Study Finds. *Washington Post* (October 1), http://www.washingtonpost.com/wp-dyn/content/article/2009/09/30/AR2009093005106.html

Stacey, Clare L. 2005. Finding Dignity in Dirty Work: The Constraints and Rewards of Low-Wage Home Care Labour. *Sociology of Health and Illness*, 27/6, 837–854.

Steil, J. M. 1997. *Marital Equality: Its Relationship to the Well-Being of Husbands and Wives*. Thousand Oaks, Calif.: Sage.

Still, Mary. 2006. *Litigating the Maternal Wall: U.S. Lawsuits Charging Discrimination against Workers with Family Reponsibilities*. San Francisco: University of California Hastings College of the Law, Center for WorkLife Law. http://www.uchastings.edu/site_files/WLL/FRDreport.pdf.

Stone, Pamela. 2007. *Opting Out? Why Women Really Quit Careers and Head Home*. Berkeley: University of California Press.

———. 2009. Getting to Equal: Progress, Pitfalls, and Policy Solutions on the Road to Gender Parity in the Workplace. *Pathways* 3–8.

Stone, Robyn. 2000. *Report: Long-Term Care for the Elderly with Disabilities: Current Policy, Emerging Trends, and Implications for the Twenty-First Century*. New York: Milbank

Memorial Fund. http://www.milbank.org/reports/0008stone/LongTermCare_Mech5. pdf.

———. 2001. *Policy Brief: Long-Term Care Workforce Shortages: Impact on Families.* San Francisco: Family Caregiver Alliance. http://www.bjbc.org/content/docs/LTC_Work-force_Shortages.pdf.

———. 2004. The Direct Care Worker: The Third Rail of Home Care Policy. *Annual Review of Public Health,* 25, 521–537.

Story, Louise. 2005. Many Women at Elite Colleges Set Career Path to Motherhood. *New York Times,* September 20, A1.

Super, D. 1957. *The Psychology of Careers.* New York: Harper and Row.

———. 1980. A Life-Span, Life-Space Approach to Career Development. *Journal of Vocational Behavior,* 16, 282–298.

Tarr-Whelan, Linda. 2009. *Women Lead the Way: Your Guide to Stepping Up to Leadership and Changing the World.* San Francisco: Berrett-Koehler.

Taylor, Brian, and Michael Donnelly. 2006. Risks to Home Care Workers: Professional Perspectives. *Health, Risk and Society,* 8/3 (September), 239 –256.

Toledano, Jessica. 1999. Health Workers for Home-Bound to Vote on Union. *Los Angeles Business J.,* February 8.

Tyler May, Elaine. 1988. *Homeward Bound: American Families in the Cold War Era.* New York: Basic Books.

United Nations. 2005. *Gender Equality: Striving for Justice in an Unequal World.* Geneva: United Nations.

U.S. Census Bureau. Fall 1995. Who's Minding the Kids? (issued October 2000). http://www.census.gov/prod/2000pubs/p70-70.pdf.

———. 2003. Grandparents Living with Grandchildren (issued October 2003). http://www.census.gov/prod/2003pubs/c2kbr-31.pdf.

———. 2009. *Statistical Abstract of the United States: 2010* (129th Edition). Washington, D.C. http://www.census.gov/statab/www/

U.S. Congress. House of Representatives. Subcommittee on Workforce Protections. 2007. *The Fair Home Health Care Act: Hearings on H.R. 3582, 110th Cong., 1st sess.,* October 25, 2007.

U.S. Department of Education, National Center for Education Statistics. 2008. *The Condition of Education.*

U. S. Department of Labor, Bureau of Labor Statistics. March 2006. Women Still Under-represented among Highest Earners. *Issues in Labor Statistics.*

———. Bureau of Labor Statistics. 2009. *Highlights of Women's Earnings in 2008.*

———. Women's Bureau. 2005.

———. *Labor Force Participation of Mothers with Infants in 2008.*

———. *Occupational Outlook Handbook, 2008–2009.*

———. *Unemployment Rates for Men and Women.*

———. 2011. Labor Force Statistics from the Current Population Survey. Downloaded July 30, 2011, http://www.bls.gov/data/.

U. S. Department of Labor Care Employee Benefits Security Administration. 2000. *Report to the Working Group on Long-Term Care.*

U.S. General Accounting Office. March 21, 2002. *Long-Term Care: Aging Baby Boom Generation Will Increase Demand and Burden on Federal and State Budgets: Hearing before the Senate Committee Special Committee on Aging. 107th Cong., 2nd sess.*

———. 1996. *Brief: Long-Term Care: Some States Apply Criminal Background Checks to Home Care Workers* http://www.gao.gov/archive/1996/pe96005.pdf.

U.S. General Accounting Office. May 17, 2001. *Nursing Workforce: Recruitment and Retention of Nurses and Nurse Aides Is a Growing Concern: Hearing before the Senate Committee on Health, Education, Labor and Pensions.* 107th Cong., 1st sess..

U.S. Government Accountability Office. April 27, 2005. *Long-Term Care Financing: Growing Demand and Cost of Services Are Straining Federal and State Budgets, Hearing before the Subcommittee on Health, Committee on Energy and Commerce, House of Representatives.* 109th Cong., 1st sess.

VanBurkleo, Sandra F. 2001. *"Belonging to the World": Women's Rights and American Constitutional Culture.* New York: Oxford University Press.

Vapnek, Lara. 2009. *Breadwinners: Working Women and Economic Independence, 1865–1920.* Urbana: University of Illinois Press.

Vonhoff, Jeanne M., and Martin H. Malin. 2004. What a Mess! The FMLA, Collective Bargaining and Attendance Control Plans. *Ill. Pub. Employee Rel. Rep. 21,* 1–7.

Vroom, V. H. 1964. *Work and Motivation.* New York: Wiley.

Walters, Suzanna Danuta. 1995. *Material Girls: Making Sense of Feminist Cultural Theory.* Berkeley: University of California Press.

Walzer, Susan. 1998. *Thinking about the Baby: Gender and Transitions into Parenthood.* Philadelphia: Temple University Press.

Warner, Judith. 2005. *Perfect Madness: Motherhood in the Age of Anxiety.* New York: Riverhead Books.

Warr, P., and G. Parry. 1982. Paid Employment and Women's Psychological Well-Being. *Psychological Bulletin,* 91, 498–516.

Waxman, Elaine. 2009. *As Good as It Gets? The Structure of Opportunity in Lower-Level Retail Jobs.* Unpublished doctoral dissertation, School of Social Service Administration, University of Chicago.

Weinert, P. 1991. *Foreign Female Domestic Workers: HELP WANTED!* World Employment Programme Research Working Paper. Geneva: International Labour Organization.

West, Robin.1988. Jurisprudence and Gender. *University of Chicago Law Review,* 55, 1–72.

Wial, Howard. 1993. The Emerging Organizational Structure of Unionism in Low-Wage Services. *Rutgers Law Review.* 45, 671–738.

Williams, Joan. 1989. Deconstructing Gender. *Michigan Law Review,* 87, 797–845.

———. 2000. *Unbending Gender: Why Family and Work Conflict and What to Do about It.* New York: Oxford University Press.

———. 2010. *Reshaping the Work-Family Debate. Why Men and Class Matter.* Cambridge: Harvard University Press.

Williams, Joan C., Stephanie Bornstein, and Jessica Manvell. 2006. *Opt Out or Pushed Out? A New Perspective on Work/Family Conflict.* San Francisco: University of California Hastings College of the Law, Center for WorkLife Law.

Wright, Bernadette. 2005. *Report: Direct Care Workers in Long-Term Care.* AARP Public Policy Institute. http://www.hcbs.org/files/75/3748/directcare.pdf.

About the Contributors

KERSTIN AUMANN is Senior Research Associate at the Families and Work Institute, and author of *Being a Stranger in a Strange Land: Person-Organization Fit and Expatriates' Success* (2008).

JAMIE DOLKAS is Staff Attorney at Equal Rights Advocates.

ELLEN GALINSKY is President and Co-Founder of Families and Work Institute, and author of *Mind in the Making: The Seven Essential Life Skills Every Child Needs* (2010), *Ask The Children*, and *The Six Stages of Parenthood*.

LISA ACKERLY HERNANDEZ is a Ph.D. student in the Sociology Department of the Graduate Center at the City University of New York, as well as a licensed attorney.

BERNIE D. JONES is Associate Professor of Law at the Suffolk University Law School, and author of *Fathers of Conscience: Mixed Race Inheritance in the Antebellum South* (2009).

SUSAN J. LAMBERT is Associate Professor in the School of Social Service Administration at the University of Chicago.

JOYA MISRA is Professor of Sociology and Public Policy at the University of Massachusetts in Amherst and editor of *Gender & Society*.

MAUREEN PERRY-JENKINS is Professor of Psychology at the University of Massachusetts in Amherst.

PEGGIE R. SMITH is Professor of Law at Washington University Law School, and coauthor (with R. Gely, A. Hodges, and S. Stabile) of *Principles of Employment Law* (2009).

PAMELA STONE is Professor of Sociology at Hunter College and the Graduate Center of the City University of New York, and author of *Opting Out? Why Women Really Quit Careers and Head Home* (2007).

JOAN C. WILLIAMS is Distinguished Professor of Law and Founding Director of the Center for WorkLife Law at the University of California, Hastings College of the Law, and author of *Reshaping the Work-Family Debate: Why Men and Class Matter* (2010) and *Unbending Gender: Why Family and Work Conflict and What to Do About It* (2000).

Index

DCAP, 112
demographics, 64, 121, 130n15
dependent care assistance plan (DCAP), 112
depression, 107
disability benefits, 110–111
discrimination: against caregivers, 166–169; against mothers, 166; against pregnant women, 7; and sexism, 51–53; workplace, 52
Dolkas, Jamie, 21, 151–175
dominance theory, 13, 22–23, 27
dual-earner couples, 62, 67–68, 70. *See also* working class families

earnings. *See* income
Eaton, Mary, 27
economic downturn, 18
educational equality, 61–62
EEOC v. Sears, Roebuck & Co., 11, 12, 29n5
effective workplaces, 77–80, 83
elder care, 20, 119, 121, 123, 158
employees: in effective workplaces, 77–79; headcount of, 94–95; health of, 71; and workplace fit, 82
employers: expectations of, 164–165; practices of, 99; and psychological contracts, 70; values of, 65
employment. *See* work
equality: educational, 61–62; substantive, 7
Equal Rights Amendment, 12
equal treatment, 4, 6, 22
equal treatment feminism, 6–7, 10–13, 15, 17, 23, 26–28
Europe: and care work, 137; employment patterns in, 138–140; and immigrants, 140–145; and public sector care, 20–21

Fair Labor Standards Act (FLSA), 120, 123–124
Faludi, Susan, 38
families: and African American women, 16; and discrimination, 166; and emergencies, 165; expectations of, 47–48; and gender roles, 69–70; life stages of, 76,

115–116; stability of, 16–17. *See also* working class families
Families and Work Institute, 57–84
Family and Medical Leave Act (FMLA), 171n22; and caregiving, 7–8; eligibility for, 109, 156; and hours worked, 100
fathers, 48, 69, 114, 161, 163–164, 168–169
federal labor protections, 124
Feminine Mystique, The, 3
feminism, 3–30; backlash against, 38; choice, 11–12; conservative, 28; critical race, 25, 27; cultural/difference, 7, 10–11, 22, 26; equal treatment, 6–7, 10–13, 15, 17, 23, 26–28; global, 25, 27; and legal theory, 26–28; lesbian, 27; and media, 38, 40–41; and military, 12–13; and opting out, 40–41; second wave, 23–24; third wave, 23–24, 28
flexibility: of labor, 94–98, 100; of workplace, 46, 152–153
flexible careers, 57, 62–66, 72–77, 83–84
FLSA, 120, 123–124
FMLA. *See* Family and Medical Leave Act (FMLA)
France, 142–145
Friedan, Betty, 3, 9, 27
full-time employment, 93, 139
full-time flex, 97

Galinsky, Ellen, 19, 57–84
Geduldig v. Aiello, 7
gender: and bias, 166; and earnings, 48, 62; and expectations, 50–51; norms, 34, 54; and work hour preferences, 89–90
gender roles, 6; attitudes about, 68; and careers, 72; and childcare, 114; and family, 69–70; and opting out, 51–53; and work, 62, 66–72; and work hour preferences, 92–93
General Electric Company v. Gilbert, 7
Generation X, 36, 59, 75–77
Germany, 142–145
glass ceiling, 26, 62
global feminist legal theory, 25, 27
Goldin, Claudia, 35–36, 44–45
government policies, 127, 145
grandparents, 157–158

headcount, 94–95, 101

health: employee, 71; insurance, 95–96

Hernandez, Lisa Ackerly, 33–56

Hewlett, Sylvia Ann, 17–18

high-income women, 14

Hirschman, Linda R., 13, 23

Hispanic women, 89, 91. *See also* race

history, of women's work, 4–5

home care, 20, 119–135; consumers of, 129n3; workers, 121–123, 125, 127–128, 132n37

hourly workers, 87–102; and headcount, 94–95; income of, 99; labor force participation of, 19; and scheduling, 97–98; women as, 91

husbands, 48. *See also* fathers

ideal worker, 51, 160

identity, 113–114

imagery, 51–54

immigrant women, 140–145

immigration policies, 142–144

income, 4, 67, 122; gender differences in, 48, 62; and hourly jobs, 99; of working class men, 164; of working class mothers, 159–160

independent contractors, 126

Independent Women's Forum, 25, 28

inflexible workplace, 152–153

insurance, 95–96

international trends, in care work, 137–147

jobs: dissatisfaction with, 122; low-wage, 19–20; pressure from, 60; security of, 62. *See also* work

Jones, Bernie D., 3–30

Kaminer, Wendy, 12

labor: flexibility practices, 94–98, 100; legislation, 5, 109, 124

labor force participation, 33–56; of African American women, 34; by age, 37; and childbearing, 36; of college-educated women, 35–36; and employer practices, 99; and hourly workers, 88,

101; of mothers, 67–68; and opting out, 41–42

Lambert, Susan J., 19, 87–102

language, 53

layoffs, 98

leave, 8, 110, 155–156

legislation, 5, 109, 124

lesbian feminism, 27

Levit, Nancy, 25

LFP. *See* labor force participation

life stage, 19, 83–84; and age, 74–75; and career aspirations, 66; family, 76, 115–116; and flexible careers, 72–77

Lochner v. New York, 5

Long Island Care at Home, Ltd. v. Coke, 120, 122–125

long-term care policy, 120

low-income women, 94, 103–117

low-wage jobs, 19–20

mandatory overtime, 108–109, 154–155

married women, 35–37

maternity leave, 110

Matures generation, 75–77

McKinnon, Catharine, 22–23, 27

media, 38–41, 43–44, 50, 151, 152, 158–159

men: attitudes of, 68, 164; career advancement of, 59; and child care, 48, 69, 114, 161, 163–164; roles of, 69; and work-family conflicts, 168

mental health, 116

middle class, 9–10, 15, 21, 34

Milennial generation, 59, 61, 75–77

military, 12–13

Misra, Joya, 20, 137–147

Missing Middle, 21, 151–175

momism, 9–10, 39

mommy: track, 46, 51, 152; wars, 10–11, 55

motherhood: bar, 18, 50; penalty, 52; and race, 54

mothers: at-home, 43; career aspirations of, 60, 61; college-educated, 37, 42; discrimination against, 166; employed, 67, 68; employment rates of, 138–140; income of, 159–160; labor force participation of, 36, 67–68; and mental health, 116;

mothers: (*continued*)
middle-class, 9–10; opting out of, 43; single, 105–106, 167; standards for, 50; work hour preferences of, 90–91; working class, 103, 104; and workplace expectations, 45–47
Muller v. Oregon, 5

National Study of the Changing Workforce, 57–84
Nevada Department of Human Resources v. Hibbs, 8
new momism, 9–10, 39
nineteenth century, 4–5, 35
norms: gender, 34, 54; sociocultural, 63, 64, 67
NSCW, 57–84

off-ramping, 52, 53
Onwuachi-Willig, Angela, 24
open availability, 98
opt-in, 94–98
opt-out: and African American women, 15–16; and choice feminism, 12; and class, 104, 116–117; critique of, 23; definition of, 41; demographics of, 39; as euphemism, 53; and gender roles, 51–53; and high-income women, 14; language of, 44–45; media portrayal of, 38–41, 43, 50, 151–152, 158–159; rates of, 43; reasons for, 44, 45, 49–51; trends in, 41–44, 50; and vulnerability, 14; and women of color, 91
Opt Out or Pushed Out? How the Press Covers Work-Family Conflict, 158–159
"Opt-Out Revolution, The," ix, 16–17, 28
organizational values, 65
overtime, 108–109, 154–155, 162–164

parents: attitudes of, 75–77; leave for, 8; new, 107; working class, 105–113; work schedules of, 106–107. *See also* fathers; mothers
part-time: employees, 87, 91–92, 96–97; work, 46
paternity leave, 110

Perry-Jenkins, Maureen, 19–20, 103–117
Personal Responsibility and Work Reconciliation Act of 1996, 54
person-environment fit, 80–83
postfeminism, 38
poverty, 105–113; and employment, 103; of home-care workers, 132n37; and part-time work, 99
pragmatic feminism, 28
Pregnancy Discrimination Act of 1978, 7
primary wage earner, 89, 92–93
print media, 38–39
privilege, 42
probationary periods, 111–112
professional women, 15, 33, 39
Progressive Era, 5
psychological climate, 81
public: assistance, 100; sector, 20–21, 142–147

race: and class, 54–55; and feminism, 25; and work hour preferences, 89–92
Radin, Margaret Jane, 28
Republican Motherhood, 4

scheduling, 97–98, 153
Schein, Edgar, 73–74
Schlafly, Phyllis, 11
Schneider, Elizabeth M., 28
school demands, 47
Schultz, Elizabeth Rose, 26
second shift, 9
second wave feminism, 23–24
SEIU, 125–126
separate spheres, 4, 34–35, 51–53
sequencing, 44, 50, 52, 53
Service Employees International Union (SEIU), 125–126
sexism, 51–53
sex roles. *See* gender roles
shift work, 107–108
sick leave, 155–156
single: mothers, 105, 106; parents, 161, 162
Smith, Peggie R., 20, 119–135
Social, conservatives, 10–11. *See also* class
sociocultural norms, 63, 64, 67

Stabile, Susan J., 26
Stone, Pamela, 18, 33–56, 103, 104, 106, 113
stress, 71
Super, Donald, 73

tag-team child care, 55, 157, 162–163
TANF, 100
Tarr-Whelan, Linda, 14
Temporary Assistance to Needy Families
    (TANF), 100
temporary worker, 97
third wave feminism, 23–24, 28
Title VII, 7
twentieth century, 34

underemployment, 87–102
unions: and arbitration, 21, 151–175; and
    care workers, 147; and home-care work-
    ers, 125–126, 128; and sick leave, 155

values, 75–77
Verchick, Robert R. M., 25
vouchers, 112

wages. *see* income
Wells, Catherine Pierce, 28
WFTP, 105–113
Williams, Joan C., 21, 151–175
Williams, Patricia J., 27
Wing, Adrien, 27
Wolf, Naomi, 28
women: African American, 15–16, 34,
    89, 91; career advancement of, 59;
    childless, 138; college-age, 24; college-
    educated, 33–37; of color, 91; conserva-
    tive, 25, 28; earnings of, 67; educational
    attainment of, 67; employment rates of,
    138–140; Hispanic, 89, 91; immigrant,
    140–145; married, 35–37; professional,
    15, 33, 39; young, 24, 60, 61. *See also*
    mothers

"Women and Work: Choices and Con-
    straints," xi
Women's Institute for a Secure Retirement,
    30n12
Women's Institute for Financial Education,
    30n12
women's rights movement, 3. *See also*
    feminism
work: barriers to, 94–98; cultural construc-
    tion of, 55; and family life stage, 115–116;
    and gender roles, 66–72; hour prefer-
    ences, 88–93; hour requirements, 100;
    nineteenth century, 4–5; preferences, 115;
    return to, 18, 49, 53; schedules, 106–107;
    and stress, 71; values about, 75–77
Work and Family Transitions Project
    (WFTP), 105–113
workers: availability of, 98; home-care,
    121, 122; and hours, 97–98; ideal, 51, 160;
    temporary, 97
work-family balance, 52; and class, 15;
    and dual-earner couples, 70; and men,
    69–70; and working class families, 21,
    151–175
work-family policies, 10
working class families, 151–175; and child
    care, 156–158; and elder care, 158; and
    overtime, 162; and tag-team parenting,
    55, 157, 162–163; and work-family bal-
    ance, 21, 151–175; and workplace inflex-
    ibility, 152–153
working class mothers, 103–117, 159–160
working poor, 105–113
WorkLife Law, 21, 151, 158–59
workloading, 98, 100
workplace: benefits, 117; effective, 77–80,
    83; inflexible, 152–153; outdated, 160;
    policies, 21, 45–47, 64, 112–113, 154; and
    women's lives, 51

Young, Cathy, 29n4